BOOTS ON THE GROUND BY DUSK

BOOTS ON THE GROUND BY DUSK

MY TRIBUTE TO PAT TILLMAN

Mary Tillman

with Narda Zacchino

MODERN TIMES

Modern Times is a trademark of Rodale Inc.

Rodale books may be purchased for business or promotional use or for special sales. For information, please write to: Special Markets Department, Rodale Inc., 733 Third Avenue, New York, NY 10017

Printed in the United States of America Rodale Inc. makes every effort to use acid-free ∞, recycled paper ◉.

Photographs provided by Mary Tillman

Book design by Joanna Williams

Library of Congress Cataloging-in-Publication Data
Tillman, Mary.
    Boots on the ground by dusk : my tribute to Pat Tillman / Mary Tillman with Narda Zacchino.
        p.   cm.
    ISBN-13 978-1-59486-880-1   hardcover
    ISBN-10 1-59486-880-8   hardcover
    1. Tillman, Pat, 1976-2004.   2. Football players—United States—Biography.
3. Soldiers—United States.   4. Afghan War, 2001—United States.   5. Afghan War, 2001—Casualties.   6. Mothers of war casualties—United States.   I. Zacchino, Narda.   II. Title.
GV939.T49T55   2008
796.332092—dc22
[B]   2008005542

Distributed to the trade by Macmillan

2   4   6   8   10   9   7   5   3   1   hardcover

CONTENTS

For Kevin, Richard, and Marie

I

When it is dark enough, you can see the stars.

—CHARLES A. BEARD

A chilly breeze rustles the leaves of an old elm, whose branches hang over me like a canopy. The sound of crackling and sizzling oak logs is all I hear as I sit wrapped in a quilt staring into the fire pit in my front yard. One log splinters and falls onto another. There is a snap and a swish as tiny yellow and red sparks scatter into the darkness, as if to join the flickering stars in the distance. I light my cigarette wondering what I would do if I couldn't smoke, if I couldn't blow out my anger, frustration, and sense of crippling loss into the night.

In forty-eight years I have never been a smoker, but now I am smoking to stay sane. Pulling the quilt around my shoulders, I wonder how it can be so cold tonight, when just weeks earlier I sat sweltering in a pink linen dress at my son's memorial service. It was important to me that I not wear black on that day. I wanted to wear something cheerful in celebration of his life and his spirit. However, as I sat in the intense heat listening to the whine of bagpipes, perspiration seeping through the light fabric, I felt vulnerable, exposed, as though people could see the pain of my loss through my sweat-soaked dress.

Ashes from my cigarette fall onto the quilt. I toss the butt into the fire and look around at what I can see of my yard from the light of the flames. In the two weeks following my son's death, this yard had been almost constantly full of people. I remember the movement of bodies and drone of voices, but I only recall a few specific faces, and I remember almost nothing of what was said. Now the yard is empty. My family members have returned to their homes to face their own void, and our friends have gone back to lives they neglected in order to support us and to deal with the shock over the death of their friend. I feel alone and frightened, wondering how I am going to live my life without my oldest son.

The fog is rolling in, obscuring the stars in the distance. I get up to place another log on the fire and stare into the blaze. My thoughts drift to another time, and I turn to look up at the elm tree behind me. My eye catches a six-inch stub, a remnant from a branch removed long ago, protruding twelve feet from the base of the sturdy trunk. A painful lump forms in my throat, and my sinuses sting as I try to hold back tears. But as my brain conjures the memory that my emotions fear to confront, a smile forms on my face, gently releasing the welling tears down my cheeks.

I see my son at nineteen, standing muscled and tan on the front stoop of our house, smiling devilishly, first at me, and then in the direction of the elm twenty feet away. I watch his smile slowly fade as his eyes stare intently at something I cannot see. Suddenly, he pushes off from the stoop and takes a running leap at the tree, planting his right foot about five feet up the trunk. His momentum propels him to grab the stub jutting at least five feet above his head and to swing himself with one solid tug onto an adjacent branch. He stands up with his arms raised and smiles down on me as if to say, "Life is great!" And then we both laugh.

It was under the umbrella of this big elm that my son played as a child. The house that stands before me, that holds so many memories, is where we lived when he was born. Patrick Daniel Tillman was full of life from the moment he came into the world at 9:39 on the morning of November 6, 1976, occipito-posterior, facing up—a stargazer.

He was brought home to this house, which is nestled in the rocky and wooded canyon of New Almaden, a California settlement developed in 1845 after a rich supply of quicksilver (mercury) was discovered there. Quicksilver was once a necessary component in processing gold and silver as well as in manufacturing munitions, which led President Lincoln to seize the mines in 1863, for the duration of the Civil War.

From the time I was ten years old, the Civil War has fascinated me; learning that New Almaden had in fact played a crucial role in that war made me feel we had moved to the perfect place. The mines operated under private ownership until the year Pat was born, when Santa Clara County purchased the surrounding property for a county park. These four thousand acres, with their twenty miles of beautiful and rugged trails, is where I would take Pat for walks as a baby.

He was not a cuddly infant. Actually, he was a little malcontent. He didn't like being swaddled and held like most babies; he preferred to be upright. I remember I would sit in a chair and hold him up so he could bounce on my knees until my arms got so tired I could no longer hold him. As an infant Pat was quite sinewy, displaying his father's quick-twitch muscles and the incredible coordination of his uncle Rich. When he was three months old, his father and I got a back carrier for him. He was really too little to sit in it properly, so I'd stuff diapers all around him so he would fit snugly. It was from the back carrier that Pat got his first exposure to Quicksilver County Park.

We would hike for hours while I described the sights. Along with the birds and squirrels, it was not unusual to see wild turkeys, families of quail, wild boar, or an occasional rattlesnake. On weekends, Pat's father and I also liked to take him on walks past the reservoir two miles up the road. We loved living in this quaint secluded place, but my husband's hour-long commute to Cupertino, where he worked, was grueling. So when Pat was seven months old, we moved to Campbell, California, where our second son, Kevin, was born.

About six months before Kevin's arrival, Pat went through a phase of regularly hurling himself out of his crib and onto the floor in protest of bedtime. He would crawl over to the bedroom door, put his hand through the crack underneath it, and howl, "O-o-o-u-t! O-o-o-u-t!" You could see the little pink balls of his fingers desperately seeking someone's attention. I would sit on the couch with a lump in my throat and tears rolling down my face. My pediatrician had told me I needed to let him cry, and eventually he would stop, and as a young mom, I still thought my doctor knew best. When Pat's crying stopped, his father and I would gently open the door to find him asleep, knees curled under him, diapered bottom in the air, and his hand still reaching through the space under the door. We would carefully lift him and place him back in the crib. After a week of this gut-wrenching ritual, we decided to get Pat a big-boy bed with a railing on it.

Pat never really crawled in the way babies do. To get around, he would hold a plastic doughnut in each hand and push them around the floor with his legs straight, butt in the air, and knees never touching the floor. He learned to walk when he was eight and a half months old.

By the time Kevin was born on January 24, 1978, fourteen-month-old Pat seemed very much a little man. Now the crib that had been so repellent to him just months before became a curiosity; it held his baby brother. Pat began climbing into the crib and carefully curling up next to Kevin, as if he had an innate sense that he could hurt the baby if he rolled over. Pat was quite pleased to have Kevin in his world and liked to help me bathe, feed, and change him. Pat did not like to nap; he hated the idea that he might miss something, but some days I needed him to take a nap, so I would sit on the floor, with Kevin in the infant seat next to me, and read aloud as Pat played. Eventually, Pat would sidle up and sit between his brother and me. Often he fell asleep holding Kevin's hand.

Pat was talking all the time by twenty-two months. If you asked him his name, he would say, "Packet Daniel Tillman." He pronounced Kevin "Nubbin." As months passed, Pat learned to pronounce his own name properly, but he continued to call Kevin Nubbin or Nub. To this day, everyone close to Kevin calls him Nub.

We had a nice little front yard at the triplex. My husband and I had put in a new lawn six months before Kevin was born, so the grass was thick and green. But I was nervous about the boys playing in the front yard close to the street, so I usually had them play in the back, where there was a tiny patch of grass alongside the cement parking area.

My mother, Victoria Spalding, who lived twenty miles away in Fremont, often came to visit us when she wasn't working. One morning she and I took the boys to the PruneYard, an outdoor shopping mall ten minutes from our house. My youngest brother, Mike, who was around eighteen at the time, was going to come to visit in the afternoon. Time got away from us, and I was worried we wouldn't get home in time for my brother's arrival. I told the boys, "We have to hurry. Uncle Mike is coming. We don't want him to have to wait for us." I strapped Pat and Kevin into their car seats and we headed home. Pat, not wanting to keep his uncle waiting, kept saying, "Hurwe, Mom! Hurwe!" As we turned the corner onto our street, Pat unbuckled his seat belt, scrambled out of his car seat, and planted himself behind the front seats, poking his head between my mom and me. When he saw his uncle's Volkswagen parked in our driveway, his face looked grave. Concerned that his uncle had been waiting, he yelled at the top of his lungs, "Here we come, Unka Mike!"

Pat was always unbuckling his car seat. In the late seventies, the car seats were easy to buckle and unbuckle. It was constant worry and aggravation. I would be driving down the freeway, glimpse in the rearview mirror, and see Pat out of his seat. I'd turn around to find him unhooking Kevin and helping him out. Both of them would start to giggle and squat behind the seats, covering their heads with their blankets. I'd have to pull over, put them back in their seats, and scold them. We would then head off down the road. Within ten minutes, Pat would be out of his seat and letting his brother loose again. It didn't matter how annoyed I got; they both seemed to think the routine was a hoot. I can't recall when this little antic stopped, but I was grateful when it did.

Just before Kevin turned a year old, we moved to another location in Campbell, where we rented a white elephant of a two-story house. The beauty of it was that it had a fairly good-sized backyard. My husband hung two ropes from some beams that at one time had supported a patio roof. The boys would wear Spider-Man Underoos with Superman capes and swing from one side of the patio to the other, clearing their world of bad guys. By the time Pat was two and a half, he could hold on to both ropes and swing into a back flip. Kevin, at fourteen months, would hold on to both ropes, lift his feet in the air, and wait for his own flip to happen. He wouldn't put his feet down until his brother clapped in approval.

At this stage, the boys looked very much alike. Strangers would often mistake them for twins. They both had blond hair with the same bowl cut. Firm, chubby cheeks padded faces of similar structure. Their skin was naturally a creamy pink, but a day or two in the sun turned them brown like berries and streaked their brown eyebrows with golden strands. The difference in their faces was in the eyes. When serious, Pat's deep, dark, almond-shaped eyes had an intensity and earnestness that could be startling as well as unsettling. When he laughed, they turned into horizontal black crescents that twinkled and teased playfully. Kevin had enormous blue eyes surrounded by feathery black lashes that made him look curious and surprised at the same time. For several years, I called Kevin my Tweety Bird. Within six months or so, Pat's jaw became much more angular, and once again, it was clear he was the older brother.

Several months before Pat turned three, on a very windy day, he and Kevin were upstairs playing while my mom and I baked cookies in the kitchen below. At about the same moment, we looked at each other, thinking the same thing: "The boys are too quiet!" As I rounded a corner to head up the stairs, there was a knock on our front door. It was my neighbor from across the street. She told me Pat had climbed out the second-story window onto the roof of the porch.

I bolted upstairs, questions racing through my mind: How had Pat unlocked a window I could barely open myself? Had I forgotten to lock it? I ran into the room and found Kevin on his tiptoes, peering outside, watching his brother. I gathered myself, my heart racing, walked to Kevin, picked him up, and handed him to my mom, who was now behind me. Kneeling down, I stuck my head outside to discover Pat had leaped from the roof to a tall, thin tree that grew about three feet from the house. He had his arms wrapped around the trunk and yelled with joy, "Here it comes!" as the wind blew the tree back and forth.

I tried not to panic. Slowly, I climbed out the window and, seated on the roof, inched my way along the length of the house. I sat on the edge, nearly paralyzed with fear, coaxing Pat to grab my arm as the wind blew him toward me. On the next gust, the tree carried him in my direction, and I frantically grabbed his outstretched arm and yanked him onto my lap. He hung on tightly around my neck as we shimmied back to the open window, where I handed him off to my mom. I took Pat by the shoulders and started to scold him, but as I looked into his intense brown eyes, so full of delight and mischief, I started to cry and simply hugged him close. Only after hours passed was I calm enough to sit down and talk to him about what he had done. He promised not to do it ever again.

We enjoyed living in Campbell. I took the boys all over town in the red wagon or the stroller, with Kevin riding in the seat and Pat standing in the back. Our adventures usually ate up a good part of the day, as the boys were never content to sit in the vehicle of choice for very long. They would get out to chase bugs, pick up leaves off the ground, pet dogs and cats, and climb on benches and fire hydrants. I liked taking them to John D. Morgan Park, which had a wonderful slide. The only way to get to the top was to climb up a ladder inside a giant cylinder. There were lots of swings and a net rope to climb, all in a sea of sand.

When the boys got hungry, we would eat a picnic lunch of peanut butter sandwiches, raisins, carrots, and apple juice. If it was right after payday, we might have ham sandwiches, grapes, slices of cheese, and oatmeal cookies. On the way home, Pat always liked steering the wagon down the descending half of the pedestrian bridge over the expressway we had to cross to get home. Kevin would sit in front of him, and Pat would hold on to the handle and steer them down as I caught them at the bottom, bracing myself for the inevitable slam of the wagon on my shins. The joy they got from this routine was worth it.

One late spring day, the boys were cranky, and I was, too. I decided it was time they learned to play baseball. I loaded them in the wagon and took them to the store to buy a Wiffle bat and ball. We went to the A&W for root beers and then home, where I taught them in the backyard how to hit a ball. Both boys were right-handed, but they naturally swung as lefties. Their dad praised me for teaching them to swing with their strong arms. Almost a week passed before I finally admitted they both instinctively hit as lefties; I had nothing to do with it.

In August 1980, the house in New Almaden was once again available to rent. A new road had been built, allowing quicker access to the freeway and shortening my husband's commute. While we were preparing for our move, my father-in-law, Hank, died of lung cancer. He had been fighting the disease with tremendous dignity since before Kevin was born. His death was very difficult, even though it put an end to his suffering. I loved Hank very much; my own father had died suddenly of a heart attack when I was eighteen, so my father-in-law was important in my life. Hank's death, though, was far more painful for my husband. He had been an extremely busy young husband and father, going to work each day and law school at night, with little time left to spend with the boys and me and virtually none for his parents. He'd made as much time as he could for his dad once we learned he was ill, but it wasn't enough; there could never be enough time.

Several weeks after Hank's death, we were back in New Almaden. I was five months pregnant with Richard and happy to be back in the rural setting so the boys could wake up to the sound of our neighbor's roosters and play in the country. It was also good for their dad to be in a relaxing setting at the end of the day.

Richard's due date was January 6, 1981. However, that day came and went, and all I did was get bigger and more exhausted. Obviously, the doctor had miscalculated, but when you have a date in your head, it's difficult to wait any longer. On the morning of January 23, I started having contractions. Patrick and I dropped the boys off at the Fergusons', friends who had two young sons, and we drove to Kaiser Foundation Hospital in Santa Clara, about fifteen miles away. Within a half hour, we were back in the car; it was false labor. The doctor suggested we go for a long, bumpy ride. My husband bought me some ice cream to wipe the pout off my face and took me on every winding, pothole-laden road from Santa Clara to Morgan Hill. Richard was born at 2:00 a.m. on January 24, Kevin's third birthday.

Patrick brought Pat and Kevin to the hospital that afternoon. I felt terrible that I had nothing with me to give Kevin for his birthday, although he was thrilled with his baby brother. I walked to an area near the elevators and handed them each a package of crackers that had come with my meal. As their dad and I stood talking, Kevin struggled to open his crackers. Suddenly, his package burst open and the crackers fell to the floor. He looked down at them with disgust and yelled, "Ah, shit!" Everyone looked at my husband, and one guy said, "Way to go, Dad."

Pat and Kevin were excited to have a baby brother. They liked helping me bathe him in the sink. I would give them each a plastic cup and let them rinse off the suds. As Richard got older and started to crawl, the boys called him Goose because in his big diaper, he had a goose butt. However, by the time Richard started to walk, Pat and Kevin decided that with his blond hair, stout body, and dark brown eyes, he looked remarkably like Winnie the Pooh. From that day on, they endearingly called him Pooh, Pooh Bear, or—when giving him a bad time as teenagers—Shit Bear.

When Richard was a baby, they didn't like to leave him alone while they played, so they took turns carrying him from room to room or from one spot in the yard to the other. We concluded that the reason Richard didn't walk until he was fifteen months old is that his brothers carried him everywhere they went. They had great fun playing in our secluded little yard, and I felt very content hanging my clothes on the clothesline on warm days as Richard crawled around on a blanket or in his playpen, and Pat and Kevin rode their Big Wheels, played cars in the dirt, or ran around in Underoos with squirt bottles hanging from their belts.

In August 1981, when Pat was four, I signed him up for soccer. The team didn't have an assistant coach, so I volunteered. I knew nothing about soccer, but I figured I could learn. Soccer practice was about two and a half miles from our house. In those days we had only one car, which Patrick needed to commute to work, so the boys and I took the city bus as far as it would take us—about two miles. Then Pat, Kevin, and I, with Richard in a back carrier, walked the last half mile to Hacienda Elementary School. Looking back, I realize that was a long way for two little guys to walk, but at the time I thought nothing of it. We did this two evenings a week. Most evenings their dad would help out with the last part of practice, and we would drive home together. On the evenings my husband had classes, the head coach drove us home.

We didn't win many games that year, but we had fun. Pat wasn't sure he liked soccer. He actually would have preferred staying home to climb trees. But Kevin loved going to his brother's practice. Midseason, we bought Kevin his own cleats, shin guards, and size-three soccer ball. At Pat's practices, I would set up cones for him on the sidelines, and he would happily dribble through the cones, over and over, alongside Pat's team. We kept telling Kevin that he would get to play on a team the following year, when he turned four. That next season Pat, Kevin, and I lined up at soccer registration to sign them both up. Kevin was so excited; every time we got a step closer to the table, he would look up at me with a big smile. Finally, we stood in front of the woman taking care of registration, and she informed us that the age of eligibility had been changed to five. Pat looked at me in horror as the delighted look on Kevin's face turned to devastation, and tears formed and fell from his eyes. Pat and I tried to console him, but words and soothing gestures were useless. The three of us got into the car. From the rearview mirror I could see Pat patting Kevin's shoulder and looking at him sympathetically as Kevin mean-mugged me all the way home.

The following year I signed Kevin up without a hitch. The team meetings for parents were held on the same evening, so Patrick went to Pat's meeting and I went to Kevin's. We learned that Kevin's team didn't have a head coach. After twenty minutes of banter about who would take the team, I volunteered. I figured I had been an assistant coach already, and I'd watched Pat's coach very carefully. That night, I went home and told Kevin I was going to be his coach. He looked like someone had punched him in the stomach; Pat started to laugh. Standing before me were a five-year-old and a six-year-old who could dribble circles around me. What was I thinking?

Several evenings later, Patrick watched the boys while I attended my first coaches' meeting, where I got my equipment and uniforms. I also learned my team's name. The league determined that the under-six teams would be named after birds. My team was to be the Hummingbirds. Kevin would hate that name, I just knew it. I asked if the team could be called the Eagles or the Hawks or maybe the Vultures, but I was informed those names were taken. "What about the Condors?" I asked. "Does any team have that name?"

"The names have been decided," the meeting coordinator said curtly.

I dreaded Kevin's reaction. At home, I presented him with his new uniform and cheerily told him the team was called the Hummingbirds. His bright, happy face immediately fell. "Oh yeah, Hummingbirds," he said, dropping his uniform in a heap in front of him. Then he turned and went moping down the hall. Pat looked at me quizzically.

"Did you pick that name, Mom? Poor Nub."

He picked up Kevin's uniform and walked down the hall after his brother.

I looked over at my husband, who was observing the scene with amusement. "Did you?" he asked as he plucked Richard out of his highchair.

"Did I what?"

"Did you pick that name?" he said, chuckling.

"No," I said wearily. "What should I do?"

"I think you should disband the team," he said with a wink.

I managed a weak smile, then walked to the bookshelf and grabbed an encyclopedia. In the boys' bedroom, Pat was trying to coax Kevin to try on his uniform. I sat between them, opened the book to a picture of a hummingbird, and pointed out that they are the fastest birds. Pat glanced up at me and then watched Kevin's reaction. Kevin stared at the picture for a few seconds, then walked away with all the dignity a five-year-old can muster.

Two days before the first practice, Pat and Kevin went outside to play, and Pat saw a hummingbird hovering around the bottlebrush plant at the side of the door. I heard him say, "Nub, look. That's a humming-bird. Look how fast it moves." I peeked around the door and watched them observe the bird as it darted around the bush. Once it flew off, the boys went about their play, but when they came into the house an hour or so later, Kevin said, "Mom, our team will be really fast." He skipped down the hall and put on his new uniform. Pat walked in the door and smiled at me, then followed his brother down the hall, happy that once again, Kevin was excited about playing soccer.

At the first practice, I gathered the kids and told them the name of the team. They—and several of the parents—all looked at me the same way Kevin had days before. I told them hummingbirds are the fastest birds: "They can flap their wings fifty times a second." I considered telling them that they flap their wings up to two hundred times a second during courtship, but thought better of it. Kevin helped me out by telling everyone that we would be the fastest team.

With a lot of practice, encouragement, creative substitution, and stickers—lots of stickers handed out for good playing—we won every game that year. Like Kevin, several of the kids on the team had older siblings they had watched for several years. Those kids were the engine of the team. They taught the others through example, while I looked important wearing my whistle. I was excited for Kevin and so proud of him. He ran around the soccer field, dribbling with abandon and passing like an expert. Two seasons of watching games and practicing on the sidelines had paid off. The first several games, I watched him through eyes welled with tears. He was so happy to be out there. When Pat's games didn't coincide with his, Pat was able to watch him play. Two years of watching his big brother, and now it was his turn. He got a look of ecstatic delight whenever he heard his brother yell at the top of his lungs, "Way to go, Nub!"

Three years later, I would coach Richard's team, again called the Hummingbirds. No longer was Richard the little tyke sucking orange slices on the sidelines and running onto the field at inappropriate times. He was an ominously big five-year-old who could move the ball with surprising grace and had the ability to score a goal from midfield. Because he had watched and played soccer with his brothers for so long, he had an amazing perspective and feel for the game. And so did Matt Kline, the younger brother of a friend of Pat. He had curly brown hair, dark brown eyes that shot tears like a cartoon character when he was upset, and little short legs with calves the size of coconuts with which he could dribble around three people before they knew he was coming. The rest of the kids on the team learned quickly from Richard's and Matt's example. That year, the Hummingbirds had another undefeated season. I framed the banner and hung it in the back room of our house; I was getting a big head.

A year later, I helped my husband coach Richard's team, the Gorillas. Patrick missed many practices because of his work, so I would conduct the practices, and he would coach the games. By the start of the last game of the season, we had won every game. Maybe, I thought, we would have another undefeated season. But it wasn't in the cards. My husband decided to make a substitution the last quarter of the game. One of the kids didn't get his fair share of playing time. I was all for the child playing, but a straight substitution was too risky. "What are you doing? You have to move some players around. He can't play that position," I protested to Patrick between gritted teeth so as not to be heard by the parents. But by the time my objection was voiced, the other team had scored. We couldn't answer back.

Only a few of the kids were disappointed; most of them couldn't have cared less if the game was won. They were just happy to exchange stickers and have their juice and treat. I was the grief-stricken one—my winning record was ruined. I tried to hide my disappointment; I knew full well how ridiculous it was. My husband and sons laughed and chided me for being a poor loser. I hung up my coaching whistle after that, though I continued to be excessively proud of my coaching success and all too frequently told people about my two undefeated teams and the season that got away. Any time the boys overheard me start to tell someone I coached soccer, they would get sly little grins on their faces and say, "Oh, don't forget to talk about the Hummingbirds and your undefeated seasons."

When the boys weren't busy playing soccer, they were occupied with school. Graystone Elementary School had a system of reward and punishment that Pat took very seriously. The school made it clear: There were good behaviors and bad behaviors, and if you were bad, you got a pink slip. Pat did not want to get a pink slip. By second grade, he was almost obsessed with it.

That same year, Kevin started kindergarten, and one day the three of us were talking after school and Kevin said excitedly, "Today I got a warm fuzzy."

"You got what?" I asked, perplexed.

"A warm fuzzy," he said.

Pat, as if trying to ease my concern, said, "It's a good thing. It's better than a cold prickly."

"A cold prickly!" I said, laughing.

"Yes, you get them for being bad," they both explained.

Patrick and I liked the idea that the kids received recognition for good deeds and behavior, but the pink slips and cold pricklies seemed to be causing a lot of anxiety, especially for Pat. That evening, their dad sat with them and told them it was okay to break a rule now and then. Pat decided to test his father's advice; at some point, he broke a rule, and lightning didn't strike. He started coming home with pink slips for walking up the slide the wrong way, walking briskly on the blacktop, and getting a drink after the bell.

After so many infractions, he decided he better use the slide properly. Unfortunately, he did so by cutting in front of people on the ladder. I got a call one day that he had cut in front of someone, and the kid bit him on the butt. Both boys were suspended for two days. Pat never cut in line again, but testing the limits continued. By the time he got out of fifth grade, we could have wallpapered our bathroom in pink slips.

Middle school was a fun time for Pat. He had terrific friends and conscientious, dedicated teachers, and he thrived on the more sophisticated environment for learning. He liked having different teachers for different classes, and each subject was stimulating to him; it was so much more interesting than staying in the same room all day with one teacher. Pat loved learning new things and discussing ideas, concepts, and opinions. I know several teachers were nearly driven mad by his constant questions, but most of them welcomed his enthusiasm and tenacity. Since he had started school, he was very conscientious about his class work and homework; he particularly liked doing presentations, projects, and essays.

In sixth grade, Pat had to do a presentation on George S. Patton. He worked for several weeks gathering information on note cards. One particularly cold night, he sat by the wall heater in the hall, methodically sorting through his index cards outlining his oral presentation. The next evening he practiced his speech in front of his brothers and me three or four times, and again when his dad got home. He then asked his dad to tie his tie for him so it would be ready to slip on the next day.

He got up early the following morning and put on black slacks, a white shirt, and the tie his dad had prepared for him. Kevin and Richard, who were still in elementary school, wished Pat luck and raced down the driveway to catch their bus. Pat ate breakfast then gathered his things. I wished him luck, and then watched as he crossed the yard and headed down the driveway to catch the city bus. He looked so grown up. He walked with assurance, knowing he was prepared; I was proud of him.

That afternoon, while Kevin and Richard were changing for soccer practice, we heard Pat's bus stop on the road below. We opened the door and watched him run up the driveway, laughing and swinging his tie over his head. When he got to the door he said excitedly, "Mom, I got a B+ over A."

It always amused me that Pat, even in grade school, would question his grades. I would chuckle to myself when I went through his schoolwork and found papers with comments that he had written to the teachers: "What's wrong with it?" "What don't you like?" "Please read it again." Many adults who worked with Pat weren't comfortable with his inclination to question authority, but his dad and I respected and often encouraged it. We didn't want our boys to be disrespectful, but we also didn't want them to be afraid to question or to obey blindly.

This was a lesson I'd learned during six years of Catholic school, when I was exposed to some remarkably gifted, kind, understanding, and dedicated nun, but also nuns who were unhappy and hateful, who expected unconditional obedience. In the early 1960s, it was not unusual for nuns to slap us, hit our hands with rulers, or otherwise humiliate us by calling us stupid, dumb, or slow. My first-grade teacher at Saint Michael's in Montpelier, Vermont, was about four foot eight, and I think she hated me for being nearly as tall as she was. One day, she kept yelling at me during phonics because I repeatedly mispronounced a vowel sound. I finally yelled back, so she stuck me in the broom closet all morning. I remember twisting my neck like a contortionist as I tried to peer through slates that angled down in order to see what was going on.

By the time I was in third grade, we'd moved to New Cumberland, Pennsylvania. While the students were filing into the pews for Wednesday morning mass, I watched in horror as a nun slapped my seven-year-old brother, Richard, in the face for not wearing a sweater in accordance with our uniform. I ran up to him, grabbed him by the hand, and walked him out of the church and four blocks to our house, tears streaming down my cheeks. I was angry about what the nun had done to my brother and frightened as to what would happen to me. My dad went to our school the next day and firmly admonished the nun who had slapped my brother and her superior who allowed her to get away with it. He also made sure I was not reproached when I returned to school.

I learned from those experiences that adults should not be blindly obeyed or automatically trusted. My husband and I tried to instill politeness and respect in our boys, but we also wanted them to be able to voice their needs and opinions and establish boundaries for those who were not respectful in return. We also made it clear to the boys that if anyone tried to hurt them or make them do something they didn't want to do, they must stand up for themselves.

I don't recall getting any phone calls about Pat's conduct in the classroom during middle school—he was generally well behaved in class—but I was consistently called about his roughhousing between periods. He was getting referrals for chasing people, wrestling in the quad, climbing on the bleachers, and talking while walking to assembly. The administrators were perplexed that a boy so conscientious about learning and generally well behaved in class could be so rambunctious outside the classroom.

I remember that the last referral he got at middle school was at the last Bronco Night, the monthly school dance. It seems that Pat turned over his ticket, got his hand stamped, then proceeded to get a running start and slide all the way across the dance floor on his stomach. Swiveling on his pelvis, he stood up dramatically, only to face his principal. Just as I got home after dropping him off, the phone rang for me to come and get him. Pat had slid himself right out of the last schoolwide dance.

Where has that life gone?

A chill comes over me. I'm suddenly aware that I'm staring into dying embers.

2

*The ultimate measure of a man is not where he stands
in moments of comfort and convenience, but where he
stands at times of challenge and controversy.*

—Dr. Martin Luther King Jr.

Friday, May 27, 2004: One month and five days have passed since
Pat's death. I sit in a small room next to my classroom at Bret Harte
Middle School wondering why I came back to work. Two and a half
weeks ago, it seemed the right thing to do. Staying home trying to comprehend what I have lost would be too painful. It seemed wise to get
back to work and keep my mind busy. With just over a month of school
left before the summer break, I believed it was important, for my students and for me, to finish the year.

Clearly, I made a mistake. The patience I once had is gone. I'm not ready
to cope with the demands of middle school students. Some of my seventh-
and eighth-grade students had met Pat, and they were devastated to learn
of his death. By now their horror has waned, but I continue to live in a state
of shock. At times, standing in front of them, I'm struck by the set of a child's
jaw, an earnest look in the eyes, the way a small hand holds a pen. I feel the
onset of nausea, and my throat tightens to a point where I cannot speak.

Memorial Day is three days from now, and I am telling my students the day is set aside to honor fallen soldiers. A wave of unbearable sadness comes over me as I speak the words "fallen soldiers," and I have to leave the room.

Pat is dead, a fallen soldier.

Sitting in this anteroom, I feel safe, shielded from the triggers that uncover grief I'm trying not to reveal. My co-workers, Carmen and Nancy, are letting the kids play bingo. I hear their laughter, and I find myself feeling angry that they can laugh and have fun, and Pat will never laugh again. I force myself to concentrate on the paperwork that mounted up during the two and a half weeks I was away from the classroom.

Nancy tells the kids to pick up and get ready for the bell. The sound of fifteen kids scrambling to turn in bingo cards and load their backpacks prompts me to gather my paperwork and go back to the classroom. They hardly notice me as they hastily grab their chairs and put them on their tables with a collective bang. The bell rings, and they stand behind their tables looking at me anxiously, awaiting their dismissal.

"Good-bye," I say, forcing a weak smile. "Have a relaxing three days." Most of them are too eager to get out the door to respond, but several little stragglers look back at me and chirp, "You, too."

Carmen and Nancy help me get the room in order. They hug me and tell me to try to enjoy my three days off. I see feeble smiles and the helpless looks in their eyes as they turn to leave. They know there is nothing they can say or do to help me. Nancy lost a brother in a car accident when she was in her early twenties; he was fourteen. She understands the pain I feel and realizes there is little anyone can do but to know when—and when not—to be present.

As I lock the door to my classroom, I focus on Kevin, Richard, and my daughter-in-law, Marie, Pat's widow, who are coming home for the three-day weekend. I haven't seen them in several weeks; it will be good to have them home. From in my car, I check my phone messages on my home answering service. A reporter from the *Arizona Republic* left a message asking that I call him. His voice sounds strange to me. Maybe he is confused because on the message machine I refer to myself by my nickname, Dannie. He may not be sure he has the correct number. But there's something else in his voice that gives me an eerie feeling. I haven't heard from reporters for nearly three weeks. I find it odd one is calling now.

I call Pat's father—now my ex-husband—and tell him about the message. He assures me the reporter probably was calling to verify some information. I feel something is wrong, but I push the thought out of my mind while I go to the grocery store to pick up some food for the weekend. Once home, I again become concerned about the phone message. I decide to call the reporter in Arizona.

"Hello, this is Mary Tillman. You left a message for me to call you."

"Yes, Mrs. Tillman," the voice sounds uncomfortable. "I'm sorry to bother you. But what do you and your family think of the news the Army has just given you?"

"What news?" I ask. I'm overcome with a feeling of dread.

"You mean the Army hasn't told you?"

"Told me what? What are you talking about?" I ask, trying to contain my panic.

"What do you have to say about the fact Pat may have been killed by friendly fire?"

His words stun me. Blood rushes to my chest, and I feel sick.

"I have nothing to say about it and I never will!" I snap.

Pushing the off button on the portable phone, I hurl it onto the table and begin pacing the floor, a dozen thoughts—all terrifying—racing through my head. Does Kevin know? Does Marie know? How do I tell them? How do I tell Richard? What will this do to Kevin?

I run out the front door and across my yard to my neighbors' house. Peggy and Syd Melbourne have lived next door to me for more than twenty-five years. They've watched my sons grow up. Syd was a calm and steady figure in their lives, someone who never seemed to know or care what they were doing but never missed a thing. Peggy, on the other hand, was obviously vigilant. She was a school yard supervisor at their high school. As a teenager, Pat thought she was a "royal pain in the ass," but as he matured, he grew to respect her and love her dearly. They were the first people I ran to upon hearing of Pat's death, and they continue to offer unwavering support.

I knock on the screen door. Peggy walks toward me, sensing right away that something is wrong.

"What's happened, Dannie?" she asks solemnly as she steps out onto her porch.

"Peg, I just heard from a reporter that Pat may have been killed by friendly fire."

Tears form in Peggy's eyes, and her arms open to hug me.

"What next?" she asks as she holds me close.

"I don't know what to do." Peg stands back to wipe away her tears. "I don't know if Kevin knows yet; I'm afraid to call him."

She looks at me intently and says, "Call Alex."

Alex Garwood was Pat's brother-in-law; he is married to Marie's sister, Christine.

"Alex. You're right. He might know something. Thanks, Peggy. I'll call him right away." I run back to my house and dial Alex's number.

"Alex, this is Dannie. A reporter just told me Pat may have been killed by friendly fire." I can barely get the words out. "I don't know what to do. How do I tell Kevin, Marie, and Richard?" Tears well in my eyes.

"Dannie. Dannie!" Alex says firmly. "They know. That's the reason they're coming home this weekend. They wanted to tell you in person before you found out this way. Kevin was told Monday morning that Pat was killed by his own guys."

Tears spill down my cheeks at the sound of those words, "killed by his own guys." I try to process everything else Alex is saying.

"Dannie, I think Kevin called Richard Monday to tell him. Everyone is coming home to tell you in person. The Army assured Kevin the press would not be informed until after he had a chance to tell you. There obviously was a leak."

I don't know what to say. Part of me is relieved that I don't have to be the one to break such horrible news, but I am also heavy with sadness imagining how my sons and daughter-in-law felt when they were told.

"Dannie, are you all right?" Alex asks.

"Yes. I'm fine." I say good-bye. Holding the receiver in my hand, I sit on the front stoop of my house in a daze, looking out at the trees. Trees always remind me of Pat. He loved trees. He loved climbing them, hiking among them, and sitting in them to think.

Several minutes pass; the phone rings.

"Hello," I answer with trepidation, not even looking to see the number on my caller ID.

"Mom?" The voice is full of concern and sounds tired.

"Kevin! Kevin, are you all right?" Hearing the worry in his voice, I forget about my own distress.

"Mom, Alex just called me. I'm sorry you had to find out from a reporter. I wanted to tell you in person. Someone leaked the story."

"It's not your fault, Kevin. How are you holding up? How is Marie?"

"We're both fine. We're flying home tonight." Kevin had returned to Fort Lewis in Tacoma, Washington, several days after Pat's memorial service. "Richard is driving home right now. Lieutenant Colonel Bailey, my Ranger commander, will be flying in to meet with us unofficially on Sunday to tell us what happened. He went over it with Marie and me already. We will get a formal briefing later."

"Have you talked to your dad? I haven't called him yet. I wanted to get more information." I tell Kevin about the brief conversation I had with his father about the reporter's voice mail message before I learned the news.

"I'll call him. Mom, are you sure you're solid?" I can hear Kevin's voice take a different, almost businesslike, tone.

"Yes, I'm fine. What time are you and Marie flying in?" I think of my lovely daughter-in-law, so young and so dignified, having to deal with Pat's death, and now this.

"I'm not sure. Don't worry about picking us up at the airport; we'll probably rent a car."

"I'll see you both when you get here." As we hang up, I look out the window and see a car arrive. It's Alex. He walks across the yard and reaches out to give me a hug.

"It's déjà vu, isn't it?" he says.

"You're right, Alex," I tell him as we sit on the front porch stoop. "This is like the evening you came over after learning of Pat's death. Richard is driving up from Los Angeles right now. I haven't talked to him yet. Do you mind if I give him a call?"

"No, go ahead."

I get up, get the phone, and dial Richard's cell.

"Hello."

"Rich, it's Mom. I know you're on your way home. Honey, I know about the friendly fire." I explain about the reporter's call.

"I'm sorry, Mom," Richard says sympathetically. "Michelle and I are halfway home."

I'm so relieved Richard is with Michelle. I don't like to think of him driving alone under the circumstances. Michelle has been Richard's friend for more than seven months. I got to know her wonderful character when she stayed here for five days right after Pat died. She knew how to just be there for us. I tell Richard I'm glad Michelle is coming and ask how he is handling this new information.

"It's fucked up, Mom. Are you okay?"

"Yes, but I'll be better when all of you are here."

"I'll see you in a few hours, Mom."

"Be careful, Rich."

When I hang up, I see Alex is making coffee in the kitchen. I call my brother Mike. He is saddened by the news but not shocked. He reminds me gently that fratricide, unfortunately, is a real part of battle. He also assures me that he will come to hear what the Ranger commander has to say on Sunday.

Pat's father calls me almost immediately after I finish talking to Mike. He is frustrated that Kevin gave him no details of what happened. I explain that Kevin did not get into any details with me, either, and that we'll have to wait to hear from the colonel when he arrives. Patrick is very angry, and I realize that I am of little comfort. I hang up feeling sad and emotionally drained.

I go out to the stoop where Alex is sitting. He asks me if I'm okay and hands me a cup of coffee.

"Alex, when Kevin called you Monday, did he give you any details of what he learned?"

"All I can say is that it seems the stars were aligned that Pat would die that night."

A chill runs through my body as I stare at the sky. I want to ask more, but right now I'm afraid to hear it. We turn toward the driveway when we hear the sound of an approaching car. Marie's parents, Paul and Bindy Ugenti, pull up. It is clear they are shaken by the news. In an attempt to comfort me, Paul tells us it really doesn't matter how Pat died; nothing will bring him back. I don't know how to respond.

My phone rings. It's Steve White, the Navy SEAL friend of Pat and Kevin who spoke so eloquently at Pat's memorial. He has just learned the news from Kevin, and he is very upset. He tells me that friendly fire happens more often than anyone knows, adding that one of his friends was killed by his own men shortly after Pat died. I thank Steve for calling and hand Alex the phone. While speaking with Paul and Bindy, I overhear him tell Steve there was a "military blunder." I immediately turn to Alex.

"What! What do you mean, 'military blunder'?" I ask, my anger building.

Alex looks at me, horrified. He quickly excuses himself and gets off the phone.

"Dannie, I'm sorry. I didn't mean for you to hear me. Kevin didn't want me to tell you anything yet. All I know is that a series of mistakes and poor decisions led to Pat's death."

"What!" I scream. I begin to cry. Later, after Alex, Bindy, and Paul leave, I sit numbly on the front stoop staring at the sky and wondering what circumstances led to Pat's death. When I first heard about the fratricide, I thought it was errant fire that caused Pat's death. Learning now that the Army made mistakes that could have been prevented makes me sick.

Suddenly, I'm aware of the night chill and go inside. Grabbing the knitted afghan draped over the couch and wrapping it around my shoulders, I go into the kitchen to make some tea. I lean against the kitchen counter and stare at a picture of Pat and Marie that hangs on the refrigerator door. I grab the whistling teakettle from the burner and pour the boiling water through the strainer of tea into a cup. Switching off the kitchen light, I walk to the family room, where I coil myself into a corner of the couch. I'm reminded of the day Pat and Kevin told me they had decided to enlist in the Army.

Mother's Day 2002 fell on May 9, which is also my brother Mike's birthday. It was the day before Pat and Marie were leaving for their honeymoon in Bora Bora. My plan was to spend a relaxing day at home with my brother and mom. Mike and I went for a hike in Quicksilver Park. We got to a fork in the road, and Mike decided to run a particular trail. We decided to split up and meet where the two trails intersect. Our attempt to meet up was like a scene out of a Three Stooges movie; we kept missing each other, walking past where the other had just been.

I yelled for Mike a few times and asked a woman who was hiking past if she had seen anyone; she hadn't. I decided to head home to shower and get dinner started. Fifteen minutes after I got home, Mike walked up the driveway, wondering what happened to me. He told me he had run into a woman, the same woman I saw, but she indicated she hadn't seen me. We laughed at an image of the two of us standing back-to-back, our hands shading our eyes, each looking out over the expanse of hills for the other.

Just before I got in the shower, Richard called to wish me a happy Mother's Day. I noticed Mike's expression change when the phone rang, but I didn't think much of it. I told Rich about the comical experience Mike and I had on our hike, and he talked about his latest trip to Santa Monica and Venice Beach with his friends. He wished my mom a happy Mother's Day, and she passed the phone to Mike. I yelled good-bye to Rich and jumped into the shower.

Later I was making dinner and talking to my mom and Mike when the phone rang again. I was hoping it was a call from Pat, Marie, and Kevin. Kevin had been released from the Burlington Indians, one of Cleveland's farm teams, just weeks before, and he was staying with Pat and Marie, who were preparing to leave for their honeymoon. As I picked up the phone, Mike looked over at me with an expression of foreboding.

"Hello," I said, not taking my eyes off Mike. There wasn't an immediate reply from the other end, and I started to tense.

"Happy Mother's Day, Ma!" Kevin said cheerfully.

"Thank you, Nub," I responded, relaxing at the sound of his voice.

"Are you having a good day?"

"Yes, it's beautiful today. Mike and I went on a hike . . . "

"Ma," he interrupted gently. "Is Mike there?"

"Yes, he's right here," I said softly, feeling something ominous was about to happen.

"Mom, you know how I have talked on and off about enlisting in the military?" My heart froze. He had talked about joining the military over the past few years. Suddenly, I realized that Kevin was telling me he was enlisting. My stomach dropped at the thought of how Richard was going to cope with this decision. Shortly after September 11, Kevin had discussed enlisting with Richard. Rich got extremely scared and angry.

I stood holding the phone, my knees shaking. "Kevin, have you really thought about this?" I felt sick, and my body was getting clammy. "Kevin, do you know what you're doing? Are you positive? What does Pat have to say about this?"

"Mom," he paused. "Pat's joining, too."

I was absolutely speechless. I turned to Mike with an expression of horror. Our eyes locked. It dawned on me that Mike already knew about this.

"Mom, I'm putting Pat on the phone," Kevin said.

Pat's voice sounded pained. "I'm sorry, Mom, to have to tell you over the phone. Kevin and I planned to tell you in person when Marie and I got back from Bora Bora. But someone recognized Kevin and me when we were in an enlistment office, and we were afraid you would find out from a newspaper while Marie and I were gone."

I clutched the table to get my balance before I spoke. "Pat," I said, my voice trembling, "I don't understand. You just got married. What about Marie? How does she feel about this?"

Mike grabbed a chair and placed it behind me, gently nudging my shoulders to prompt me to sit down. I listened as Pat told me how in November 2001, he and Kevin had started talking about enlisting. He told me they believed it was the right thing to do because our country had been attacked, and Marie was involved in the decision. Characteristically, Pat had done a lot of research, particularly about the Army Rangers. He had read about them and traveled to Utah to talk to a former member of the Marine Reconnaissance units to learn more about special operations forces. He introduced Pat to a general, who answered many of Pat's questions. Pat and Kevin did not do things impulsively, and this was no exception: They had been preparing to enlist for six months.

I asked Pat if they had told Richard; they had. My heart was breaking for him. His greatest fear had been that Kevin might enlist; now both of his brothers were signing up.

"Pat, I don't know what to say right now. You and Marie are leaving on your honeymoon tomorrow, and I don't want to take anything away from that. We all have to talk when you get back."

"We will."

"Pat, have you told your dad?"

"We haven't reached him yet, but we're trying. I'll talk to you soon. . . . Ma?"

"Yes, Pat."

"I love you."

"I love you, too," I said, trying not to cry. "Say good-bye to Kevin and tell him I'll call him tomorrow after he sees you and Marie off. Have a great time in Bora Bora."

"We will. Bye, Mom."

My heart was racing, but my movements were leaden. Mindlessly, I turned off the phone and placed it on the table. My mom sat down across from me and gently took hold of my hand. I raised my head slowly to meet Mike's grim expression.

"Dannie," Mike said solemnly as he pulled up a seat next to me, "Pat and Kevin called me yesterday to tell me. They wanted to make certain I was here with you when they called. I tried to talk them out of it over the phone, but I really need to speak to them in person." I could tell Mike felt terrible for not telling me, but I knew Pat and Kevin had to tell me themselves, and I was grateful Mike was with me.

"I can't believe they're doing this," I said numbly. Yet, even as I said the words, a part of me wasn't shocked.

A feeling of dread had lingered in me since the September 11 terrorist attacks, knowing that horrible act could move Pat or Kevin to enlist. My immediate fear was for Kevin, as he had previously expressed an interest in going into the military. When his rotator cuff surgery hadn't healed properly in January and he was released from the baseball team, I feared he'd have even more incentive to join. It hadn't occurred to me to worry about Pat as much; both he and Kevin were outraged and saddened by the violation against our country, but Pat was about to get married, and he was five years into a professional football career.

Mom, Mike, and I ate our Mother's Day birthday dinner in relative silence. After cleaning the dishes, I made coffee, and we gradually started to talk about the circumstances that were unfolding. Mike and I had concerns about the Bush administration. Invading Afghanistan in October 2001 had seemed the right thing to do. The president had appeared to act cautiously before sending troops into that region, which seemed a good sign then. However, six months had passed, and there was something about Bush's cockiness and lack of empathy, which seemed borne of the fact that he had avoided battle during the Vietnam War, that made me uncomfortable. I was uneasy about what future decisions he might make.

Several times that night, Mike repeated, "I'm proud of Pat and Kevin's decision to defend the country, but I don't want them fighting for this commander-in-chief." He said he planned to go to Phoenix to talk with Kevin while Pat and Marie were away.

After Mike and Mom left, I called Richard. I wanted to give him all my attention when I spoke to him. As I dialed the number, a knot formed in my stomach.

"Hello." He sounded cautious.

"Richard, it's Mom. I know about Pat and Kevin."

"When did they call you?" he asked sullenly.

"Several hours ago, but I wanted to talk to you after Mike and Mom left. . . . This is just fucked up, Mom," his voice cracked. "I don't think I can talk about it right now. I'll call you tomorrow. Is that all right?"

"Of course," I said, trying to stay strong for him.

"How are you doing with this, Mom?"

"I'm not sure, Rich," I said. "I'm in shock. It's probably better we talk tomorrow; I'll have a better idea of how I feel."

"I'll call you when you get home from work," he told me.

"Good. Hang in there, hon," I said.

"You too, Mom."

I hung up feeling overwhelmed but unable to move or cry. I began to wonder what my father would think if he were alive. Like Mike and me, I knew he would be proud of Pat and Kevin for wanting to serve their country. Yet I wondered whether he would share my doubts about the administration. Thirty-five years ago, he and I had been at odds over Vietnam. He'd died before seeing the outcome of that involvement. Would he have encouraged Pat and Kevin? Or would he have feared, as I did now, that our family had glamorized the honor of military service?

Discussions about the military had been part of the boys' childhood—why people fight for their country; why they should; when it is right to do so; the effect of war on people; how it crushes them tragically or enables them to do heroic things. At dinnertime and at holiday gatherings, our conversations had often turned to the military and its place in history and in our family. My sons were influenced by these stories and of our family's military past.

My younger brothers, Richard and Mike, and I had inherited an appreciation of history from many relatives, but our fascination with military history came directly from my father, Richard M. Spalding, who had served as a Marine in the Korean War, and from my mother's brother, John Conlin, who had served in World War II and the Korean War, and then the National Guard.

I'd majored in history at San Jose State University, and my ex-husband, Patrick, who was an economics major, had also studied history. My interest in military history, particularly the Civil War, developed during my frequent childhood visits to Gettysburg National Military Park in the mid-1960s. I was ten to twelve years old when we lived in New Cumberland, Pennsylvania, less than forty miles away from the historic battlefield. My father and mother took my brothers and me there nearly every weekend. With great poignancy, Dad would make the history of that war come alive for us. We could picture the Confederate troops advancing down the Chambersburg Pike on July 1, 1863, the first day of the battle, and those Southern forces charging the Union position on the third day.

To help us understand the tragedy of the valiant but futile Pickett's Charge, Dad told us the story of the encounter at Cemetery Ridge on July 3, 1863, between Confederate Brigadier General Lewis Armistead and Union troops led by Major General Winfield Scott Hancock. These two men had met and became friends at West Point and served together in the same infantry in California before the Civil War. Armistead was wounded on Cemetery Ridge. He asked if he could see his adversary and once-good friend, General Hancock, but was told Hancock had been wounded just minutes earlier. Although Armistead's wounds had not appeared to be life-threatening, he died the morning of July 5 in a Union field hospital. It was haunting to know that these two friends had fought against each other, both had been wounded in the same skirmish, and one had died.

We often had picnics on a knoll between Little Round Top and Devil's Den and dangled our feet in a creek near Spangler's Spring. My father bought us Confederate and Union hats that we wore as we ran through the fields, climbing rocks and trees in the vast historical park. The statues, monuments, and cannons that memorialize the soldiers who fought there demanded reverence, and Dad made it very clear that climbing on the monuments was disrespectful. But sometimes we forgot ourselves, and Dad would catch us and get angry. I vividly remember being yanked firmly from an equestrian statue of Major General John Sedgwick and feeling ashamed and embarrassed. The museums, the cemetery, and the home of Ginnie Wade, the only civilian to be killed at the Battle of Gettysburg, fascinated me.

My ghoulish little brothers were particularly intrigued by the replica field hospital, where bloody wax arms and legs were thrown into a barrel by the window. They referred to it as the "arms and legs museum." My father earnestly and patiently talked to us about battles, strategies, and tactics. I remember him telling us that prior to the Battle of Gettysburg, Robert E. Lee often had split his troops into sections. He did it out of necessity, and he got away with it because of the incompetence of Northern generals. However, my father cautioned that it was never a good idea to do that because troops can lose communication with one another, resulting in confusion and chaos.

During the time we visited Gettysburg, former president Dwight David Eisenhower was living at his Gettysburg home. We once walked into the Gettysburg library and saw him sitting at a table, reading. I remember being in awe of this honored and respected World War II general, even though he was by then a frail old man. From 1944 through 1945, Eisenhower had been responsible for planning and directing the successful invasion of France and Germany by Allied forces, and still he'd cautioned against governments using military strength and resources to achieve political and commercial gain.

As children, we'd played military games while visiting my uncle John. I knew that during World War II he had been the last soldier to parachute safely out of a crashing plane, and he had been so shaken by that experience that he never boarded another plane once he got out of the military. Uncle John had no children of his own, so his nieces and nephews were like his kids. Often, when we would visit him in Newark, Ohio, he would set up his military tent for us in the backyard in the summer and in the living room in the winter. We would sit in the tent eating Army rations, which were pretty terrible, and garlic popcorn. While Uncle John rarely spoke to us of his military experiences, he would take us to military cemeteries and army bases. Once when he and my grandmother visited us in Nyack, New York, they took me to West Point. I was only three years old, but I still remember the ornate swords and rifles displayed behind glass in one of the buildings. My parents took my brothers and me back to West Point when I was thirteen and living in Tenafly, New Jersey. The statues and buildings were old, formidable, and impressive. I didn't notice the plebes my first visit to the campus, but ten years later, they were the main attraction.

Military service was part of the life of my husband's family as well, which of course became familiar to my sons. Their paternal grandfather, Hank Tillman, and two great uncles had served in the Navy, and all were stationed at Pearl Harbor when it was bombed by the Japanese; all three survived. My father-in-law did not talk about his painful wartime experiences, but he occasionally spoke about the fun times and camaraderie. I found his stories fascinating. One New Year's Eve, my husband, Patrick, and I went to a party and left two-month-old Pat with my in-laws. After several hours I left the party to go nurse the baby, intending to return before midnight to celebrate the New Year. But I ended up talking with my mother-in-law, Mary, my husband's youngest brother David, and Hank, who started telling stories about hitchhiking, drinking, and just hanging out with his Navy buddies.

My dad, like my father-in-law, didn't talk much about the specifics of his military service or any horrors he might have seen. It wasn't until after he died that I learned his best friend had been blown up by a land mine just yards in front of him. When he talked about the Marines, he talked about friendships, drinking and brawling in seedy bars, hitchhiking from town to town, being stationed on the USS *New Jersey*, swimming with dolphins in the Pacific Ocean, and boot camp.

Dad had been stationed at Camp Lejeune, North Carolina. With a wistful expression, he would recall how he and his fellow Marines had to run miles along the beach on the thick sand in their combat boots. The exercise was grueling and the drill sergeants, merciless. Yet, when the drill was over, even though they all complained and grumbled, everyone who completed it experienced a sense of achievement and solidarity. My brothers liked the story my dad told of a group of Marines maneuvering under barbed wire on their bellies as they were being shot at with live rounds. One Marine kept sticking his butt in the air. The drill instructors continually yelled at him to get his butt down, but he continued to jut it out until it took a bullet. The guy was out of commission for weeks, but he had a great time holding court in the infirmary. To this day I wonder if the story is true.

From the time I was very little, I was aware of my father's pride in being a Marine. When I was three years old, in the days before children's car seats, I would stand between my parents, feet digging into the soft leather of the big front seat, and sing the entire Marine Corps Hymn at the top of my lungs: "From the Halls of Montezuma . . . " My father would sing with me. My brother Richard served in the Marines in the late seventies, and my brother-in-law Jim served in the Army around the same time. Military service was prevalent in my family and my husband's family, and we were taught to respect it.

The 1960s and '70s produced good war movies, and I saw most of them: *Battle of the Bulge, The Great Escape, Patton, The Devil's Brigade, The Dirty Dozen, A Bridge Too Far,* and many more. When my boys were old enough, my husband and I shared these old films with them, and we also watched and discussed contemporary war movies: *Platoon; Apocalypse Now; Good Morning, Vietnam;* and *The Thin Red Line.*

We talked about how war best exemplifies the camaraderie of men, especially when in battle, and puts people in positions to think about what they value, making them put their integrity on the line. The subject fascinated me. I had always believed that war brings out the best and the worst in people. This belief would come to dominate my life in a way I never would have imagined at the time.

My own thoughts about war evolved over the years. The United States' involvement in Vietnam had begun before I was born. By the time I was thirteen, I already felt very conflicted about it. My father supported our presence there and believed we were doing the right thing. I loved and respected my dad, so I was deeply influenced by his opinions. But I had teachers I also respected who were telling me our involvement in Southeast Asia was wrong. By the time I was in high school, I had decided that Vietnam was not at all a moral war and we didn't belong there. I got into an argument with my father about it. I had never shouted at him before, and I remember becoming very angry and running out of the room in tears. After that, we never spoke about Vietnam again. Looking back, I can understand the conflict he must have felt. The senseless destruction, loss of life, and government deception clashed with his belief that ours is a righteous country.

The first Gulf War started when Pat and Kevin were in their early teens and Richard was ten. I felt it was an unjust war. As with Vietnam, we had not been attacked, nor had we been threatened; a motivating factor was oil, and I believed it was unacceptable, outrageous, and inhumane to put lives on the line in a fight over oil. I also was appalled when President George H. W. Bush told the people of Iraq to rise up against Saddam Hussein and then backed out, leaving the Kurds to be slaughtered by Hussein's men. No one knew what was going to happen in the region. I wondered at the time if tensions there would escalate due to our involvement.

My sons were getting closer to draft age by then; there might come a time when the draft would be reinstated and they would be called. Because we had talked so much with the boys about the honor of military service, I wanted them to understand that this was not the kind of war to get into. I did not glorify this war. The briefings to the public by Generals Norman Schwarzkopf and Colin Powell did not stress the serious nature of what was happening, and it disturbed me that the daily visuals from the war zone looked like a video game. My sons spoke of the war as cool. They had trouble understanding that people were dying. My husband and I would remind them, "You're not seeing the death there."

Curled up on my couch, securing the blanket over my shoulders, I recoil. All of those discussions of the military and the honor of serving come back to haunt me. Through tear-filled eyes, I look out the picture window into the darkness.

3

I sought my soul, but my soul I could not see.
I sought my God, but my God eluded me.
I sought my brother, and I found all three.

—UNKNOWN

The lights of an approaching car cast a hazy light onto my front yard. Richard gets out and walks toward the front door. His arms reach for me, and he holds me close. Michelle hangs back for a moment, and then she comes up to give me a hug. We walk into the house, where I put out some light snacks. They look exhausted.

"How are you holding up, Mom?" Rich asks.

"I'm okay, how about you two?"

"I don't know. I never did believe the story about Pat charging up the hill to the enemy. Pat wasn't that stupid."

"I know. There was something off about that story."

"Did Kevin tell you anything about what really happened?" Michelle asks.

"No. But I learned from Alex that his death was the result of military blunders." My eyes well up, and I can't say any more.

"Yeah, that's all we know," Rich says. "Kevin didn't fill us in much. He just told me to head home. It's good to be here, Mom."

"I'm glad you're here." I get up and walk behind him to wrap my arms around his shoulders as the phone rings. It's Kevin; he tells me the Army can't fly him and Marie home until tomorrow.

"Is Rich home yet?" Kevin asks.

"Yes, he and Michelle got here about fifteen minutes ago."

"Good. I'm glad you're not alone. I just got off the phone with Dad. He sounds better than he did earlier in the day. Mary is with him," Kevin says.

My ex-husband's girlfriend, Mary Badame, has been with him for more than five years. She is a very kind and gentle person who has been very supportive of all of us, before and after Pat's death.

Rich and Michelle get their bags from the car. Rich grabs two sleeping bags out of the closet and lays them out in the family room.

I straighten the kitchen as they get ready for bed. I give them each a hug, then go to my room. I read for about an hour, then lie rigidly on my back. I'm very tired but unable to sleep. Staring up, I focus on a patch in the ceiling that's illuminated by the hall light coming through the crack in the door. I think back to a stormy evening more than ten years ago.

My husband's nephews had a wrestling tournament in Union City, a town about thirty miles north of San Jose. Patrick and Richard left early in the morning for the tournament. Pat and Kevin had a function of their own in the morning, so they'd arranged to take my car and meet up with their dad and Rich later in the day. I stayed home to get housework done.

It was dreary and rainy; by early evening the wind had picked up and the rain was coming down in sheets. Our family room had flooded several years earlier, so I checked out the back window a few times to see if I needed to go outside to dig trenches. The ground was obviously absorbing the rain, so I went about my business. I walked into my bedroom to put some folded clothes in my dresser. When I switched on the light, I noticed dimples in my ceiling. "Oh, shit," I said under my breath. My husband had been putting a new roof on the house. I had forgotten he had not quite finished and had secured a section by covering it with a tarp. The wind must have blown the tarp off.

I dropped the clothes on my bed and raced outside to get the ladder. I rummaged around the shed trying to find it, but it wasn't there. I came back in the house and grabbed towels, a bucket, and a kitchen stool, which I positioned under the crawl-space door in the hallway. I managed to open the door, but the stool wasn't tall enough for me to be able to hoist myself up. I could hear the rain coming down harder and had visions of my ceiling caving in. Just as I started to panic, I heard the front door open.

"Hello! Can you believe this awesome rain?"

"Pat, is that you?! Where are Dad and your brothers?"

"They're still at the wrestling tournament. I have homework to finish." Pat looked down the hall and saw me standing on the stool. "Ma, what are you doing?"

"The roof is leaking. Look at the ceiling in my bedroom. See the dimples? The tarp blew off the roof, and I can't find the ladder."

Pat looked up at my ceiling. "Damn!" He ran out to the shed to locate the ladder. A few minutes later he yelled that he found it at the side of the house. I ran outside to find him on the roof securing the big blue tarp.

"Be careful!" I yelled as the wind whipped around.

With the tarp in place, Pat came in the house, threw off his jacket, and hoisted himself on the stool to look into the crawl space. Water that had come in through the exposed roof was still dripping from the soaked rafters and seeping into my ceiling. Standing on the stool, Pat took off his shoes and socks, threw them in the open bedroom door, and pulled himself up into the crawl space.

"Hand me the towels and bucket, Mom."

I held them up. Grabbing them, he disappeared into the dark space under the roof. I could hear him rumbling around trying to sop up water as I got more towels out of the linen cabinet.

"Mom, there's one spot that's leaking a lot. I'm going to put the bucket under if I can get to it. It's hard walking on these skinny . . . *holy shit*!"

A thud came from above my bedroom. "Pat, are you all right?" I yelled as I ran into the room. I heard a thunderous laugh as I looked up to see a size-twelve bare foot sticking through a hole in my ceiling.

The memory is so vivid, I close my eyes with the hope of reliving it as I fall sleep. Waking up early, I put on some coffee. Richard and Michelle sleep until about ten. As they shower, I make breakfast. We sit around and talk for several hours while waiting for Kevin and Marie to get home. They pull up the driveway in a rented car at around two. We help them carry their things from the car, and I make them sandwiches that they hardly touch. We sit in the family room for an hour or so, deliberately avoiding the reason we are together.

But gradually, our talk leads Kevin to get a notepad. He crouches in front of my chair and begins to sketch a map of the region where Pat was killed. Richard and Michelle sit on the floor on either side of us. Marie stays curled up on the far end of the couch. Her flawless skin looks particularly pale as she stares distantly out the window, revealing her apprehension about listening to details the Ranger commander had reviewed three days earlier, details too painful to fully absorb.

Marie's fair and delicate beauty belies her quiet strength. For five weeks, with tremendous dignity, she has coped with Pat's death and struggled with the reality of facing life without him. As Pat's wife, the burden of making many painful decisions and dealing with overwhelming amounts of paperwork has fallen on her young shoulders. Watching her so bravely try to fathom the information she recently has been given fills me with sadness and pride.

Kevin starts his narrative by writing the date "April 21, 2004" on the bottom right corner of the paper. My stomach tightens with anxiety, anticipating what I am about to hear. Kevin then points to a circle he has drawn just above the date. He labels it "Magarah." He begins, weaving his own memories of what happened that day into his recollection of what Lieutenant Colonel Jeffrey Bailey told him just days before. His and Pat's platoon, part of 2nd Battalion, 75th Ranger Regiment, had been ordered to conduct "clearing operations"—essentially, sweeping villages for Taliban fighters—in a region of southeastern Afghanistan near the Pakistan border. As they were getting ready to begin operations, one of their vehicles, a Humvee[1] mounted with a .50-caliber machine gun, wouldn't start. The unit mechanic determined that the vehicle needed a new fuel pump, and one was flown in by a supply helicopter. But the pump didn't solve the problem. Kevin's vehicle towed the Humvee using tow straps.

By the morning of April 22, the vehicle had been further disabled by being dragged around. The platoon stopped in a little village called Magarah and sat for nearly six hours while a decision was made about how to continue the mission.

Requests by the platoon leader, Lieutenant David Uthlaut, to airlift the vehicle out were denied. Because the vehicle was holding up the mission, a lot of the soldiers in the platoon kept saying, "Blow the bitch up," but the chain of command would not permit them to destroy it or leave it behind. It was decided that a local truck driver would tow the Humvee on the back of a jinga truck.[2]

---

1 HMMWV—High Mobility Multipurpose Wheeled Vehicle, used primarily for personnel and light cargo transport.
2 Also known as a jingle truck, a flatbed truck used for local towing.

Uthlaut received orders from a commander at the tactical operations center (TOC) in Khost, about sixty-five miles away, to proceed with their mission without further delay. He was told the commander wanted "boots on the ground" in Manah before dark. Because of the disabled vehicle, the only way to accomplish this was to split the platoon into two sections, Serial One and Serial Two. Serial One was supposed to go directly to the village of Manah and prepare for clearing operations. Serial Two was ordered to escort the disabled Humvee to a link up point near the Khost highway to a village called Tit, where it would meet with a recovery team from Khost and drop off the Humvee with the maintenance team so they could fix it back at the forward operating base in Khost. Once Serial Two delivered the Humvee, it was to travel along a pre-determined route and link up with Serial One in the village of Manah.

Uthlaut vehemently objected to this plan. He didn't want to split his troops in dangerous terrain on the border of Pakistan and risk losing communication in the canyon. He also was concerned because he had only one .50-caliber machine gun, which meant one of the serials would be without a big gun. But he was told again that there must be no more delays.

There were six vehicles in Serial One. Pat was in the second vehicle. Serial One left Magarah about fifteen minutes ahead of Serial Two, which included Kevin. On the paper, Kevin draws a path showing the route Pat took with Serial One. Pat's serial headed west along a route that would take them through steep canyons and difficult terrain. Kevin's group took a northerly route to deliver the disabled Humvee to the drop off point. Kevin's vehicle was the last in a convoy of five, not including the disabled Humvee that was towed by the jinga truck. He watched the tail end of Pat's serial as it split west and disappeared into the canyon.

When Kevin's group, Serial Two started their movement, a Humvee was leading the convoy, followed by the jinga truck which was towing the disabled Humvee. But when the jinga driver realized he couldn't negotiate the intended route due to poor road conditions, the driver adamantly refused to continue along the planned route. It was decided by the Platoon Sergeant, the Serial Two would back track to the point where Serial One traveled into the canyon and pick up the same route.

As Serial Two re-adjusted their route, the lead Humvee also backed up and fell in behind the jinga truck, making the jinga truck and the disabled Humvee the lead vehicle for Serial Two. As the convoy entered the canyon, Kevin remembered looking at the canyon walls and thinking it was crazy to be taking this route in daylight, especially after they'd sat in Magarah for six hours, making their presence known to any enemy in the area. He remembered thinking they were going to get whacked.

Serial One moved through the canyon safely. It was supposed to take a left turn and head south to get to Manah, but the serial mistakenly turned right and headed north. The soldiers in Serial One quickly realized they made a wrong turn and stopped their movement and began to turn their vehicles around and get back on the right route. As Serial One started to re-adjust their vehicles, Serial Two, traveling along the same route, but minutes behind Serial One, came under attack by what soldiers thought were RPGs—rocket-propelled grenades—or mortar fire and small arms fire from the northern and southern ridgelines. At first they thought one of their vehicles had hit an IED—improvised explosive device—so they stopped and dismounted, as they were trained to do. Within seconds, they realized they were in an ambush. They quickly got back in their vehicles, started firing, and tried to maneuver out of the canyon. The MK-19[3] on Kevin's vehicle failed to fire and his rifle also was jammed. He started shooting with his pistol. The situation was extremely confusing. Serial Two returned heavy volumes of fire. Soldiers were firing every weapon system to include their 60mm mortar and AT-4s. The canyon walls were high and made it difficult for the soldiers to fire at the enemy who occupied higher ground. Bullets were ricocheting everywhere. But at no time did anyone in Serial Two receive any injuries from enemy fire.

Back at the intersection, the Serial One soldiers heard the explosions

---

3 A 40 mm grenade launcher or grenade machine gun.

and gunfire coming from the canyon. They immediately identified the machine gun fire as friendly forces. Lieutenant David Uthlaut attempted to contact Serial Two, but was not able to make contact. Everyone in Serial One was surprised to hear gun fire since they knew Serial Two was not supposed to be moving along the same route. They stopped their vehicles close to a cluster of houses near the road, and were ordered to dismount. A group of soldiers moved on foot past the houses. Pat moved to the eastern slope of the spur with Private Bryan O'Neal; an Afghan Militia Force (AMF) soldier followed them. Sergeant Matt Weeks and his squad moved on the west side of the tiny village. Uthlaut, the platoon leader, stayed by the village with his radio operator, Specialist Jade Lane, in an attempt to communicate with Serial Two.

Ordinarily, Pat would have been maneuvering with his squad leader, Sergeant Jeffrey Jackson, but Uthlaut assigned Jackson to Serial Two. Uthlaut was trying to compensate for the lack of the .50-caliber gun by giving Serial Two more men. Pat was acting as a team leader due to the circumstances. He noticed the enemy on the southern ridgeline. Because he had no radio, he ran across the crest to the ridge Sergeant Weeks was occupying. Pat asked Weeks if he could take off his body armor so he could move faster and assault the enemy. Weeks told Pat he could not remove his body armor, but he could assault the enemy. Pat ran back to his position to explain his plan to O'Neal and the AMF soldier.

In the meantime, Serial Two vehicles could not move forward because the jinga truck had stalled in the middle of the road. At some point Sergeant Greg Baker, the squad leader in charge of the lead Humvee, was able to get the stalled jinga truck out of the way so his driver and the other vehicles could get around it. Now positioned where the canyon road opened up, Baker got out of his vehicle. A crew member on the vehicle shouted, "Contact three o'clock!"

Baker saw the bearded Afghan soldier near Pat with an AK-47[4] 200

---

4 A gas-operated assault rifle that can fire up to 600 rounds per minute.

to 250 meters away. It looked to Baker as though the Afghan was shooting at his vehicle. He shot him about eight times and watched him fall. The soldiers in the lead vehicle started shooting where their team leader had shot. Meanwhile, Serial One soldiers on the ridgeline were trying desperately to signal that they were friendlies. Pat and O'Neal, who were just several meters behind the fallen AMF soldier, frantically waved their arms and yelled, "Cease fire! Friendlies!" They tried to take cover behind two rocks that were being sprayed with machine-gun fire from the lead Humvee. Pat may have shot off a flare; he definitely threw a smoke grenade in an attempt to signal there were friendlies on the ridgeline.

After Pat threw the smoke, there was a lull in fire. Pat and O'Neal, believed the shooters in the lead vehicle saw the smoke and recognized that friendlies were on the berm. They thought it was safe at this point and got out from behind the rocks. Pat came around the rock and started to head toward the enemy position when the soldiers in Baker's vehicle opened up their weapons again. O'Neal was able to take cover. Pat was shot in the legs and dropped to a squatting position, yelling "Cease fire! Friendlies! I'm Pat fucking Tillman!"

Seconds later, O'Neal heard pain in Pat's voice. The soldiers had opened up on Pat again. He was hit three times in the head.

Kevin pauses for a few seconds; he continues the story.

Baker's vehicle drove down the road shooting up the ridgeline and the houses. Uthlaut and Lane were hit with shrapnel—Uthlaut in the face and Lane was shot in the knee. Kevin is now silent. His tired and glassy eyes stare into mine as he places the notepad with his diagrams in my hands. I gaze numbly at the "P" Kevin wrote on the paper, indicating Pat's final position. Gently, I run my fingers over it, as if by stroking it softly I'm able to soothe the horror of Pat's last moments of his life.

My son knew his own men were killing him.

I see Kevin's pained and helpless expression and wonder what images swim in his head and haunt him. The memory of Pat's face the last time he saw him? The sight of the last vehicle in Serial One fading into the canyon? The final view of a helicopter's silhouette as it lifted his brother's body into the Afghan sky?

Richard sits on the floor with his back against the wall, staring across the room. His face is pale and his eyes are bloodshot. I can see his defenses building. The anger he has carried the last five weeks is palpable. My heart sinks at the thought of what this new reality will do to him. I glance down at Michelle, who is sitting at my feet. Her face is stricken and also watchful of Richard's reaction. I see Marie's slender frame curled up on the couch, eyes dull and fixed on the floor.

The five of us sit quietly in our own thoughts for many minutes. Hesitantly, I ask Kevin how he was informed that Pat may have been killed by friendly fire. He tells us his platoon arrived at Fort Lewis from Afghanistan late Sunday or early Monday. The first time he saw anyone was Monday morning. He hadn't seen the men in his platoon since Pat was killed, and he had no idea at the time of Pat's death that he had been shot by a fellow Ranger. Kevin had been in the last vehicle of Serial Two, and by the time he reached the scene, no one was talking about fratricide. He didn't even know for about forty-five minutes that the soldier who was killed along with the Afghan was his brother. Then he was flown out shortly afterward to escort his brother's body home.

Kevin returned to Fort Lewis after Pat's memorial in early May. He was happy to see the soldiers from his platoon, particularly the guys from his and Pat's units, return home. "Those were the guys that served with Till," Kevin says, referring to Pat by the nickname he had given him in college. Kevin says he went through physical training exercises with his unit early Monday. At some point after that, Sergeant Baker walked up to Kevin and told him he had shot the AMF soldier in the chest. Kevin had no idea what Baker was talking about and looked at him blankly. Kevin knew an AMF soldier had died when Pat was killed, but he never heard the facts of the situation. It never occurred to him that the deaths of Pat and the AMF soldier were related. Baker must have seen from the look on Kevin's face that he was confused and walked away. Kevin found Baker's behavior a bit strange, but he didn't dwell on it.

A short time later, Kevin was approached by his squad leader, who told him to report to First Sergeant Thomas Fuller, whom Kevin hadn't seen since Pat was killed. Kevin assumed Fuller just wanted to see how he was coping with Pat's death; once seated in Fuller's office, however, Kevin got the sense he was called in for another reason.

Sergeant Fuller gently began to explain that Pat may have been killed by his own men. Kevin was stunned.

"That doesn't make any sense. Pat was shot by the enemy in the forehead running up a hill," he said, repeating the story the family had been told about Pat's death. "His own guys were behind him. It doesn't add up."

The sergeant patiently explained what he knew. He said there were numerous shells from a .50-caliber machine gun found all around the area where Pat's body was recovered. He told Kevin the Army was conducting an investigation to find out exactly what happened. He informed him that his Ranger commander, Lieutenant Colonel Bailey, would be talking to him the next day to give him more details.

Kevin thought the information he had just received was ridiculous. Pat couldn't have been killed by his own guys. Kevin left the sergeant's office and spent the rest of the day in a fog. Finally, it was time to go home. He would have to tell Marie what he had learned.

Kevin drove to the little sage-green house where he, Pat, and Marie had lived so contentedly, the house he and Marie would continue to share until his obligation to the military is over. Marie took the news stoically. It was difficult for her to comprehend or to see how it mattered; Pat wasn't coming back.

On Tuesday, Kevin was called in to talk to Lieutenant Colonel Bailey, who briefly reviewed the events surrounding Pat's death. The following day, Bailey made an official visit to Marie and Kevin's house, where he went into great detail describing what happened on April 22. Bailey told Kevin and Marie the media would be given no information until the rest of the family had been informed, and he indicated that he would be flying to San Jose over the coming weekend, Memorial Day weekend, to tell us the story.

By now it's about five. We are emotionally and physically exhausted. Marie has fallen asleep on the couch. Michelle places a pillow under her head as Rich covers her with a blanket. Kevin gets up when he hears a vehicle coming up the driveway. It's my brother Mike. We go outside to greet him, then Michelle and I go into the kitchen to prepare vegetables and salad. Kevin, Rich, and Mike get the barbecue ready. We let Marie rest until it's time to eat.

After dinner, Marie takes the rental car to her parents' house. She's going to spend the night there and return in the morning. Michelle and Rich go for a walk. Kevin and Mike sit at the table to drink coffee and talk politics while I wash and put away dishes. Once it's dark, all of us sit around the fire pit. Michelle and I quietly sip our wine. Mike listens gravely as Kevin tells him what he has learned about the day Pat died. When he is done, he sits back in his chair. Mike's stricken face peers into the dying fire.

"Jesus Christ," he says. "This is unbelievable!"

4

To betray, you must first belong.

—Harold Philby

My eyes open just as the neighborhood roosters start their crowing. I tiptoe down the hall, trying not to wake anyone. As I walk gingerly into the kitchen, I see Kevin is asleep on the living room couch. Michelle and Richard are curled up inside sleeping bags on the family room floor, and Mike, with a pillow over his head, is crashed on the couch beside them. I pour coffee beans into the grinder but then realize I'll rouse everyone in the house if I turn it on, so I pull the plug from the socket and return to my bedroom to grind the coffee. Back in the kitchen, I look into the family room and see Michelle is lying on her back with her eyes wide open.

"Good morning," she whispers drowsily as she stretches and slips out of the sleeping bag.

"Good morning," I whisper back.

She pads up to the table in her stocking feet and sits down. Her blond hair is endearingly rumpled. She yawns, and her dark brown eyes water as she breaks into a smile.

"Did you sleep all right on the floor?" I ask quietly, knowing full well Michelle always has difficulty sleeping.

"Well, I slept okay once I got to sleep." Her smile widens.

I take two coffee mugs from the cupboard and sit with Michelle to wait for the coffee to finish dripping. We chat quietly for an hour or so as Mike, Kevin, and Rich reluctantly get up and take turns in the shower. I make French toast for everyone as Kevin and Rich get ready to leave for their dad's house. They're going to meet Lieutenant Colonel Jeffrey Bailey at Patrick's house so Bailey can present the information to them before he comes to see me. Kevin and Rich drive off at about eight thirty. Bailey won't be at Patrick's for several hours, but Kevin wants to prepare his father for some of the details he will hear.

Michelle and I clear the breakfast dishes and get showered and dressed. Marie pulls up in the driveway around noon, and Mike, Michelle, Marie, and I sit in the yard, talking and nervously awaiting the Ranger commander's arrival. Several hours later, the phone rings. Kevin is calling to tell me Richard is riding to my house with the colonel in his rental car. Kevin says he's going to sit with his dad for a while to make sure he deals all right with all he has had to absorb.

Within twenty minutes, Colonel Bailey and Richard pull up. Bailey emerges from the driver's side, a tall, fit man wearing a uniform. He greets Marie, and she introduces him to the rest of us. He graciously shakes our hands and expresses condolences. Handsome and fair-haired, with striking blue eyes, the colonel must be in his late forties but looks much younger.

Seated at the dining table, Colonel Bailey looks me in the eye and apologizes for the way we had to learn of Pat's death. He tells me he had investigated the area where Pat was killed the day after his death and was pretty certain Pat had been killed by his own men. No one from the Army had said anything about this to us because they wanted to conduct an investigation first. I think his explanation is a bit odd—why couldn't they have done both?—but I don't say anything. I tell him that Kevin already has given us a detailed description of what took place, so we have an idea of what to expect.

We make small talk for several minutes, waiting for Kevin to arrive from his dad's. But then we decide Bailey should begin. He asks for a piece of paper; I take several from my printer and hand them to him. Although I absorbed every detail of Kevin's presentation, my stomach constricts in anticipation of information I'm afraid to hear.

Bailey draws a map identical to the one Kevin drew for us. He explains the platoon's mission, the problem with the Humvee, and how the platoon had stopped in Magarah. I ask him pointedly why the platoon had to drag a broken vehicle through such a dangerous region.

"Couldn't it have been run off the road? Couldn't it have been destroyed?" I ask. "Kevin said a lot of the soldiers believed it should have been blown up."

The colonel stares at me.

"Ma'am, they couldn't leave the vehicle. Locals could get on the vehicle and take pictures. The pictures could then be used for propaganda purposes, which wouldn't look good."

I can't believe what I'm hearing. "Pictures of local Afghans in U.S. vehicles don't look good, but killing two men and wounding two others is acceptable? That doesn't make any sense," I tell him.

He looks at me without responding.

"Why couldn't it have been destroyed?" I ask in frustration. "Couldn't they have blown it up? It was a $50,000 vehicle; that's nothing."

"That goes against Army policy, ma'am," he says, looking at me as if I'm crazy to even consider destroying the vehicle an option. He said the platoon leader, Lieutenant David Uthlaut, radioed the commander in

Khost and asked if the Humvee could be lifted out by air, but his request was refused. It appears that the MH-47 helicopters[1]—which could do the job—were not available.

Kevin quietly comes in and sits at the end of the table. Bailey explains, as Kevin had, that a fuel pump was flown in but didn't fix the vehicle, so a local truck driver was hired to evacuate it with his flatbed truck. He tells us that Uthlaut had no direct order to split his platoon but did so because the chain of command in Khost wanted "boots on the ground" in Manah, a village on the other side of the canyon, by dusk, and he wanted no further delay. Bailey reiterates that Uthlaut aggressively objected to being placed in a position to have to split his men into two sections, for the reasons Kevin stated. But his protests were futile.

I am appalled at what I hear. I look across the table at my brother; his face is somber. My gaze turns back to Bailey. "Why wouldn't the officers in Khost listen to the officer in the field? He is the one who best knows the situation. If he was protesting his predicament, why wouldn't they respect his concerns?"

Bailey explains that Uthlaut had misunderstood his orders, which were not to have his troops in Manah by dusk but rather by dawn, a crucial difference. The commander in Khost didn't realize Uthlaut thought he had heard "dusk" and not "dawn."

I feel myself becoming incensed.

"That makes no sense at all!" I say harshly. "He was concerned about moving during daylight, yet he never specifically questioned the time to get clarification? Wouldn't he logically say to his superiors that he doesn't want to move before dark? What about military time? Kevin and Pat referred to military time when they talked about going to breakfast. Why weren't they using military time?"

I feel myself wanting to cry, but I hold back the tears.

---

1 A long-distance, heavy-lift helicopter.

Bailey says he doesn't know how the misunderstanding occurred, then tells us there was a doctor in the village of Magarah who passed a note to one of the soldiers during their long wait. He says no one knows what the note said and no one followed up on it. Some of the soldiers were angry that the note wasn't investigated, as they believe it could have been a warning of some kind.

Kevin, Marie, and Richard look numb. They have heard this before and have nothing to say. Mike and Michelle are obviously taken aback. I feel like I am going to burst out of my skin. How could there be so much incompetence? These are Rangers. I thought they were so well trained. I want to scream, but I contain myself and allow the colonel to continue.

Mike, as if reading my mind, tells Bailey that he had real fears about Pat and Kevin being in the regular Army but believed the Rangers to be better trained. He asks, "How could everyone be so inept?" Bailey says he doesn't know everything that went on between Uthlaut and CENT-COM.[2]

"CENTCOM?" Mike says, looking astonished. "You mean Florida?" Colonel Bailey stares at Mike, who looks at me with a furrowed brow. Clearly, he assumes, as I do, that Bailey's lack of response means orders had come from Florida. My head starts to pound; I look desperately around the table to see if everyone is as outraged as I am. Kevin and Mike's eyes are fixed on Bailey as if their intent looks will move him to explain. Marie looks at me, dismayed. Richard gets up from the table, and Michelle watches apprehensively as he walks out the door.

It's unconscionable that commanders in Khost, sixty-five miles away from the situation, were passing along orders originating half a world away while disregarding the concerns of the field officer. Bailey

2 One of nine commands in the Department of Defense, the central command (CENTCOM) oversees operations in twenty-five countries, including Afghanistan and Iraq. It is headquartered at MacDill Air Force Base in Tampa.

continues with his explanation of the chain of events, how the serial was split and how Uthlaut felt such a sense of urgency that he did not think he had time to inform the whole platoon of what was happening, so he gathered his sergeants to let them know the plan. Most of the soldiers had no idea where they were going or what they were supposed to do.

Bailey stops talking as Richard returns to the table. He can see that Richard is trying to suppress his agitation. Kevin goes to the kitchen to get several bottles of water out of the refrigerator. He places them on the table. Bailey thanks Kevin as he opens a bottle and takes a drink. He seems to appreciate Kevin's gesture, which defuses the tension a bit. He then continues with the account, describing, as Kevin had done, how Serial One got through the canyon just about the time the jinga truck driver, towing the disabled Humvee, realized he could not maneuver up the northern road to Tit. Soon after that, explosions and gunfire were heard from the canyon.

My brother interrupts, "Did anyone question the jinga truck driver? Maybe he was involved."

"We took him in and questioned him," Bailey responds. "He didn't have any involvement."

Bailey goes into detail about how Pat ran up the hill with Private Bryan O'Neal and the Afghan Militia Force soldier. Bailey thinks the Afghan was just following Pat. He tells us O'Neal was frightened by the mortars, the gunfire, and the chaos. Pat had to calm down O'Neal, who was only eighteen years old. Pat positioned him near a rock and told him where to shoot. Bailey repeats what Kevin told us about how Pat tried to drop his protective gear and improve his position and how Sergeant Greg Baker, standing outside his Humvee, shot the Afghan in the chest, killing him.

Bailey pauses, turns, and looks directly at me. His expression appears pained. He tells us that when he questioned Baker about killing the

AMF soldier, Baker told him, "He was just a *haji*," an offensively negative term for an Afghan. He tells us he was appalled at Baker's callous and bigoted remark.

Bailey explains that the Afghan soldier was shooting upward, toward the enemy across the road, so that Baker's vehicle might have passed safely. "Regrettably, from Baker's angle, it appeared as though the Afghan was firing at them," he says. He adds that Baker's vehicle was not taking fire from anyone at this point, and he is uncertain why they behaved as they did. We are dumbstruck by the lack of communication, the misunderstandings, and the blunders.

Calmly, I say, "You said the Afghan soldier was one hundred meters away; you can see a person one hundred meters away easily, especially if he is on elevated ground. We have a ridge behind this house. I could identify the boys at one hundred meters when they would play up there as kids. Was it too dark?"

Bailey explains that it wasn't dark. He reminds us he walked the site of Pat's death twenty-four hours after it occurred, and the light conditions were the best of the day because there were no shadows. He says the distance may have been two hundred meters; he can't be sure.

"Didn't you measure the distance?" I say, my distress growing.

"No, ma'am," he says. "Actually, the distance was anywhere from one hundred to two hundred and fifty meters."

"Don't you know? You're a colonel in the Rangers! You were conducting an investigation!"

Looking annoyed, Bailey waits to see if I have anything else to say. Without responding to my comment, he continues to explain what happened after the Afghan soldier was shot and how the soldiers in Baker's vehicle started firing on the ridgeline where the soldiers were waving their arms and yelling, "Cease fire! Friendlies! Cease fire!"

He discusses how a barrage of bullets came at Pat and O'Neal as they crouched behind the rocks, bullets and shrapnel flying. Although Pat waved his arms and kept yelling, "Friendlies! Cease fire!" the soldiers in the vehicle were unable to hear because of all the gunfire. Pat managed to throw a grenade that produced purple smoke, a feat Bailey says was remarkable under such intense fire. He tells us Pat did everything he should have done and more. Bailey says he found the residue of a flare as well, but he wasn't sure if Pat set it off.

Seconds after Pat threw the grenade, the firing stopped. Believing the soldiers in the vehicle recognized the smoke, Pat and O'Neal got up, and Pat came out from behind the rock to run up the hill toward the enemy. Again, the guns from the vehicle started firing. Pat again was yelling, "Cease fire, friendlies! Cease fire! I'm Pat fucking Tillman, damn it!"

I look at Bailey through tear-filled eyes, and my body starts to shudder. Bailey pauses, gauges our reactions, and then continues: Pat was hit in the legs and fell in a crouched position. There was another lull in fire. O'Neal could hear Pat trying to speak. The soldiers in the vehicle suddenly opened up again as they drove down the road, shooting at the houses in the village, hitting the radio operator and Uthlaut before coming to a halt.

O'Neal heard what sounded like running water coming from the rock, and then he realized he was covered in blood.

Pat had been shot three times in the head. Kevin had already gone over the last moments of Pat's life. I knew what to expect. Yet the details, coming from Lieutenant Colonel Bailey, are utterly jarring.

For several minutes we sit, unable to speak, then Richard and Michelle get up and go to the kitchen to make coffee. Colonel Bailey drinks the rest of his water and looks warily at Kevin, Mike, and me. Marie returns to the table and sits down. I feel sick thinking about what this is doing to her.

Appearing uncomfortable, the colonel begins to tell us that Uthlaut was hit in the face with shrapnel, and the radio operator was hit in the knee. He says he thinks they were hit as the vehicle drove past the houses just before stopping. However, he says, it's possible they were shot while the vehicle was stopped in front of Pat's position. Further questions will have to be asked. He said Uthlaut was devastated by Pat's death and felt responsible.

"Why?" I ask. "He protested the splitting of the troops. It seems like his superiors are more to blame. What about the soldiers in the vehicle? Are they going to be punished? No one was firing at them. They killed Pat and another man and wounded two more of their own, and no one was firing at them!"

"Ma'am, I'm sorry," he says gently.

"Why didn't the soldiers stop firing when they saw the smoke Pat threw?"

"They didn't see the smoke," he tells me.

"Why was there a lull in fire?"

"Ma'am, I believe they were reloading their weapons."

"You mean they reloaded and started firing without looking at who they were shooting! Are you kidding?" Tears start to run down my face, and I try to keep myself from shaking.

Bailey looks close to tears himself. He says he thinks that's what they were doing, but we will have to wait for the official report to be certain what happened. Again, he tells us he's sorry.

I look Bailey in the eye. "Colonel, what would you want your wife to do if this happened to you?"

He is taken off guard by the question. He tells me he would expect her to realize mistakes happen in battle. There was a lot of confusion. Bailey says that in his view, Uthlaut should have had more control of the situation, even though he admits the lieutenant determinedly tried to prevent splitting the troops. He says he is disgusted with Sergeant Baker, who, in his mind, is very much to blame. He was in charge of that vehicle, and he allowed his men to lose control. Sergeant Baker told him he had tunnel vision when he shot the Afghan soldier, but he can't really explain what happened. Several soldiers, he says, may be punished, but Baker is most culpable. Bailey is adamant that he will make sure the people responsible for Pat's death are punished.

He then remarks that a lot of mistakes were made and that he told the platoon that everyone must take responsibility for what happened. Mike and I both see the confused and injured expression on Kevin's face. I shoot an indignant look at Bailey. I know what he was trying to do by telling his soldiers they are all accountable; he doesn't want to assign blame and cause enmity. But it's ludicrous to blame everyone. I remind him, "Five vehicles of soldiers weren't even out of the canyon when this happened, and the soldiers on the ridgeline were getting shot at by men they were trying to save. How is it their fault?"

"Yes, ma'am," he says, not wanting to upset me further.

"Was anything accomplished on this mission?" my brother asks, in part to break the tension. "Were any enemy killed? We read an Associated Press story about Pat's death by a reporter in Afghanistan which said that nine enemy were killed."

"No, sir," Bailey responds. He tells us a few Afghan men were picked up in Manah, but they turned out to be insignificant to the incident. He also admits there was faulty intelligence, along with a false sense of urgency.

My heart sinks and my stomach feels sick. Words get caught in my throat and I look down at the table.

"Are there going to be any changes in training procedures because of this incident?" Mike says.

Marie and I make it clear to the colonel how important it is that nothing like this happens again.

"Yes," Bailey says earnestly. He indicates that they will use the situation in training soldiers to prevent the same kind of accident. He stands up from the table and tells us again how very sorry he is that Pat was killed in such a senseless manner and says he takes full responsibility as the battalion commander. He says we will get more information with the official report in several weeks.

I gather myself and stand up.

"You know," he says, "I liked Pat." He tells us that he got to know him a little when he went to Pat for advice about an injured ankle; Pat, who was familiar with sports injuries to ankles, was very helpful.

Staring out the window, as if in a trance, I say, "He was an amazing person."

We all start drifting around the room as the colonel prepares to leave.

"Do you mind if I change into my civilian clothes?" he asks.

"No, that's fine," Kevin tells him. He walks him to his car to get his duffel bag, and then shows him to one of the bedrooms.

After more than three hours in the house, it's getting claustrophobic. We go out into the front yard to wait for the colonel to change out of his uniform. The day is warm, and the air is clear and fragrant. I wonder how the day can be so beautiful when Pat is gone.

Richard and Mike are smoking by the elm tree. Marie, Kevin, and Michelle stand in a huddle and talk. After a few minutes, Bailey comes out of the house. He looks very different out of uniform, a bit younger and less serious. We thank him for coming out and taking so much time with us. After shaking our hands, he gets into his car. Richard guides him as he backs out of our driveway, turns around, and heads down the road. We wave as he leaves.

For several minutes we stand around and stare at each other, not knowing what to say, afraid to say anything. Finally, cautiously and cynically, Mike says, "If that was an unofficial visit, why was he wearing his uniform? I think it's strange."

"I'll tell you something more strange," Richard says, lifting his face as he blows cigarette smoke out the corner of his mouth. "After listening to this bullshit at Dad's, I said to Bailey on the way here, 'I don't care what anyone says, I think my brother was fucking murdered.'"

Kevin looks at Richard and asks apprehensively, "What did he say?" Our eyes shift back and forth, ready to weigh each other's reactions.

"He said, 'You may be right.'"

5

A half-truth is the most cowardly of lies.

—ANONYMOUS

It seems like months since Lieutenant Colonel Jeffrey Bailey came to my house, but it has only been seventeen days. As Pat's father, my brother Mike, and I board the plane to Seattle to hear the official briefing on Pat's death, I momentarily feel badly that I won't be attending the graduation of my eighth graders. Many of them appeared disappointed that I wouldn't be there. However, it's for the best. Since Pat's death, I've been in a constant state of anxiety; I would never be able to sit through a ceremony.

Seated by the window, I look through the thick glass and watch the luggage being loaded on the plane. A heavy feeling comes over me, followed by a wave of nausea as I realize the last time I boarded a plane to Seattle was just before Pat and Kevin were deployed to Afghanistan. I continue to stare out the window, trying to stifle the tears that are welling in my eyes. I'm grateful Mike and Patrick are talking and don't notice my state of mind. If one of them were to say something, I would crumble. The plane takes off, and I try to blow my nose discreetly. Mike glances over at me with a knowing look.

What would I do without my brother? Mike has always been so

supportive of all three of his nephews and me. He was sixteen when Pat was born; they were very close. Mike helped look after Pat when he was a baby. As Pat got older, Mike watched movies and played soccer, baseball, basketball, and football with him. As the proud uncle, he cheered Pat on through high school, college, and professional football games. He and Pat shared an interest in history, politics, and economics and a love of arguing over all three. They also shared a sense of humor and an earnest quality I rarely have seen.

Pat's death has taken a toll on Mike. The evening Pat was killed, I wanted him to know right away, but it took nearly an hour for my neighbor Peggy to reach him. He was at his job at United Airlines in San Francisco, where he works in maintenance. Peggy couldn't reach him on his cell phone, so she called United and asked for Mike Spalding. "Mike" is actually his middle name, and there was no Mike Spalding there. I told her to use his first name, Stephen. She finally called United's security department to find him. Once his department was reached, an announcement echoed over the intercom:

"Stephen Spalding! Call security!"

Mike told me that as soon as he heard the shrill announcement, his gut tightened. He knew something was wrong; he had never given the phone number of security to anyone. He called security.

"You'll have to hang up the phone, and I'll call you back to connect you with the caller," said the voice on the line.

"Hang up the phone! What's happened?" He hung up, the phone rang, and he grabbed it.

"Hello, Mike. Mike, this is Peggy." Her voice sounded shaky. "Go to Dannie's right away!"

"Peggy, what happened to Dannie?" There was silence on the other end.

"Peggy, what's happened to Dannie!" he yelled.

"Nothing has happened to Dannie," she said delicately. "We lost Pat today."

Immediately, he felt hollowed out. "I'm on my way," he stammered. He robotically clocked out and walked to his truck. What he had learned was too big for tears. All he was thinking was that he had to get to my house. He could only imagine what I was going through, and he feared for me.

On the freeway, it was forty miles of bumper-to-bumper traffic. As Mike finally broke free, his anxiety and impatience increased. He was desperate to reach me. Finally, he drove the last sixty yards up my driveway. By then it was dark. Two figures stood in the shadows by the front stoop. He walked past them, as if in a trance. I was seated on the couch in my living room. Any doubts he may have had about the reality of what happened dissipated the instant I looked up at him. My eyes were faraway, lost in grief, and my face was red, swollen, and streaked with tears. I got up as if in slow motion and hugged him.

"Pat's dead, Mike," I said softly and I started to cry.

Holding me tightly, he said, "I know."

Tears are now running down my cheeks. I quickly wipe them away. The memory of that night is unbearable, and I try to erase it from my thoughts. I look over at Mike, and he and Patrick are reading. I see the flight attendant approaching. She's taking drink orders from a young couple across the aisle. They have a little boy, blond, about four or five years old. Seeing him saddens me, and I look away. I start rummaging through my bag for my book as the flight attendant asks me for my drink order. I tell her as I open my book to begin reading.

When she returns with our drinks, my eye once again catches a glimpse of the fair-haired little boy. His hair is the same shade Pat's was at that age. He's a cute little fellow but very fragile looking. Pat was sturdy and muscular, even at four. He always seemed older than his chronological age, always wanting to push himself, to move on to the next level. Pat was especially excited about starting school. He was four years old when he began kindergarten. A week before Pat's first day, I still wasn't ready for him to go. He hadn't attended a preschool other than one brief but disastrous stint at age two and a half, when several of my friends convinced me that he should go to preschool to be around other children his age. They told me I was being selfish to keep him home with me.

I located the Winnie the Pooh School, which was close to my husband's job, and arranged for Pat to go for three hours a day, three days a week. I dropped him off after I drove Patrick to work, then I took Kevin to a park nearby until it was time to pick up Pat. On school mornings, I would leave him in the brightly colored classroom wearing his little green backpack that held his morning snack, and I'd drive away in tears; three hours later I would return to find him sitting on the lap of a teacher or assistant, looking miserable and trying desperately to hold back sobs. Two weeks of that was quite enough. Neither Pat nor I was ready for him to be a student.

When he was about to enter kindergarten, I had nightmares that when the school bus driver brought him home, someone would kidnap him before I got to the end of the driveway. I feared he would like school better than home. I feared I was sending him too soon. After all, he had a November birthday; he was going to be young in his class. Maybe he wasn't ready. Never mind that he'd had his new backpack loaded and ready to go for a month, and he was proudly and boastfully telling anyone who would listen that he was starting school; I was convinced I was making a horrible mistake.

The first day of school I made French toast, the boys' favorite breakfast, and Pat's dad took pictures of him standing in front of the house in his brand-new school clothes. After Pat strapped on his backpack, the whole family piled into the car to take him to his first day at Graystone Elementary School in San Jose. We walked him to a busy and bright classroom full of four- and five-year-olds and left him in the care of a warm and down-to-earth teacher named Sue Gutierrez.

As I walked out the door, I turned to take one last look at him. He had a big grin on his face as he waved a confident good-bye. My husband drove Kevin, Richard, and me home before heading to work and, with an understanding smile, asked if I was going to make it. Tearfully, I chuckled and told him I guessed I would live.

After that first day, Pat took the school bus. It stopped right at the foot of our driveway. Kevin, Richard, and I waited with him and waved as the bus pulled away; it went to the end of the road and turned around, and we waved again as it passed.

Pat was very happy and confident the first three or four weeks of school, but then I noticed a gradual change in his attitude; something was bothering him. I sat him down one afternoon and asked him what was wrong.

"I'm dumb," he said. "All the other kids can read and I can't. No one wants me in their reading group. Why didn't you teach me to read?" I had made sure he knew the alphabet, learned his colors, and could count to twenty-five, but I hadn't taught him to read. I was horrified. I should have taught him to read. I should have left him in the Winnie the Pooh School. All the other kids had gone to preschool while I kept him home to play. Now I was paying the price.

With earnest brown eyes, my four-year-old son bore a hole right through me because I had failed to prepare him for kindergarten. The following morning, I went to school to talk to Mrs. Gutierrez. I told her what Pat had told me, and she smiled. She said a number of the children weren't able to read; Pat wasn't the only one. But he wanted to be in the highest reading group, and some of those kids told him he couldn't read, so he couldn't be with them. My heart sank. I had set my son up to be an outcast. Mrs. Gutierrez could see that I was feeling responsible for Pat's first academic failure, and she told me I shouldn't worry—most children read at the same level by second grade anyway. I walked away feeling somewhat better. Pat, however, was not as easily assured.

"Dan. Hey, Dan!"

I look up to see Patrick eyeing me curiously.

"Dan, put your tray table up."

"Oh, okay," I say, startled to see that we are already landing.

We step off the plane. Walking through the Seattle airport makes me queasy. We pass an area where Patrick, Richard, Marie, and I stood on Thanksgiving morning, seven months ago, waiting for Pat and Kevin to arrive home from Ranger School. We were so excited to see them. They'd been away for three months, and we were allowed no communication. Closing my eyes, I can picture the two of them walking hurriedly up the airport corridor to the lobby in their Army uniforms, big grins on their faces, proud of having earned their Ranger tabs and thrilled to be home.

I can see the delighted and amused look on Pat's face when he saw Marie, usually so conservatively dressed, wearing her new, retro pink-and-brown plaid coat with the pink fur collar. The blush on her cheeks and a wide dimpled smile conveyed her joy at seeing him far more expressively than words. A rascally grin formed on Kevin's face, and his blue eyes lit up as he caught sight of Richard, who was standing tall and proud and smiling in satisfaction at them.

I feel a firm hand on my back. I look up into Patrick's sad and blood-shot eyes. He knows the image I have conjured; he gently pushes me along so we can both flee the memory.

Patrick rents a car for the hour-and-a-half drive south to University Place, a little town outside Tacoma. I feel dread mount in my stomach as we turn the corner to the charming house where Pat lived with Marie and Kevin. Pat had loved that house, situated on a hill overlooking the Tacoma Narrows, with a majestic view of the Olympic Mountains. I immediately glance at the spot where I last saw Pat standing, less than three months ago, as he and Kevin waved good-bye to their father and me as we drove away.

We park the car and grab our sparse luggage from the trunk. Kevin greets us as we walk up the stairs to the front porch. He's with a family friend, Tony Doran, who has been visiting for several days. Kevin tells us

Marie is still at work at an employment agency but will be home soon. We follow him into the house.

In the entry are two very large boxes. Intuitively, I know they hold Pat's belongings, recently shipped from Afghanistan. I swallow hard as I walk past them and into the front room. Everywhere I look in this house, I'm staggered by memories. I see Pat in every corner and in every doorway. Kevin watches me with moist eyes as I apprehensively look around. All of a sudden, I notice something that makes me smile and my eyes fill with tears of warmth and affection. On a metal easel next to the television hutch is a white board. Written on it is the phrase "Word of the Week," and below that, "acrimony," meaning "bitterness of temper." I look at Kevin and smile.

"Remember, Mom, Pat always said he wanted to put up a whiteboard and have words of the week like you do in your classroom, but he never got around to it. Marie and I decided it was time, and acrimonious is how we feel," he says with a weak smile.

"I think it's great that you and Marie carried out Pat's idea." With a wink I tell him, "*Acrimony* is the perfect Word of the Week." We both laugh.

Kevin and Tony lead Mike and Patrick into the kitchen to get beers, and then they all walk out to the front porch. I stay in the house to look at Pat's books on the shelves and appreciate his special keepsakes displayed in the dining room hutch. As I'm looking at the mementos, I find a small newspaper clipping I've seen before. The article is about Rachel Corrie, the 23-year-old peace activist from Olympia, Washington, who was crushed to death by an Israeli bulldozer on March 16, 2003, trying to protect the home of a Palestinian doctor and his family.

I remember picking up the article from the same spot more than a year ago and asking Pat, "Who's this?"

"That's my hero," Pat said. "She was a stud; she had a lot of guts."

I read the article with tears in my eyes then; now, I quietly cry.

Marie's car pulls up in the driveway, and we all greet her as she walks to the porch. We sit and talk for about an hour, and then we leave to get something to eat. Most of the evening is spent in light conversation. We go to bed early to be ready for the official briefing the next day.

Kevin has to go to work before our meeting. The rest of us head for Gig Harbor, across the narrows, to kill a few hours. I love Gig Harbor, but I'm nervous as we approach the waterfront town. The last time I was here I was with Pat, Kevin, and their dad, weeks before Pat was killed. We park the car, then look at the boats docked in the harbor and wander around in several antique shops and boutiques.

I swallow hard and brush back tears as we pass by No Dearth of Books. I remember so vividly the smell of musty pages and the cramped yet cozy feeling of the one-room bookstore. Pat was wearing jeans and a blue plaid shirt. He walked around the small room closely examining the used books displayed on the center tables and ceiling-high shelves. I watched him and Kevin as they spoke so respectfully and with such interest to an old gentleman who sat at a desk by the window, surrounded by aged books and periodicals waiting to be shelved.

I remember suddenly being gripped by a feeling of absolute dread as I watched the soft and earnest expression on Pat's face. There appeared to be an unsettling aura around him. I was so shaken by it that I left the bookstore and waited outside. Minutes later, Pat, Kevin, and Patrick came out of the store, and we started walking down the street to the car. Pat glanced in the bag he was carrying and took out the receipt to look at it. His eyes widened and he appeared distressed. He turned and started running back to the store. Kevin called out, "Where are you going?"

"We didn't pay for one of the books. I have to run back and pay the old guy!" Pat yelled back.

"Pat, it's okay," Kevin said loudly. "I paid for my book separately. We paid for all the books."

Pat stopped, then slowly walked back toward us, rechecking his receipt; he compared it with the one Kevin held in his hand. Relief spread across his face, and then he broke into a smile that revealed his embarrassment. I recall being very touched by his concern, but I felt something else—paralyzing fear for Pat.

"Dannie," Tony says, pulling me from my thoughts, "you all right?" I look up and see everyone looking at me.

"Yes, I'm fine. Can we get some coffee?"

After stopping at the nearest coffee shop, we return to the house and receive a call from Kevin that the meeting has been pushed back a few hours. Kevin comes home to wait with us. Tony leaves for the airport, and the rest of us drive to the Army base at Fort Lewis. We're all very quiet. I stare out the window, recalling the times I drove this route with Pat and Kevin. I glance at Kevin, then at Marie, wondering if they are having similar thoughts.

As we pass by a wooded area, I recall a story Pat and Kevin told me about the last time they drove this route before being deployed, when they saw two raccoons at the side of the road. One had been hit; the other hovered mournfully over his dead companion. Kevin told me the sad little buddy made eye contact with them as they passed. Pat and Kevin looked at each other; both were very unsettled by the experience.

When we arrive, Kevin escorts us into the headquarters of the 2nd Ranger Battalion, 75th Regiment. Lieutenant Colonel Bailey greets us and introduces us to Colonel James C. Nixon, the regimental commander. They lead us to a large room, where we're met by about twenty soldiers of various ranks. We're introduced to several of them and then seated at a large table at the corner of the room situated in front of a screen. The soldiers sit on chairs that have been set up several feet behind us. It's clear they will be listening to the presentation, but I wonder why.

Colonel Bailey stands in front of the screen, facing us, and Colonel Nixon sits at the head of the table. In front of each of us is a copy of the

PowerPoint presentation we're to be shown. My ex-husband asks Bailey where the narrative report is. Bailey tells him it's not ready to be distributed. Patrick, who asked weeks ago if he could have the report in advance, is clearly angry that it is still not ready.

Bailey begins his presentation by admitting that he made some errors in his earlier briefings to us. He tells us that Sergeant Greg Baker actually did not get out of the vehicle. In fact, he said, the vehicle never stopped. He said the vehicle came out of the canyon, and Baker saw the Afghan soldier in a prone position, not standing, and, thinking he was the enemy, shot him in the chest eight times. The other soldiers, following the lead of their officer, fired up the ridgeline, killing Pat and wounding Lieutenant David Uthlaut and the radio operator Jade Lane.

This makes absolutely no sense. How could a man in a prone position get shot in the chest eight times? We are astounded by this information, but we let Bailey continue. He tells us that visibility was not as good as he had thought originally. Patrick reminds him that he told us he walked the site of Pat's death at the same time of day Pat was killed and had said light conditions were good. Bailey looks my ex-husband in the eye and tells him the soldiers who were present at the time told him visibility was poor.

We all look around uncomfortably at each other. Something isn't right about this. Bailey doesn't even seem to be the same person. His demeanor has changed completely from the last time we saw him. At my house, he appeared genuinely disturbed by Pat's death, and his briefing, although upsetting and full of unsettling details, seemed to be presented with sincerity. Now he seems haughty, superior, and disingenuous.

He puts an image on the screen of the site where Pat died, which very much upsets Marie. She says under her breath she hates that Pat has been reduced to a PowerPoint presentation. Her face and lips are white, and I worry about her sitting through the whole briefing.

Bailey points out illustrations of vehicles placed where he believes they were positioned during the shooting. The vehicles look like Tonka trucks and are not at all to scale.

"Why do you have drawings of vehicles?" I ask. "Why didn't you position real vehicles there so things could be seen to scale?"

"Ma'am, we didn't have the vehicles. It was too dangerous to use real vehicles."

"How did you get there?" I ask. "Didn't you have a vehicle?"

"I was flown in," he says, and quickly changes the subject.

We are confused about the changes in the story. We don't understand how, two weeks ago, Bailey was so sure that Baker was out of the vehicle, shooting a standing Afghan, and now he's telling us that the shooters drove by without stopping and Bailey shot a prone AMF in the chest. Kevin looks dumbfounded and helpless. These are his superior officers, and he is suspicious that they are lying about his brother's death. My brother asks Bailey how much time had elapsed from the time the AMF was shot to when Pat was killed. Nixon tells Mike they were shot simultaneously. He talks about how chaotic and confusing it was and compares the situation to the opening scene in *Saving Private Ryan*. I look at him in disbelief.

"What about the lull in fire?" Mike says. "Lieutenant Colonel Bailey told us there was a lull. Pat wouldn't come out from behind the rock while they were shooting."

Bailey stares at my brother and says he was mistaken; there was not a lull in fire.

"But you said there was a lull in fire because the soldiers were reloading," I remind him.

"I was mistaken, ma'am," he says, looking at me as if to dare me to dispute his words.

"I still don't understand why they didn't see the purple smoke," Patrick says.

"We thought the smoke was purple, but it was actually white. The soldiers thought the smoke was dust stirred up from bullets hitting the dirt."

Again, we look at each other in disbelief.

"By the way," Bailey says, "I suggested earlier that Pat may have released a flare, but we think it was actually Sergeant Weeks who did that."

"I still don't see how the soldiers could have missed the smoke, no matter what color it was," I say. "I've seen that smoke; it was used at the ceremony during boot camp graduation. It's like theatrical smoke. You can't miss it."

"Yes," Nixon says, "that's what it looks like."

"Well then, how could it have been mistaken for flying dirt?"

Both Bailey and Nixon stare at me. Neither one attempts to respond. I change the subject.

"Why were orders to split the troops coming from Florida?"

"There were no orders given from Florida, ma'am," Bailey tells me in a patronizing tone. I'm beginning to hate being called ma'am. I hear it as an insult.

"When my brother asked you at my house if by CENTCOM you meant the Florida headquarters, you didn't disagree."

"Yes, when I questioned if CENTCOM meant Florida, you remained silent as if to confirm my belief," Mike says.

Bailey, once again, makes use of his steely stare and tells us CENT-COM is in Salerno, in Khost. Mike and I look at each other. We are at a loss as to what to say.

Patrick then tells Bailey and Nixon that Pat did not earn the Silver Star. We are all silent, taken aback by his words. Kevin and Mike look at him, stunned. Marie, jolted by his statement, quietly walks out of the room.

I become furious at his words. I know Pat was heroic. The fact that he was a victim of fratricide and by definition should not get a Silver Star doesn't mean he wasn't brave. I'm angry at the way my ex-husband has worded his statement, as if Pat was to blame.

Colonel Nixon tells Patrick that he has several Silver Stars, and Pat was far more heroic than he had ever been.

"Pat did what any other Ranger would do," Patrick says.

"I think what he means is that you made Pat's Silver Star suspect because you awarded it knowing he may have been killed by friendly fire. That award isn't usually given to victims of fratricide, is it?" I ask.

"Pat was very heroic out there," Nixon says. "He did everything he was supposed to do."

Marie comes back in the room. I don't want her to hear any more of this talk.

"When are families supposed to be informed that their soldier was killed by friendly fire? You were all pretty certain from the beginning that he was killed by his own men," I tell him.

Bailey says, "Ma'am, we suspected he may have been killed by friendly fire, but we wanted to investigate before we said anything and gave the wrong information."

"Colonel, we were given the wrong information," I say angrily. "If the Army knew he was killed by friendly fire, why were we and the media told he was killed by the enemy and that there were nine enemy dead and all that rubbish? The Army could have easily said it was a special ops mission and there was no information available. Why was this fraudulent story given to us and to the press?"

Bailey and Nixon look at each other, and then Bailey eyes the soldiers seated behind us. He asks that someone find the protocol for telling families about suspected fratricide. One of the soldiers jumps out of his seat and strides out of the room.

"Ma'am, we didn't want to give you false information," Bailey says. "No one has deliberately tried to hide anything."

I glance at my family. Everyone looks shell-shocked. The soldier sent to get the information on Army protocol returns. His findings make no sense. First he says families are to be informed within two weeks; next he says something about five weeks. Everyone appears to be lying. I don't know what to believe. Bailey then casually tells us the driver of Baker's vehicle saw the Afghan and recognized him as an Afghan militia soldier before Baker shot and killed him.

We are stunned.

"What! Why didn't he do something?" Patrick yells.

"He tried to stop everyone, but they couldn't hear him because they were deaf from all the firing in the canyon," Bailey tells him.

Patrick's anger mounts. "Why didn't he swerve the vehicle or put on the brakes? The guy is a goddamn Ranger!"

Bailey and Nixon stare at Patrick, not knowing what to say.

My heart breaks as I hear this information. Patrick is right. Why didn't the driver stop the vehicle or swerve out of the way? What kind of Ranger allows his own men to be killed? Kevin is incredulous. He looks as though he is living a nightmare. Mike is clearly having difficulty absorbing what he is hearing. Marie sits silently, overwhelmed by the senselessness of everything. Patrick once again demands to have the written report. Again, someone hustles out of the room.

It's obvious we won't get straight answers from these officers. I decide to ask no more questions, but I have a statement to make: "Colonel Bailey, I want to tell you something that I think is ludicrous. Two weeks after Pat was killed, Colonel Chen, who was at Pat's memorial service, sent two books to my house. One was for Patrick and one was for me. The books were on Ranger training. There was a cover letter that indicated the books were sent so we would know how well trained Rangers are. Well, I thought it was ridiculous such a book was sent to us in the first place, but now that I know Pat was killed by his own men and you all knew it right away, I think sending those books was disgusting."

"Yes, ma'am," Bailey and Nixon say simultaneously.

We ask if there will be a court-martial of the soldiers who killed Pat; they tell us they aren't sure. Nixon says we can call him anytime, as he is taking over command of the 75th Regiment. Bailey has been promoted and will be leaving for a different post. I'm thinking: Pat's dead, killed by his own guys, and now Bailey gets a promotion. Something is wrong.

I want to ask Bailey about his alarming remark to Richard indicating Pat may have been murdered, but I don't want to ask him in front of all these soldiers, certainly not in front of his superior. I also don't want to make things more uncomfortable for Kevin, who's in a delicate position. If something isn't right with what happened to Pat, what can this mean for Kevin?

The soldier who left to check on the written report returns with a stack of documents and passes them out. The packets are warm, fresh off the printer. Bailey walks around the table as Nixon stands up, signaling the end of the meeting. It's as if they want us to get out before we can read anything. We gradually rise from our seats, not sure what to do. The soldiers and officers seated behind us stand, and we start mingling. Some of the men offer their condolences. I feel like I'm going to suffocate.

I walk out of the room and down the hall. Nixon catches up to me. He tells me how sorry he is about what happened and reminds me that I can call if I have questions. He puts out his hand. I shake it, feeling angry, confused, and flustered. I walk outside to wait for everyone else.

We drive home in near silence. We are thoroughly bewildered and exhausted. At home, I try to look at the documents I was given, but I'm gripped with fear, afraid I'll come upon information I'm not ready to see. Hearing pots and pans clanging in the kitchen, I place the documents in my bag and offer to help Marie with dinner. After the meal, we discuss the troubling briefing.

"How could they make a mistake about Baker being out of the vehicle?" Mike asks. "Or whether the Afghan was standing? That just seems like horseshit!"

"Bailey was very clear on those facts each time he told the story of what happened," Kevin says. "I heard his briefing four times. There is something suspicious about this change of story."

I turn to Marie. "Didn't Bailey tell us he walked the site of Pat's death twenty-four hours after he died, and light conditions were good?"

"Yes, that's what he told Kevin and me when he was here, and that's what he said at your house," Marie responds. "He was very clear about that."

"Didn't he also say the smoke was purple?"

"Yes," Marie says.

"What do you think about him saying the Afghan was in a prone position? That must be how he got shot eight times in the chest," Patrick says sarcastically.

"That's ridiculous," I say. "There is something very peculiar about all of this. And what about what Bailey said about the driver seeing the Afghan before Baker shot him?"

"Yes," Mike says, outraged. "How could he realize Baker was shooting at a friendly and not respond more aggressively? Obviously, there could have been more friendlies in the area."

"Baker should have known there could be friendlies nearby," Kevin says. "All the sergeants in our serial knew Serial One was no more than fifteen minutes ahead of us."

"Hell," Mike says, "even if they weren't concerned about accidentally shooting at members of Serial One, you would think they would be saying to themselves, 'Where is Serial One? We need their help right now.' It would seem they would be looking for them."

"These guys are playing us for fools," Patrick says. "We need to go over these documents very carefully."

All of a sudden we are all very quiet. It's getting late, and we need to get to bed. Mike, Patrick, and I have a plane to catch early in the morning, and Marie and Kevin have work.

At four-thirty we are all up. Patrick, Mike, and I see Kevin off to the base and say good-bye to Marie, who has a long commute to Seattle. We eat breakfast rolls and drink coffee, then pack. Patrick and Mike walk out before I do and head to the car. Just as I'm locking the door behind me, I look at the boxes of Pat's belongings in the entryway.

Hesitantly, I return and peek inside the top box. In view are Pat's coffeemaker, two brown Army T-shirts, several boxes of Irish Spring soap, and one running shoe. My throat aches and I feel tears welling as I look at the shoe. Quickly, I grab one of the shirts and a box of soap and place them in my bag. 'I'll tell Marie later,' I say to myself. I hesitantly close the door behind me.

6

No love, no friendship can cross the path of our destiny
without leaving some mark on it forever.

—François Mauriac

Sitting in the backseat of the car, I listen to the drone of Patrick and Mike's voices as we drive north on Interstate 5 to Seattle-Tacoma International Airport. I pull Pat's brown T-shirt from my bag and clutch a section of it in my fist. Resting my forehead on the cool glass of the window, I look out at the SR 509 bridge, the cable-stayed bridge that connects the 5 to downtown Tacoma. Gazing out at the maritime city, I remember the last time I was here with Pat, Kevin, and Marie. We sat talking for hours in Tully's Coffee on the ground level of a quaint triangular building that was once the Hotel Bostwick. The coffee and conversation were pungent and stimulating. A smile forms on my face as I recall how our raucous laughter incited embarrassed giggles and sideways glances from the patrons around us.

The car slows and my purse slides off the seat. I see we have come upon morning commuter traffic. I lean over to pick up my bag and find that my wallet has fallen out. It's open to Pat and Marie's wedding picture. I'm engulfed in sadness as I observe the happiness reflected on their faces. Their eyes radiate joy and contentment that they will be sharing a future together, and their smiles reveal excitement about all the possibilities that future holds. I stare at Marie's lovely face: her large, bright blue eyes, her flawless skin, and her warm, vibrant smile framed by endearing dimples. Her life with Pat was so full of promise: living the military life, feeling good about the service and sacrifice they both made, beginning new careers, having children, good times with family and friends, traveling, building dreams, and enjoying the simple things in life, like conversation over coffee, long walks on windy days, and car rides to unknown destinations.

Marie appears to be very delicate and fragile, but she is remarkably brave and resilient, always carrying herself with grace and dignity. I'm struck by how strong she has been over the last seven weeks and how strong she must continue to be in order to rebuild her life.

Marie Kathleen Ugenti was born on November 20, 1976, two weeks after Pat. The first time I became aware of her, she was four years old. She and Pat played in the same soccer league, against each other. Later, her father coached her younger brother Paul's Little League team at the same time Pat's dad was coaching Richard's team. Marie would attend the games occasionally with her sister Christine or her cousin Gina. I don't recall ever being introduced to her or speaking to her, but I noticed how pretty she was. Pat, on the other hand, was oblivious. Except for a crush he had on blond, curly-top Stacey Landucci in kindergarten, he was more interested in climbing trees and playing sports than in girls. However, when Pat came home from school the first day of his freshman year, 1991, he said, "Mom, there is the most beautiful girl in my biology class, and her name is Marie."

I remember suggesting that he ask her out, but he said, "No, she likes older guys. Besides, she's taller than me."

Several weeks later at a football game, Pat ran up to me before his warm-up as I was walking to the stands. He had his helmet in his hand and an excited look on his face.

"Mom," he said, discreetly pointing, "there she is. That's Marie."

I looked up at the stands. "That's Marie Ugenti," I said with a surprised grin.

"Yes, Mom," he replied, grinning back—and almost hyperventilating— then turned to run back to the field. I walked into the stands and made a point of saying hello and smiling at Marie.

Pat spoke of her frequently, but he didn't ask her out until their senior year, when he was finally taller than she was. Their first date was at the Crow's Nest in Santa Cruz, and a week or so later they went to homecoming together. From then on, they were a couple. Many people said Pat and Marie were the perfect example of opposites attracting, and in some respects that was true. Pat's build was lean and muscular; his face, chiseled and square-jawed; and his eyes, dark, almond-shaped, and intense. He was extroverted, tenacious, athletic, and driven. In contrast, Marie was slender with soft, delicate facial features and enormous, warm, and gentle blue eyes. She was shy, creative, and modestly goal-oriented. These differences may have ignited the spark, but it was their similarities that lent comfort and clarity to the relationship. Both were smart, intellectually curious, quick-witted, and independent, and when it came to each other, they were playful and private. They shared a love of travel, and they appreciated simple joys.

Pat and Marie had been seeing each other less than a month when they were invited to a classmate's eighteenth birthday party at a hotel in downtown San Jose. There was drinking, and Pat and others got unruly and were asked to leave. Pat, Marie, and many of their friends ended up at a local pizza parlor in a small strip mall. As everyone talked, ate pizza, and waited for their alcoholic buzzes to dissipate, one of Pat's friends, Jeff Hechtle, left to get something at a nearby convenience store. As he headed across the parking lot, he was confronted by a group of older guys, who started harassing him, pinning him against a wall. Another friend, Eric Noble, walked outside and recognized that Jeff was in trouble.

Eric ran back inside the pizza place and yelled that Jeff was getting jumped. Pat and his friends bolted out of their seats and ran outside. When the guys surrounding Jeff saw his friends coming, they started to flee. Pat chased one down and beat him up pretty badly, knocking out his front teeth. The police were called, but Pat was not cited that night. Pat gave the young man his phone number and watched as he got into a car with his friends, who drove home to Sacramento.

The following day, Pat's dad took a call from the young man's father, who said his son had a concussion and was in the hospital. When I told Pat, he looked horrified and walked outside. Pat's father had an appointment, and after I saw him off, I looked for Pat and found him sitting in the eucalyptus tree at the side of our house. I told him I needed to talk to him. He climbed down, his eyes red and watery, and sat next to me on the ground. Tears fell down Pat's cheeks as he told me he may have over-reacted in the parking lot. He told me he thought he kneed the guy in the head once he grabbed him and that the guy, who was twenty-two years old, said he was fine. I explained that head injuries can be deceiving; a person can receive a blow and appear fine but hours later have serious symptoms and even die.

My grandmother had left me an inheritance several months earlier. I told Pat we would drive to Sacramento to visit the young man in the hospital to apologize and offer to pay his medical bills. Pat was relieved that we were going to do something proactive. But when we told Pat's father—an attorney—our plan, he felt it was unwise. He said if Pat admitted guilt, we would be setting him up to get charged, and later we could get sued. Reluctantly, Pat and I took his advice and waited to see what would happen. The legal system moved slowly, but eventually Pat was charged with felony assault and several months later pled guilty at his hearing. The judge allowed him to complete his senior year, but the day after graduation, June 19, he turned himself in to juvenile authorities for thirty days. He also was required to fulfill 250 hours of community service. Pat knew he was lucky that he was seventeen.

One of the probation officers at juvenile hall sat me down and told me he knew Pat had a football scholarship waiting for him at Arizona State and would have to report to school in mid-August. He said he feared Pat might not be able to complete his community service obligation on time, as the bus that delivered inmates to their various assignments wasn't reliable. He told me I could pick Pat up each day and take him myself. I was so grateful—not only would it ensure that Pat completed his hours, but it allowed me to spend time with him.

Every morning of his stay in juvenile hall, I packed two coolers, one filled with Pat's breakfast and one with his lunch. I picked him up at seven thirty and took him to the Julian Street Inn, a homeless shelter for mentally ill patients, where he was to work off his hours. Marie was scheduled to leave on a senior girls' trip to Mexico a week or so after Pat went to "jail," which is what we called the detention facility. Before she left, however, she rode with us several times to the work site. I had her duck down in the car in case bringing her was a violation of some rule. Seeing Marie lifted Pat's spirits. About two days before her trip, Pat called me on a pay phone from the facility and asked that I get flowers the color of her eyes. That afternoon I drove to a flower shop and picked out an assortment of blue, violet, and white delphiniums and had them wrapped in tissue paper and tied with a delicate bow. I took the flowers to Marie right away. I will never forget the way she looked when I held them out to her and said, "These are from Pat." Her eyes lit up and a natural blush colored her cheeks. She was delighted but simply said, "Thank you," smiled broadly, and closed the door to appreciate her gift in solitude.

After Marie returned from Mexico, she continued to stow away in my car every other morning or so, alternating with Pat's brothers and friends. I enjoyed her company, and after we dropped off Pat she often came by the house to visit. I took pleasure in chatting with her. With Pat away, I was able to get to know her better and found out myself how witty and smart she was. Pat often told me that Marie was one of the smartest people he had ever met.

After Pat completed his community service and time in custody, the felony charge was reduced to a misdemeanor. Pat didn't like being in custody, but he served his time without much complaint. He later confided that while he was not proud of what he had done, he was proud that he had learned more from that one terrible decision than all the good decisions he ever made.

It was difficult for Pat to miss out on all the fun that summer and being with Marie, his brothers, and his friends. He also nearly missed seeing the visitors that haunted New Almaden while he was away. Maybe it was the lack of winter rains, or maybe the ground grubs and berries were particularly tasty. Whatever the reason, the summer of 1994 was the season of wild boar. Kevin, Richard, Marie, and I were talking in the front room one night when we heard—and felt—what seemed like heavy hooves mingled with grunting and rooting noises. We were all startled. The boys jumped up and put their faces to the window to look out into the darkness. "Can you see what it is?" I asked as Marie and I scurried over. All we could make out were large blurry shapes. Kevin ran to turn off the lights so we could get a better look.

"Holy shit!" Richard said quietly. "It's a bunch of giant pigs!"

Kevin peered out anxiously as Marie giggled nervously.

"Damn! They're wild boar," he said.

The four of us watched in amazement as the giant boars cultivated half of the yard.

"Look at how cute the baby pigs are," Marie said.

"Yeah," Kevin said, "but that dad is the ugliest dude I've ever seen."

"You don't want to mess with these pigs," I said, "especially with the babies around. The males will charge and slash upwards with their tusks."

"The females don't have tusks?" Richard asked.

"No, but they will charge you with their mouths open," I answered. "They can hurt you."

Suddenly, we saw the lights from a car coming up the driveway.

"Dad's home!" Kevin yelped.

Richard ran to the front door to caution his dad about the nocturnal visitors. Patrick got out of the car and obviously heard their presence before Richard could speak up. We watched him walk quietly but briskly across the lawn. The pigs weren't disturbed in the least. They just kept rooting and grunting.

"Hey, my car is parked in front of Peggy and Syd's," Marie laughed. "How am I going to get to my car?"

It was as if the pigs heard her question. Within seconds they gathered together and lumbered down the driveway.

A few days later, I was browsing at a little shop and found a handmade, antique-looking stuffed pig with button eyes. I wrapped it in colorful paper and gave to Marie as a souvenir of the exciting evening, not imagining that the pigs would continue to pay almost nightly visits.

For weeks, boar families frequented our little "hamlet." Kevin, Richard, or their dad would come home at night and announce, "The boars are rooting around in front of the Pelosis' fence" or "The pigs are rototilling the Bairds' yard" or "The suckers are hauling ass down Almaden Road." The boys' friends who came over at night had to wait in their cars for the boars to wander away.

Pat heard all the stories about the boars and was eager to finally see them when he got home. Days passed after his return from juvenile hall, but no pigs appeared. Finally, one night he and Marie were lying on a quilt they had spread on the floor, watching *Lonesome Dove*. Marie jerked her head up at the faint sound of hooves. Pat watched as a delighted smile appeared on her face.

"It's the pigs," she said teasingly.

"No shit!" Pat chuckled. He bounded off the floor and ran to the window. They watched the intruders turn the soil in my excuse-for-a-flower-bed garden, marveling at how such ugly creatures could produce such cute piglets. After many minutes, they settled back down in front of the TV, hearing the snorting and grunting in the background.

After the show ended, Marie had to get home. The pigs, however, were still grazing in the yard. Pat grabbed a baseball bat and walked Marie to her car. They giggled as they moved cautiously across the yard, defying danger, unaware that the pigs could not have cared less. I smiled as I watched their playful innocence, happy to see them together again.

A week before Pat left for Arizona State, I threw a big going-away barbecue. Planning it had kept me sane while he was in jail. Because Pat was headed for Arizona, and because he liked the movie *Tombstone* as well as *Lonesome Dove*, the party had a western theme. We had bales of hay delivered to use as seating and for mounting a target for archery. My friend Nikki McLaughlin and I made headstones with goofy sayings, and we strategically placed them around the yard along with potted cacti. Pat's dad bought a Ping-Pong table and set it up in a prominent place to ensure its use. The boys and their friends, we would soon discover, provided beer they stashed in various bushes. The party officially ended around midnight, but Pat, Kevin, Richard, and their closest friends sat around the barbecue chatting until the sun came up.

Several days later, along with my husband, Marie, Richard, and his lifelong friend, Collin Berger, I flew to Arizona to escort Pat to Arizona State to report for practice. Kevin couldn't go with us because of his high school football practice schedule.

Pat had been to Tempe on a recruiting trip, but this was the first time for his dad and me. The weather had been cool during Pat's earlier visit, but when we arrived, it was about 110 degrees, and the area looked like a moonscape. We were pleasantly surprised when we saw Arizona State's beautiful campus. I kept thinking, "If only it weren't so hot."

We arrived at the football offices and were shown around the facilities. That's when we learned that Pat's dorm wouldn't be ready for three or four days, and we decided to stay with him until he could move in. We had time to kill, so I suggested we drive to Tombstone in our rented car, since the kids enjoyed the movie so much. They weren't wild about the idea and let that be known, but I kept telling them it would be interesting. I don't think my husband really cared to go, either. Looking back, I realize he was being a good sport.

The six of us piled into the Lincoln Town Car and headed south. After two hours of driving one of the most boring stretches of highway on the planet, I could feel the kids' dirty looks burning a hole in the back of my head; we were only halfway there. Once we arrived, I thought they would be so fascinated with the place that I would be forgiven. Wrong. I was subjected to sighs, rolling eyes, and sulky expressions. Even Marie and Collin were openly mean-mugging me. My husband, feeling a bit sorry for me, pretended he was having fun. After an hour or so of reluctant sightseeing, we had a mediocre meal, which gave the kids an opportunity to send sarcastic one-liners about misery my direction. At that point it seemed they were starting to have fun, but I should have had better sense than to think that was how they wanted to spend their time. Pat had been in juvenile hall most of the summer; he and Marie just wanted to spend time alone before we had to leave. Richard and Collin wanted to hang out at the hotel pool and eat at the burger joint down the street, and my husband wanted to relax in an air-conditioned room. I offered no more brilliant ideas the rest of the trip.

Pat's room was ready two days later. We shopped for some items he needed, had lunch in downtown Tempe, and took Pat to his dorm. Then it was time to catch our plane to San Jose. It was so difficult to leave him. Pat was the one who tended to get homesick. I had to remind Kevin and Richard that they lived at our house; they could have moved in with any number of their friends indefinitely and just paid visits to us when the mood struck. But Pat was only content away from home for short periods of time, and now he was moving to a place where he knew no one. We said our good-byes to Pat, then walked away so he and Marie could part in private.

Everyone tried to keep from crying. We could see how sad Pat was to watch all of us leave, but it was gut-wrenching seeing how painful it was for him to part from Marie. On the way to the airport, Richard, Marie, Collin, and I cried silently to ourselves. Pat's dad drove with a heavy heart.

Pat battled homesickness for several weeks, but as football got under way and classes started, he began to settle in. Marie was able to visit him several times before her classes began at UC Santa Barbara, which made all the difference for both of them. Throughout Pat's years at Arizona State, Marie attended nearly every home game. During the off-season, Pat would travel to Santa Barbara as often as he could to take part in Marie's world. Once they graduated from college, Marie moved to Chandler, Arizona, to live with Pat.

It was actually a pretty stressful time for both of them. Pat had been newly drafted to the Arizona Cardinals, and Marie was having trouble adjusting to Arizona. Not only was the weather hard to take, but she missed her friends and family and also was having a hard time finding a job in her field of biology. She considered going to graduate school, but the best programs were at the University of Arizona in Tucson, about an hour and a half away, and she didn't want that commute several days a week. She decided to take a computer graphics course and got a job at the *Arizona Republic*. After that, she started to adjust to Arizona.

During the off-season of 2000, Pat and Marie traveled to Europe for five weeks. They took the train, backpacked, and stayed in hostels in Germany, Italy, France, England, and Ireland. The last two weeks of the trip, they met up with Marie's sister and her husband, Alex. The four of them spent time in Paris, London, Dublin, and County Derry in Northern Ireland, where Pat's paternal grandmother had been born. Pat was training for a marathon, and he enjoyed running in the quaint cities and towns he and Marie visited. When Alex and Christine joined them, Pat and Alex ran the streets of London and Ireland's country roads.

They had a wonderful time. Several photographs of their trip stand out in my mind: Marie and Christine doing a little dance on a road in the Irish countryside; Pat and Alex drinking a beer at the Guinness brewery; Pat and Marie smiling into the camera, deliriously happy, as they ride a bus through London; Pat walking into the North Sea.

Pat thoroughly loved the trip. He was fascinated with the history and various cultures. He was impressed by the food, the beauty of the different landscapes, and the hospitality of the people. He kept telling me I had to go to Europe and visit Ireland. He said he'd pay my way when I was ready to go. He raved about the cozy pubs and inviting teahouses. No one appreciated a good cup of tea more than Pat.

Before the 2001 football season started, Pat and Marie moved to Los Gatos, about ten miles from New Almaden. They rented a little apartment within walking distance of the picturesque town. Marie's sister was expecting her first baby, and Marie wanted to be close by. While they were living in Los Gatos, Pat took Marie on a drive to the coast, to the Crow's Nest, where they went on their first date. It was there that he presented her with a ring encased in a tiny wooden chest and asked her to marry him.

Because of football, Pat had to return to Arizona before Alex and Christine's baby was born. The evening after Ryan's birth, many of Marie's relatives were in Christine's hospital room admiring the baby. Suddenly there was a commotion in the hallway; the door burst open and Pat charged in, yelling, "Every day's Sunday, baby!" He had caught a plane right after practice in order to see the new baby, Marie's godchild. He flew out the next morning to be at practice on time.

September 11, 2001, had a profound impact on our family. I was aware that Pat and Kevin were especially disturbed by what happened. They talked about it a lot, but Pat was beginning another football season, and Kevin was preparing for surgery on his shoulder in hopes of healing before his baseball season with the Cleveland Indians farm team began. We all got on with our lives, but in the ensuing months, the September 11 attacks were never far from our thoughts and often a topic of discussion when we were together or talked on the phone. However, we were also preparing for the wedding, an event we looked forward to with joy.

Pat and Marie's wedding day was set for May 4, 2002, at the Ruby Hills Country Club in Pleasanton, about forty miles northeast of San Jose. By February, I was still unsure about where to hold the rehearsal dinner. Pat's father and I had separated six years earlier, and by this time we had divorced. I called him to get his thoughts on where he wanted to hold the dinner, and he gave me several ideas. Then I called Pat to run them by him.

"Ma, I would like the rehearsal dinner to be at your house."

"My house? Are you sure, Pat? My house and yard are awfully small."

"I liked the party you had for me when I left for college," he said. "Remember the bales of hay and the barbecue?"

"Of course I remember," I said with a smile. "We can have something like that, but I think it should be a bit more elegant."

"I don't really want it to be elegant, Mom—and I can pay for it."

"No, Pat. Your dad and I want to pay for this. If you want the dinner to be at the house, then that's where it will be."

"Good. Thanks, Ma."

I planned the dinner for Thursday, May 2, two days before the wedding, so things wouldn't get too hectic. In the preceding months, I made several arrangements: with a caterer who would bring his giant barbecue and cook up tri-tip and chicken; with the ranch down the road to order bales of hay; with a catering company that would provide linen table-cloths; and with the New Almaden Community Center to rent tables. I arranged for one close friend to pick up the wine and beer and asked other close friends to prepare side dishes.

The house was a whirlwind of activity the Monday before the rehearsal dinner. Pat, Kevin, and Richard were all home. Their friends were in and out, and everyone was running around picking up tuxes and gifts for the best men and ushers, buying new shoes, and getting hair-cuts. That evening we had some time to ourselves, and we sat around talking. Everyone was excited about the next several days.

Tuesday morning, Richard went outside to cut the grass and came right back, saying there was a terrible smell coming from the side of the house. Pat went out with him to see what the problem was. I assumed a raccoon had died or something. When he and Rich walked back in the house, they did not look happy.

"Mom," Pat said as calmly as he could, "the septic tank has burst."

"What?" I asked stunned, hoping I had heard him wrong.

"The septic tank is leaking into the side yard," Richard said.

"Are you kidding me?" Kevin yelled, almost laughing, as he came into the room.

"That's just great," I groaned. I was ready to panic. I knew I needed to call someone, but I became paralyzed as I saw dollar signs floating before my eyes.

"Pat," I said, nearly dropping the phone book, "I don't know how I'm going to pay for this."

"Don't worry, Mom, I'll pay for it," he said reassuringly. "We don't have time to worry about the money right now, anyway. We have to get the damn thing fixed."

With that, I called a septic tank maintenance company. The man who answered said he could have someone out the next day. That was Wednesday, the day the boys and I had planned to drive to Carmel to visit my cousin David and his wife, Louise, along with my aunts Lannie and Katie and Katie's husband, Tom, who had flown across the country for the wedding. David thought it would be fun for us to get together at his home before the chaos of the wedding events. My sons hadn't seen my aunts since the boys were small, and I was excited for them to meet as adults.

We decided that Kevin and Richard would drive to Carmel, and Pat and I would stay home to supervise the septic tank crew. The septic tank was a dilemma, and the whole situation was complicated by the fact that no one in the crew spoke English. Pat had to keep running into the house to call the supervisor and ask him to translate. Pat also helped the crew dig. In the end, I ended up with a temporary septic tank, which we were told would be good for five years. That was fine. All I wanted was assurance that it would hold out until after the rehearsal dinner. The crew left, and Pat and I cleaned up the yard. Fortunately, all the digging had been done in the side area, so my lawn wasn't touched.

Days before, I had borrowed little white lights from Peggy and Syd to hang on the hedges for the dinner and placed them in my shed. Thursday morning we woke up to find Syd arranging the lights where I'd planned to put them. Kevin and Richard went out to help him, then they went with Pat in Syd's truck to pick up the tables at the community center. Richard came up with the configuration for the tables, and when the hay was delivered, he placed the bales around them. Pat realized a lot of guests would have to park down the road because our driveway wasn't big enough. As he stared at the hay Richard was arranging, it occurred to him that it would be fun and convenient for guests to have a hayride transport them from their cars to the house. Syd graciously offered use of his truck, and Pat and Richard hurled three bales of hay into its bed.

We placed inexpensive quilts over the hay so it wouldn't be scratchy for people to sit on. Later in the morning, I picked up the white tablecloths I had rented and then met my ex-husband's girlfriend, Mary, at the flower shop to pick out assorted wildflowers for the tables.

Before long, the evening was upon us. Members of the wedding party started to arrive, and Pat's dad and Mary pulled up the driveway behind Pat and Marie. Pat got out of the car to start his hayride shuttle. He picked up guests at the end of the road and drove them to the bottom of the tree-lined, whimsically primitive brick stairway leading to my house. Laughter, the hum of conversation, and the scent of mesquite filled the air. As I stood on the front stoop and looked out at the lawn, I was taken with how pleasing everything was. The tables, covered with simple white cloths and wildflowers cascading out of mismatched vases, looked dreamy contrasted with the brightly patterned quilts covering the hay bales that surrounded them. The tiny white lights twinkling in the dusk made the scene appear enchanted. The simplicity and naturalness of the evening seemed to mirror the simplicity and sincerity of Pat and Marie's relationship.

I watched Pat closely that night. I was struck by how happy he was. He thoroughly enjoyed everyone and everything, and in his exuberance, he was more content than I'd ever seen him. Thinking back, after months of research and discussions with Marie and Kevin, Pat must have felt such a sense of relief at finally having made the decision to join the military. He was comfortable with his choice, and he was looking forward to sharing this new phase of his life with Marie and Kevin.

After the meal, everyone gathered around Pat while he presented each of his best men—Richard and Kevin—and his ushers with an axe. Pat always had been intrigued with the lore and superstition surrounding the axe. Axes symbolized thunderbolts and were used to guard buildings against lightning, as it was believed lightning never struck twice. A thrown axe was believed to ward off hailstorms, and when placed in crops with the cutting edge to the skies, it would protect the crops. Pat told me the axe was once the tool of everyman. It is used in forestry, carpentry, combat, and sport. The head of each axe was engraved with the recipient's name and the inscription:

Pat and Marie
May 4, 2002

Friday morning, we cleaned the yard, and then I packed for my mother and me and we left for the hotel in Pleasanton. The whole point of getting there early was to relax before the next day's festivities. But when I arrived at the hotel, I realized I had a flat tire. I checked my mom into our room, then spent the next several hours getting my tire fixed. By early evening, Pat, Kevin, Rich, Mike, and most of the ushers had arrived at the hotel. Mom went to sleep early, and I stayed up to write cards to Pat and Marie, hoping to express what I felt in my heart.

In the morning, Pat came to my room. He said he had a bit of a stomachache. Maybe he had eaten something that didn't agree with him, maybe he had a bit too much to drink the night before, or maybe it was just a case of nerves. He lay down on the bed for a while and talked to Mom and me. Before he left, I handed him a card I had written.

"Thank you, Mom," he said as he gave me a gentle hug.

I watched Pat walk down the hall, heading back to his room. Just before he got to the doors that led to the elevator, he turned around, smiled, and waved with a giant stroke that appeared to be in slow motion. I smiled and waved back, then slowly shut the door as he disappeared from sight.

Mom and I visited with friends and family by the pool for a little while, then went to get ready. I helped bathe and dress my mother, whose Parkinson's disease sometimes got in the way of her mobility. But she certainly didn't appear to have Parkinson's once she was dressed for the wedding. The cut of her muted gold dress gave her the appearance of height and had a slimming effect. Peggy had hemmed Mom's dress and surprised her by making her a darling little purse with the same fabric. With her hair done and just a touch of mascara and rose color on her cheeks, Mom looked beautiful. As a girl, with her dark hair, exotic eye shape, and tiny stature, my mother looked very Asian. Since there were no Asian children at Saint Francis de Sales Catholic School in Newark, Ohio, during the 1930s, my mother was chosen to play a Japanese doll in a school play. As she stood in front of the full-length mirror, I looked at her admiringly. Tears formed in her eyes when I said, "Mom, you look just like a Japanese doll."

Once I was dressed, my aunts and Tom drove Mom and me to the country club where the wedding was to take place. As we drove up the winding driveway, the spectacular setting came into view. Vineyard-covered mountains bordered a villa-style clubhouse surrounded by a rolling green golf course. My aunts took Mom to find her a place to sit. I approached the main foyer of the clubhouse and saw Pat, his father, Kevin, and Richard standing on the steps. They all looked so handsome. I had my picture taken with Pat, then went to the dressing room to see Marie. She was breathtakingly lovely, serene, and confident. Before I left, I gave her the note I had written to her the night before. She read it, then thanked me with her radiant smile.

In the area where the reception would be held, the atmosphere was that of understated elegance. Surrounding the dance floor were round tables draped in white linen and adorned with centerpieces of wine and burgundy hydrangeas.

Everyone was gathering on the garden patio for the ceremony. Chairs were set up on either side of an aisle strewn with deep red rose petals. As I stood appreciating the landscape beyond the patio, Pat's paternal grandmother, Mary Tillman, walked up and gave me a hug. She looked so happy and proud. I complimented her on her tailored blue suit, and she chuckled and blushed. I have always delighted in the fact that even Mary's laugh seems to have an Irish inflection. Richard and Kevin then came over to tell us the ceremony was about to begin.

The grandmothers were escorted to their seats first. Richard took my arm and walked me to mine. I sat looking out at the majestic view as Pat and Judge Kevin Murphy took their places for the ceremony. When the music began to play, everyone turned to watch the ushers and bridesmaids walk down the aisle. Richard and Kevin followed, escorting Christine. The guests giggled as the three-year-old flower girls—Pat's goddaughter, Alex Hechtle, and my goddaughter, Meg Tillman—walked down the aisle determinedly scattering petals from their delicate baskets. Meg smiled sweetly at the rows of onlooking grown-ups as she conscientiously slowed her pace to wait for Alex, who sauntered mischievously several paces behind.

As the French doors opened, the guests stood to watch Marie and her father emerge through the archway and walk down the aisle. Marie was beaming as she gracefully approached Pat, who stood with pride. He smiled as he watched his lovely bride move toward him and take her position by his side. A soft breeze lifted Marie's veil, and it fluttered around her head. Pat gently caught it and held it tenderly against her small waist.

I'm suddenly aware that the car is slowing down and the light inside has dimmed. Looking up, I see we are entering the airport's car-rental garage. I glance again at Pat and Marie's picture, then slowly close my wallet. I take Pat's T-shirt and rub it lightly against my cheek before placing it carefully in my bag.

7

Anyone can become angry. That is easy. But to be angry with the right person, to the right degree, at the right time, for the right purpose, and in the right way ... that is not easy.

—ARISTOTLE

Patrick, Mike, and I return the rental car and pick up our tickets for the flight home. Mike and I are traveling together; Patrick is scheduled to fly earlier on a different airline. The three of us have coffee at Starbucks before we part. Patrick looks drained and tired as he leaves to catch his flight. At the souvenir shop, I buy bottled water and Mike gets a book. Onboard the plane we sit in near silence until we are in the air. Then Mike puts on his glasses, takes out a Patricia Cornwell novel, and begins to read. I stare out the window at the billowing cloud formations. I wonder what it must be like to parachute through the floating vapor.

Several years earlier, Patrick had taken the boys and me to the nearby community of Morgan Hill to go skydiving, but I decided not to participate. Pat and Kevin at nineteen and eighteen were old enough to take the course, but Richard was fifteen, so Patrick signed paperwork stating he was older. I was sick to my stomach about all of them jumping out of an airplane, but I was especially concerned about Richard.

"There are age restrictions for a reason," I said. Patrick assured me Richard would be fine, as he would get training and jump with two "spotters," who would stay with him until his chute opened. For several hours, I watched Pat and the boys go through the training. At several points, I felt inclined to go, too, but each time I chickened out.

After Patrick and the boys were deemed ready to go, they suited up and were escorted to the plane. Richard was supposed to go with his dad on the second trip, but he wanted to go with his brothers, so Patrick and two other student divers and their spotters waited for the next turn.

I was given directions to a field where I could watch them make their descent. I stood there, palms sweaty, waiting with one other observer for the plane to fly overhead. We heard the hum of the engine before the plane appeared. As it came into view, I saw three figures dive from the plane. The first jumper and his spotters fell together until the jumper's parachute opened. A few seconds later, the parachute of the spotters opened, and the next jumper and his spotters descended. Once their chutes released, another set bounded out of the plane. As the first jumpers came closer to earth, I could tell from the color of their suits that it was Pat and Kevin.

While they floated toward the ground, I kept my eye on the third set of divers, who were still in a freefall and rapidly approaching Kevin and his spotters' position. I could tell that Richard was the jumper. I was petrified. His chute wasn't opening; I felt helpless. Suddenly, the ripcord was pulled and he began to drift gently down. Richard was in his freefall so long that he ended up landing before Pat did. All three boys touched down safely. They wrapped up their chutes and walked the two hundred meters to where I was waiting. They wore huge smiles, and their eyes were as big as saucers.

"What the hell happened up there, Rich?" Pat asked.

"Yeah," Kevin said.

Richard laughed nervously. "I forgot to pull the ripcord."

I closed my eyes, breathed deeply, and told myself not to come unglued.

"Holy shit, Rich!" Pat and Kevin bellowed at the same time.

"You're damn lucky it wasn't too late to open the thing or you'd be a grease spot on the ground," Kevin added.

"I know," Rich said. "It was just so awesome up there, I zoned out."

I must have gone pale because Pat gently touched my arm and said with a grin, "Mom, Rich's chute would have opened automatically after so many feet."

After I mockingly smacked the three of them, Pat and Kevin walked over to their spotters and thanked them for their help. Rich and I jokingly thanked his spotters for saving his life, and then the four of us waited for the plane to return with the next round of skydivers. Kevin yelled as the plane came into view. We watched several sets of jumpers leap from the plane. Once the chutes opened, Rich announced that the second jumper was Dad. We watched him glide through the sky and land solidly on the ground. The boys ran over to him and helped him gather his parachute. The four of them were exuberant about their adventure, and they yammered excitedly all the way home.

I'm sure that experience somewhat prepared Pat and Kevin for jump school in the Rangers. But I recall vividly that Pat had his father, brothers, Marie, and me in hysterics during our first visit with him and Kevin at Fort Benning, Georgia, as he recounted his first several jumps. For some reason, the harness he wore tugged tightly once his parachute opened, painfully pinching his private parts. He said he howled in agony the whole way down, gyrating in vain as he tried to readjust himself while his noncommissioned officer, or NCO, hollered at him through a megaphone, "Put your feet together!" If Pat hadn't been positioned properly when he hit the ground, he could have injured himself badly.

That visit to Fort Benning in late October of 2002, after the boys' boot camp graduation, was so much fun. Marie hadn't seen Pat and Kevin for eight weeks, and the rest of us hadn't seen them for nearly four months. We spent our first afternoon together laughing in a motel room in Columbus, Georgia, listening to stories of their boot camp experience. We had dinner in a little Italian restaurant with a wonderful throwback atmosphere and bold Chianti. The next morning, we ate a hearty Southern breakfast at a little café in downtown Columbus, then leisurely chatted as we strolled in and out of antique stores and walked the promenade that runs along the banks of the Chattahoochee River.

We didn't see Pat and Kevin again until a month later, when they got an early Thanksgiving leave from the Ranger Indoctrination Program (RIP). I once again had a few bales of hay delivered to the house, and we had our turkey feast outside in the autumn sunshine among the fallen leaves. I was sad when they had to leave, but they both assured me they would be home for Christmas.

A month later, Marie picked Pat and Kevin up at the San Jose Airport. I can still hear the honking horn as Pat barreled up the driveway. He and Kevin bounded out of the car, both of them wearing crazy Christmas sweaters they had picked up in the women's department at Target. Marie got out of the car laughing, her eyes sparkling and her nose and cheeks rosy from the crisp, cold December air. Pat and Kevin ran immediately to Peggy and Syd, who stood on their front porch to greet them. Rich arrived that evening after driving up from Los Angeles. We had a wonderful holiday. The boys and Marie spent time shuttling from my house, to the home of Marie's parents, to Alex and Christine's, and to their dad's place. There was decorating, gift giving, eating and drinking, laughing, and playing lots of rounds of Trivial Pursuit. But during that time, we also spent hours discussing Iraq.

It was widely reported that Bush wanted to invade that country, and it appeared he was looking for any excuse to do so. We all knew Saddam

Hussein was a brutal dictator, but we also knew there was no connection between him and Osama bin Laden or the terrorist attacks, despite the administration's efforts to convince the American people otherwise. Bin Laden was a militant fundamentalist, and Saddam was a secular leader, and for that reason bin Laden hated Saddam and considered him a traitor to Islam. It didn't make sense that they would ever work together on anything, and it shocked me that more than 70 percent of the American people believed Bush and Dick Cheney. In addition, if the administration knew the location of Saddam Hussein's weapons of mass destruction, as claimed, why not tell international weapons inspector Hans Blix and his team in Iraq where to find them?

We discussed many of the books we had been reading—*Bush at War,* by Bob Woodward; *9-11,* by Noam Chomsky; and *Bin Laden: Behind the Mask of the Terrorist,* by Adam Robinson. We were all trying to understand the reasons for 9-11 and our government's response to it.

During the month of November, Marie and her parents looked for a house in the Tacoma area, near Fort Lewis, where Pat and Kevin would be stationed after Ranger School. Marie and her mother found the perfect house situated on a knoll overlooking the Tacoma Narrows and the Olympia Mountains. From the photographs Marie showed me, I knew Pat would love it. The little house was cottagelike, with a fireplace, wooden floors, a basement, and a welcoming Dutch door in the back. A few days before the New Year, Pat and Marie packed their Volvo with Christmas presents before setting out for Tacoma. Kevin had intended to go with them, but he came down with a bad case of the flu and ended up driving up with his father a few days later.

Pat was a bit sad to leave home. His eyes welled up with tears as he hugged me good-bye. He told me he hated to leave home—the little cabin, he called it. Marie and I glanced at each other and smiled. We knew once he saw the home she had found for them, he would be just fine. The next morning the phone rang. I read Pat and Marie's new number on the caller ID.

"Hello," I said coyly.

"Mom! This place is fucking awesome! Marie did a great job. We can look out over the water and see the mountains, and the place has wooden floors and a fireplace."

We talked for a few minutes, then I spoke to Marie, who was more thrilled than ever with her lucky discovery. I hung up the phone delighted, knowing Pat was in a "little cabin" of his own.

The plane suddenly hits turbulence. I glance over at Mike and notice he has just tucked his book in the pocket behind the seat in front of him.

"Bad book?" I ask.

"No," Mike says rather uncomfortably.

"Isn't Patricia Cornwell's main character a forensic pathologist? Seems like the book should be interesting."

"Yes, but this is a bit more graphic than I expected."

"What's it about?"

"Oh, it's not worth talking about."

I look at him quizzically.

"Well, okay," he says reluctantly. "The plot centers around the University of Tennessee's Decay Research Facility, which is used in the study of forensic anthropology. You know, the study of the decomposition of human bodies."

I instantly comprehend Mike's uneasiness. But I'm struck by the fact I'm not repulsed by the topic; rather, it seems Pat's death has made me curious about it. In fact, I've found I'm strangely comforted talking about the dead.

The flight attendant asks for our drink preferences. Mike orders a coffee, and I order a Bloody Mary. As I dig around in my purse for the money,

Mike decides to continue reading and settles back with his book. I pay the flight attendant, pull down my tray table, and then take my copy of the 15-6¹ report from my bag and place it on the tray. I sit for many minutes staring at the first page, dated May 28, 2004, more than two weeks ago.

Memorandum For
Commander, _____,
Afghanistan APO AE 09354
Commander, U.S. Army Special Operations
Command, Fort Bragg, North Carolina 28310
Commander, Special Operations Command Central,
MacDill AFB, Florida 33621-5101

SUBJECT: Report of Fratricide Investigation

My eyes scan the next few lines and focus on the last paragraph: "All requests concerning the report made pursuant to the Freedom of Information Act and/or Privacy Act should be Forwarded to USCENTCOM, attention FOIA² officer."

It is signed by John F. Sutter for John P. Abizaid, general, U.S. Army. I wonder if it's typical that all requests for documents be forwarded to CENTCOM. I turn the page and begin to go through the 110 pages of narratives and question-and-answer statements taken from the soldiers who were present when Pat was killed. The documents are redacted, meaning names, places, and sensitive information are blacked out. However, I'm able to identify some of the soldiers based on information I learned at both briefings and in conversations I've had with Kevin.

As I read through the first several pages, Colonel Jeffrey Bailey's shock-

---

1 An administrative investigative procedure implemented to find out what has occurred in military situations that are under question, which can determine if a criminal investigation should take place.
2 Freedom of Information Act

ing statement plays in my head: The driver recognized the Afghan as an allied soldier, and he saw friendlies on the ridgeline before Sergeant Greg Baker shot and killed him. I again wonder why he couldn't prevent Baker and the others in the vehicle from shooting at their fellow soldiers. I begin searching for the driver's statement. I come upon several lines in a narrative that read, "I screamed 'no' and then yelled repeatedly several times to cease fire. No one heard me." My stomach is churning. This has to be the driver, Sergeant Kellett Sayre. I start the narrative from the beginning, and then I come upon the disturbing testimony that confirms it's him.

> As soon as we had enough room we went around the Jinga truck. Immediately after that, about 200 meters, we rounded a corner where I saw the [vehicles] from the first convoy. (I was the driver the entire time.) I looked to my right and saw one pax[3] with an AK-47 which confused me for a split second, but I also saw the rest of section one on top of the ridgeline. I yelled twice "we have friendlies on top." They (GMV[4] crew) must have not heard me because my GMV opened fire on them (section one on the ridgeline). I screamed "no" and then yelled repeatedly several times to cease fire. No one heard me. By that time, I believe everybody was deaf from all the gun fire that had been shot off. Finally, they stopped after a few bursts on the .50 cal. After that, things started calming down and security perimeter was established. Nothing follows.

"Nothing follows?" That's all he has to say after the men in his vehicle kill two of their own and wound two others? He seems to have no disgust at himself for not doing more to stop them or outrage at the men who were shooting. I look over at Mike to vent my frustration, but he has

---

3 Paktia militia fighter
4 Ground mobility vehicle (sometimes called a Humvee)

dozed off. Peering momentarily out the window, I take a deep breath. How could Sayre recognize the Afghan soldier, the vehicles parked down the road, and the friendlies on the ridgeline, but the others could not?

Rage burns in my throat. I think back to when Colonel Bailey came to my house and told us that Sergeant Baker was out of the vehicle when he shot the Afghan and that the vehicle had stopped. What if that story was true? Why couldn't the soldiers see that they were firing on a friendly position? The platoon had been with the Afghan Militia Force soldiers for several weeks. Their uniforms, according to Kevin, were very similar to the ones the U.S. soldiers were wearing. If the Afghan was indeed standing, as Bailey said at first, why didn't Baker recognize him? And if he was prone, as Bailey now contended, how could he get shot in the chest? He would have had to have been a contortionist. I think of Pat, frantically yelling and signaling his presence. He had such distinctive body language; he was big compared to most Rangers and certainly bigger than the enemy. He was wearing an obvious U.S. uniform, and he was carrying a SAW[5] gun. Even at 100 to 150 meters, he would have been hard to miss.

How can we make sense out of all this? I lean my elbows on the tray table and rest my head in my hands.

"Dannie," Mike says groggily as he raises his seat, "are you all right?"

"No," I reply. "Mike, I'm really concerned. I think Bailey and Nixon lied to us, and I'm having trouble believing Pat could not be seen. Maybe they couldn't tell it was Pat, but they had to see it was an American soldier, I don't care if he was one hundred or more meters away."

"I think you're right," Mike says. "I believe they lied, too. I also think Pat was a lot closer than what they're saying. Put the report away for now. I'll go over it with you after we have our drinks."

---

5 Squad automatic weapon

One of the flight attendants hands us a pack of pretzels, and the other serves our drinks. I stick the pretzels in my purse, then pour the vodka and Bloody Mary mix into the plastic cup. Mike and I sip our drinks quietly. When we finish, we each take out our copies of the report. I have Mike read Sayre's statement.

When he finishes, he looks up in disgust, expressing the same concerns I have. "Why didn't he do more to stop the shooting? And why is he the only one who sees the friendlies?"

"I don't know," I say, shaking my head. As I thumb through the pages, I come upon a statement I know is Private Bryan O'Neal's, the young soldier positioned just feet away from Pat when he was killed. My hands start to tremble as I scan the narrative. I'm gripped with anxiety at what I am about to read and close the pages. I look out the window in order to gather myself, and then I open to O'Neal's statement again. Stumbling over the redactions, I read about Pat and O'Neal's actions prior to Baker's vehicle coming out of the canyon, and the fateful shots that took Pat's life.

While on route to our objective,——and I talked about Ranger School and how beautiful the country was when we hear an explosion. We called for——to stop, but he didn't hear us. So we kept moving [from] about 10 to 15 meters before stopping. After we stopped——and——pulled security while I moved out with SPC Tillman who was in the Hilux[6] behind us. We first moved through and up the village linking up with—— squad led by——. We received no contact in the village so we moved out, splitting up——— team who linked up with——from SPC Tillman and I. SPC Tillman and I moved up some sort of ridgeline then down into a draw where we link up with an AMF guy. We secured some lower here we could put some fire down on a high ridge area where we

---

6 Toyota 4 × 4 pickup trucks outfitted for military use.

saw some movement of what looked like to be enemy pax. SPC Tillman was forward and to the right of me at this time when I moved down to him behind the same rock. He then (Tillman) told me he was going to link up with [illegible] to find out what was the plan. So I moved into his position to lay down some fire for him while he moved out. At this time I was controlling the AMF guy on where to fire because he wanted to move out. But he lost focus of the ridge to our front [from] some action from the ridgeline to our right side shooting across the road. It took SPC Tillman a few moments to return back to our position with a plan of action, and when he moved down to my position on the side of the rock he took a hold of the top, laying down fire on the ridge. Not long after did a friendly cargo/GMV come down the road toward our direction. When they made eye contact with us, they opened fire with small arms. They rolled through very quickly. After they came, a GMV with a .50-cal rolled into our sight and started to unload on top of us. They would work in bursts, .50-cal for 10-15 seconds, 240B 10-15 seconds (back and forth) for a few minutes. SPC Tillman and I were yelling stop . . . stop . . . friendlies . . . friendlies . . . cease fire!" But they couldn't hear us. Tillman came up with the idea to let a smoke grenade go. This stopped the friendly contact for a few moments and that's when I realized that the AMF soldier was dead. At this time, the GMV rolled into a better position to fire on us. We thought the battle was over so we were relieved, getting up stretching out and talking with one another when I heard some 5.56 rounds[7] coming from the GMV. They started firing again. After only a few 5.56 rounds the .50 cal started fire again. That's when I hit the deck and started praying. SPC Tillman at this time was hit with some small

---

7 This caliber of round would have been shot from a SAW (squad automatic weapon).

arms fire. I know this because I could hear the pain in his voice as he called out "cease fire, friendlies, I am Pat fucking Tillman damn it." He said this over and over until he stopped. Not long after the firing stopped the GMV moved out. I was lying next to the original rock I used for cover when I heard what sounded like water pouring down . . . I then looked over at my side to see a river of blood coming down [from] where he was. I had blood all over my shoulder from him and when I looked at him, I saw his head was gone.

My eyes fill with tears and I feel trapped in my seat as I'm overwhelmed with nausea. I close the pages and lean back in my seat as tears fall down my cheeks.

"Dannie," Mike says not lifting his head from the documents in front of him. "Have you read O'Neal's responses to the questions?"

"What?" I ask numbly.

"Did you read O'Neal's responses to the questions he was given?"

I'm afraid to speak, afraid I'll be sick. Mike looks over at me and sees I'm upset.

"What's wrong? What did you find?"

"I read O'Neal's statement, page seventy-one," I say, barely audibly.

Mike opens to O'Neal's narrative. When he finishes, he leans back in his seat and remains silent for many minutes.

"Dannie, remember how Nixon said there was no lull in fire, that the vehicle shot continuously down the ridgeline?"

"Yes," I respond.

"Well, on page seventy-three, O'Neal is asked, 'How did CPL Tillman get killed?' and O'Neal says: 'He was yelling "cease fire" to the GMV that was shooting at us. He got up and left his position to throw a smoke grenade. Once the smoke grenade was thrown, the firing briefly stopped. We both stood up, and then the firing resumed again.' Dannie, O'Neal is saying there was a lull in fire."

I sit up in my seat. "Bailey told us there was a lull in fire when he came to the house. He said they stopped to reload. Mike, we need to go through these statements carefully to see if any other soldiers testify there was a lull in fire. If there was, then why couldn't Sayre stop them?"

"Good point. Another thing: Remember a few minutes ago I said I believe Pat was a lot closer to the shooters than they're saying?"

"Yes, why do you think that?"

"In part it's a gut feeling," Mike says. "But I don't think Pat would be yelling his name so desperately if he was that far away. I think Pat was shocked they weren't seen. Even O'Neal makes reference to the guys in the vehicle making eye contact with them."

"I know, that remark stood out to me, too," I say. "The thing that is odd about his statement, though, is that he indicates there was a cargo GMV that passed their position before Baker's vehicle came along. No one has mentioned a vehicle passing by the position before Baker's."

"If another vehicle did pass by the position and went by safely, then that would make Baker's vehicle look even more negligent. As it is, they admit they weren't aware of being fired upon other than the Afghan firing over their heads."

"Mike, do you think the jinga truck driver had anything to do with the ambush? I know Bailey said he didn't. What do you think?"

"I don't know. At this point, I just don't trust what they're telling us. Did you see anything yet about the note that was given to the platoon while they were in Magarah? Remember? Bailey told us about it at your house."

"Yeah, I remember him telling us that, but I haven't seen anything yet."

Mike and I pore over the statements together and find another one where a soldier indicates there was a break in fire: "What I thought was mortar fire from Tillman's position was the smoke he popped off which slowed down the fire." Another statement says Baker's vehicle stopped after exiting the canyon. As we read, I become frustrated by the redactions. It is very difficult trying to figure out who is talking and who they are talking about. Pat's name is the only name not blacked out.

We come upon a document of questions and responses. The responses are from the SAW gunner in Baker's vehicle. Kevin told me his name is Trevor Alders. One question asks, "Why did you fire at waving arms?" He replies, "I saw the arms waving, but I didn't think that they were trying to signal cease fire."

"What!" I gasp. "He saw waving arms and he just kept firing. Isn't it against the rules of engagement to shoot at the enemy if he's waving his hands?"

'Yes," Mike answers. "This is insane."

Several questions down it reads, "At this point in time, were you taking enemy fires?" Alders answers, "I couldn't tell. Others were firing and I wanted to stay in the firefight."

"Jesus!" Mike says. "They weren't even taking fire. This guy didn't even know what he was firing at; he just wanted to shoot."

Mike and I are getting increasingly angry, but we continue to search the documents. We find a statement by the XO,[8] whom Kevin identified as Captain Kirby Dennis, who testified, "The Commander wanted the platoon leader [to] have 'boots on the ground' by daybreak to clear the Manah village per the Battalion's tasking." Others testified that the commander wanted the platoon in the village by dusk.

"Why all this confusion with dusk and daybreak?" I ask. "It makes no sense that platoon leader Uthlaut believed he had to be in Manah by dusk. Why didn't he clarify the time of day? I don't understand why the orders were so confused. I wish I knew who the commander was."

"Doesn't Kevin know?" Mike asks.

"No. He has asked other soldiers, but none of them knows who the commander was in Khost."

---

8 Executive officer

Mike looks back at the document. "Look at this," he says. "Captain . . . what's his name again?"

"Captain Dennis."

"Captain Dennis is asked, 'What's the policy on —— movements?' There are indications in the documents that he is referring to daylight movements. Dennis answers, 'I didn't know that there's a direct prohibition against them. It was my understanding that the battalion commander strongly discouraged them and that they were to be avoided whenever possible.'"

"Sounds like Bailey didn't want the troops to move during the daylight or dusk hours," I say. "Why would the commander in Khost go against that policy? Why was there such a sense of urgency for this mission?"

"Dannie, I don't know who this is—it might still be Dennis—but he says the company commander gave the order to split the troops and he thinks that order came from the S-3,[9] who I believe is the head commander, yet this guy implies the S-3 had no idea the troops were split."

I remember listening to my father's Civil War lessons about the danger of splitting troops. The splitting of Pat's platoon resulted in the chaos and confusion that led to the devastating outcome of April 22. Who is going to be held accountable for that irresponsible order?

"Oh look, Mike. On page forty-four, this is the S-3. He says, 'I did not know the platoon was split into sections. I first found out during the AAR [after-action review] process that followed the incident. I did not order the splitting of the platoon. My only comment to the company commander was, 'This vehicle problem better not delay us anymore.' How could he not know the troops were split! And I don't understand why they didn't blow up that damn vehicle or just leave it behind. That's what all the soldiers wanted to do."

9 A battalion commander's principal staff officer concerning operations and plans.

Mike, reading ahead of me, says, "Uthlaut apparently requested fire support, but it was denied."

"Fire support?"

"Air support, I believe," Mike says.

"It was denied? I thought all Special Forces missions had air support."

Mike, disgusted, replies, "Not this one."

"In looking at these documents, I can see that the ambush was frightening and a bit confusing in the canyon, but there was no carnage. The vehicles even came out unscathed. Why was the reaction of Baker and his men so hysterical? No one was even shooting at them once they exited the canyon."

"I don't know, Dannie. And it makes no sense that Baker wasn't looking for the first serial. Didn't Bailey tell us that Uthlaut informed his squad leaders that Serial One would be taking the canyon route?"

"Yes, and Kevin said he heard his platoon sergeant tell Baker and the other squad leaders the plan. Plus, everyone saw Serial One enter the canyon ahead of them."

"Where the hell was his situational awareness? These Rangers are trained to go back to help each other," Mike says, his anger rising. "Baker should have known to control his fire team."

"Baker was Kevin's squad leader in Iraq. He and Pat both observed him to be pretty competent. I can't understand how he could have been so incompetent that day."

"Do we know who the company commander was?" Mike asks.

"I believe Kevin said it was Captain [William] Saunders. Marie worked with Saunders's wife in Seattle."

"Okay, so it's the S-3 we can't identify?" Mike asks.

"Yes. Kevin said he would try to find out."

Mike and I are both exhausted after looking at the report. We put the documents away and lean back in our seats. I close my eyes and go back to thinking about Iraq and how worried I was when Pat and Kevin were there. This was a war Pat and Kevin did not enlist to fight and one that everyone in our immediate family considered illegal. Before departing for the Middle East, Kevin and Pat could not tell us when they were leaving, and because they were with a special operations unit, once they were there, they couldn't communicate with us at all. I knew there was going to be an invasion, and I was very worried. I was mistaken on this count.

The American invasion began March 20, 2003. In the early stages, the Marines were getting hit hard. My heart was breaking for the families of those Marines. I was on edge all the time. Kevin told me later that being in Iraq was difficult for Pat. While he and his brother were usually separated on mission, Kevin recalled a time when they had been in the same armored vehicle. As it moved down the street, Pat saw a frightened old man and a child, maybe his grandson, standing against a chain-link fence. There was a look of terror in the old man's eyes. Pat yelled in Arabic over the roar of the vehicle: "We will not harm you!" He felt so awful for the man and child.

Because I was unable to write to Pat and Kevin while they were gone, I started writing to them in a composition book that I would give them when they returned. It comforted me to do so, even though I couldn't share the thoughts at that time. My sons had departed sometime in late February or early March, and by early May, I felt as though they had been gone for years.

Mother's Day that year fell on May 11. I invited my mother to stay with me that weekend. On Saturday, she and I were talking when I noticed a red flag on my e-mail. I checked to see who had written and found this wonderful message, now embedded in my memory, sent from a base in Saudi Arabia.

From: Pat Tillman<*pattillman@comcast.net*>
Date: Sat. 10 May 2003 18:23:27-0400
Subject: Mother's Day

Happy Mother's Day Ma!!!!! Unfortunately we must apologize for our absence on this glorious occasion, however, know that
we are thinking of you and cannot wait to get home. Marie sent
some pictures from her trip back home, which reminded us just
how bad we miss you and your little cabin. All is well and please
spend today reflecting on all the positives of the past and [the]
bright future that lays ahead as opposed to worrying about us.
We love you, Ma . . . Happy Mother's Day!!!!
Pat & Kevin

I'm startled as the flight attendant asks me for my trash. I wipe tears
from my cheeks and hand her my plastic cup. Mike and I put our tray
tables up, and I look out the window as we begin our gradual descent into
San Jose. Staring down on the tops of trees, building rooftops, and commuter traffic, I think about Pat and his honorable and loving character
and also about the contradictions in the two briefings. I am angry and
confused by the conflicting stories. It will take a lot of concentration and
time to carefully read each word of testimony. I know less about what
happened to Pat today than I did the day he was killed.

Colonel Bailey and Colonel Nixon told us two different stories, one
that Bailey told us when he first came to the house, and another later.

8

*Those we have held in our arms for a little while, we hold
in our hearts forever.*

—Anonymous

Mike and I return to my house from the airport. He relaxes for a while and then heads home to Fremont. After I unpack, I pour myself a cup of coffee and sit on the front stoop. The sun is shining through the leaves of the surrounding trees, illuminating their many shades of green. The sky is clear and the air is warm and pleasant. It's a beautiful June afternoon, so much like the day, nearly two months ago, when I learned Pat was never coming home.

Thursday, April 22, I had been at school early, around five thirty a.m. I had a parent meeting scheduled for seven thirty, and I wanted to make sure my lessons for the day were organized in case the meeting went longer than expected. I remember walking from the office back to my classroom looking at the mountains and thinking, "What a gorgeous and peaceful day."

At two forty-five I had another parent meeting. It ended about four. I walked across the street to my car feeling vaguely light-headed, but the sensation passed. When I pulled into the driveway and saw Peggy sitting on her porch, I sat and chatted with her for about fifteen minutes and then walked to my house. As I went through the front door, I was immediately conscious of how tired I felt, as if all energy had left my body, much like air being released from a balloon.

I started to walk toward my bedroom so I could change into more comfortable clothes when I noticed a message on my answering machine. It had been left about an hour earlier, at three thirty. It was from Richard. He sounded agitated and said he needed to talk. I dialed his number right away, but he didn't answer. I took the phone off the cradle and carried it with me to my room while I changed. I had every intention of sitting down and grading some vocabulary tests, but I felt so exhausted that I got into bed and pulled up the covers, clutching the phone in my hand.

Before I fell asleep, I remember wondering why I was so drained. It wasn't like me. I must have been asleep for a couple of hours when the phone rang. I looked to see if it was Richard, but it wasn't; it was my mom. Because I felt so tired, I let the call go to my message machine and laid my head down again, but after a few minutes, since I was awake, I called her back. She told me Alex, Pat's brother-in-law, had the operator interrupt her phone conversation with my aunt. She said he was looking for Mike. I still felt disoriented and wasn't sure I was processing what she was saying to me.

"What do you mean he interrupted a phone call?" I asked, my voice groggy.

"An emergency interruption—you know, Dan—by the operator. Alex said he needed to talk to Mike. He sounded weird. I asked him if Pat and Kevin were all right."

My chest froze. "Of course they're all right, Mom," I said curtly. But something didn't feel right. I was suddenly queasy as I got quickly out of bed.

"Alex left a number, Dannie," Mom said.

I hurriedly jotted it down. "That sounds like Alex's number, Mom. Thank you. I'll call him now. I'll talk to you soon."

My heart was racing as I hung up. I walked to the front room and looked quickly at my address book to make sure the number Mom gave me belonged to Alex. I dialed it nervously, my stomach turning. Alex answered right away.

"Hello."

"Hi, Alex," I said trying to sound calm. "My mom said you called her . . . "

"Dannie," he said abruptly, "call Marie at home." He hung up.

Fear churned my insides. I started pacing the floor, trying to talk myself out of thinking the worst. It disturbed me that Alex told me to call Marie at home. It was a little before seven p.m. Marie was rarely home before seven thirty or eight. I paced the floor for several minutes. Finally, I dialed Marie and Pat's home number.

Marie answered. "Hello."

I was so relieved. Her voice sounded like it always did. Instantly, I relaxed.

"Hi, Marie. It's Dannie. Alex said to call you. What's up?"

There was no response.

"Marie," I said softly, "what is it? Is something wrong?"

No response.

Desperate fear gripped me, and I felt I was engulfed in a haze.

"Marie! What is it?! What's wrong?!"

"He's dead," she said numbly.

"Dead! Who's dead?!" I screamed.

"Pat's dead."

I felt as if a giant fist plunged into my stomach and hollowed me out, producing a sound I had never heard before; it was guttural, primitive, the sound of an animal. Holding the phone out in front of me, I rushed out my front door, running away from the words. I screamed for Peggy as I stumbled across my yard, falling out of my shoes. At some point my legs gave way and I began to fall. Everything around me was a blur, but I was faintly aware of a figure dropping in front of me to grab me as I went down.

"My baby! My baby! My baby's dead! Oh, my God! Pat's dead!"

Through tear-filled eyes and a fog of shock and disbelief, I realized

Syd was holding me. Peggy walked up behind him, and I handed her the phone.

Someone in the distance, from a neighboring house, was yelling, "What's wrong? Are you okay?"

My body heaved as I cried on Syd's shoulder.

"It's okay," he said gently through his own tears. "Let it out. Cry. Let it out."

From the corner of my eye, I saw Peggy standing in my driveway talking on the phone. She was crying, and she looked as though her knees were going to buckle. It struck me that I must get hold of myself. Marie needs me to be strong. Kevin and Richard need me to be strong. Kevin! Where is Kevin?

With Syd's help, I pulled myself up. Peggy ended the call with Marie. She walked over to me, grief distorting her face. I looked at her questioningly and asked, "Kevin?" Peggy said Marie hadn't heard from him yet. She was still waiting.

I was crying again. Peggy was holding me close when we heard the sound of a car coming up the driveway. It was Alex. He must have left his house the minute I got off the phone with him. He looked pale, and his eyes were red-rimmed. He leaned over and hugged me and apologized for the abrupt way he had gotten off the phone. At that moment, we heard another car slowly approaching. It parked between the Melbournes' house and mine. A young female soldier, looking confused and flustered, got out of the car. Syd and Alex held me steady as I waited for her to put on her dress jacket. She was visibly nervous and fumbled getting it on. Finally, she approached me, her soft, black eyes reflecting compassion and discomfort.

In the doorway, the soldier spoke hesitantly.

"Ma'am," she said solemnly, "I'm sorry to inform you . . . "

"It's all right," I said listlessly through a cloud of tears. "I already know." I turned slowly and walked across the yard, picking up my shoes before walking through the door. Alex, Peggy, Syd, and the young soldier walked respectfully behind me.

Once in the doorway, the soldier spoke hesitantly, "Ma'am, I'm sorry, it is my obligation to inform you officially."

I turned to face her, and both of us choked back tears as she fulfilled her duty. She told me Pat was shot in the head getting out of a vehicle. She said he died an hour later in a field hospital. "Did he suffer?" I asked, afraid of what I would hear. The young woman looked at me stunned, not sure what to say.

"He didn't suffer, Dannie," Alex said gently, in an effort to comfort me and aid the young soldier. "He was shot in the head. He wouldn't have been aware of anything."

"Where is Kevin?" I asked as I broke down crying again. "Is Kevin all right?"

She told me Kevin was safe and that he was with his brother when he was killed. I looked at Peggy and saw the horror on her face. I could feel my face contort at the thought of Kevin seeing his brother killed.

"When can I talk to Kevin? Where is he?" I pleaded gently.

The young soldier looked at me helplessly. "I don't know," she replied.

"Dannie," Alex said, tenderly touching my shoulder, "all she has is a casualty report. She doesn't have much information about anything else."

"Pat's dad has to be told," I said to the soldier. "Has he been told yet?"

"No, I don't think so. We have had trouble finding him," she said.

My eyes scan Alex, Peggy, and Syd. "I have to call Patrick."

I walked unsteadily to the phone and dialed Patrick's cell number. He answered quickly.

"Hello." I could tell by his voice he knew nothing.

"Patrick," I said firmly.

"Dan," he said in his usual ironic tone.

"Patrick." I hesitated. "Patrick, Pat's dead. He has been shot in the head."

I was trying to tell him without getting hysterical, but as the words left my mouth they sounded so abrupt, so stunning. I thought I could feel Patrick's shock, and I wanted to take the words back and tell him differently. I should have just asked him to come over, but that would have made him suspicious. He would have forced me to tell him anyway. To my bewilderment, he responded as though I were delusional.

"What? Where did you hear that?" he asked calmly. I tried to tell him when he cut me off. "Dan, I'll be right over."

I hung up, and I looked up at Alex through swollen eyes. "He's coming over right away."

"Is he all right?" Alex asked.

"Yes," I said. "I don't think he believes me."

I sat on the couch with the soldier and Alex while Peggy and Syd went to their house to call my brother and closest friends. I told Alex I was worried about Richard. He was in Los Angeles. There was no way I could give him this news over the phone. I told Alex about Richard's phone message and how he sounded distressed.

"When did he leave the message?" Alex asked.

"At three thirty."

"Well, he couldn't have known then, but it concerns me that this will be on the wire soon."

"I know," I said, staring ahead dazed, terrified of how Richard would be affected by his brother's death. He had been so distraught when Pat and Kevin enlisted, although he had tried so hard over the course of their service to think positively and be supportive. Tears streamed down my face again. The first Christmas after Pat and Kevin enlisted, Kevin had presented Richard with a journal he'd kept of their experiences in boot camp. Pat had written the foreword, and then Kevin had filled the black, leather-bound book with narrative, descriptions, illustrations, and commentary. The journal was so heartfelt and so full of acknowledgments to the people in Kevin's life who meant the most to him that for a while I'd felt a frightening sense of foreboding for him.

Alex and I finished our conversation as the young soldier next to us listened helplessly. After about twenty minutes, Patrick came up the driveway. Alex stood and watched from the window as he walked toward the house. I could see he was perplexed by the cars outside, but I also could tell he hadn't believed what I told him. However, when he entered the house and saw the soldier sitting with me on the couch, his eyes turned wild with horror and shock. Alex and the soldier left the house so we could be alone. Patrick fell to his knees in front of me, crying loudly at first, then softly into my lap. It broke my heart to see his pain. I gently stroked his head, but I was so numb, I had no words of comfort.

After long minutes, Patrick raised his head and gradually composed himself. The soldier came back in with Alex and told Pat's dad what she had told me. He, too, was worried about Kevin and wanted to know where he was and when we could talk to him. Alex explained that no one was sure when we would hear from Kevin, but he assured him Kevin was all right—physically, anyway.

I told Patrick about Richard's message, and he wondered if our son already knew when he made the phone call. I told him I didn't think he did—his voice sounded agitated, not frantic or hysterical—and I didn't want him to be told over the phone or hear about it from the news.

"Now that Marie and you and I know, this is going to go public very soon," Patrick said. "I'm going to fly down there now to tell him. We won't get a flight out of LA because it will be too late, but I'll bring him home as soon as I can."

"Thank you," I said, unable to adequately express my gratitude. "Will you be all right? You're in shock and you're tired."

"I'll be fine," he said. "I just hope I get to Richard in time."

"Be careful," I said, not even wanting to consider he would get to Richard too late. I gave Patrick a hug and watched him get into his car and back out the driveway. I will be forever grateful for his act of love for Richard, and for Pat.

It occurred to me to call Richard's friend Michelle. I would tell her about Pat's death and ask her to try to keep Richard away from the television and computer until his dad arrived. I called her cell several times, but she didn't answer; finally, I left a message asking her to call me back.

I don't recall seeing the soldier leave. She must have driven away when I was talking to Patrick about Richard. What a sobering and difficult job for someone so young. I was certain Alex had seen her off and had expressed gratitude on my behalf.

Alex told me Peggy and Syd were having a difficult time reaching Mike. He wasn't answering his cell phone, and they were having trouble getting connected to his department at United Airlines. Alex went next door to see if he could help.

My face was numb from crying. I walked around the house in a stupor for several minutes, not knowing what to do. I suddenly realized I had to tell my mom. How could I tell her that her grandson was dead? I feared telling her over the phone, but I didn't know what else to do. I picked up the phone and dialed; I got the answering machine. I waited about five minutes, then tried again. This time she picked up, but her voice was barely audible.

"Mom," I said, trying not to cry.

"Dannie, what's going on? Did you reach Alex? Is everything all right?"

"Mom," I said, my voice shaking.

"What's wrong, Dannie?" she asked uneasily.

"Pat's been killed, Mom."

"Oh, God!" she gasped. "Dannie, I had a feeling that's why Alex called. I had a feeling."

"Mom, are you all right?"

"Oh, Dannie. My God, our Pat!"

"I know, Mom," I said, holding back sobs. "Mom, I'll make sure someone picks you up and brings you to my house as soon as I can arrange it. Peggy is trying to reach Mike right now, and he will probably come straight to my house. Can you have a neighbor come sit with you until I can send someone to get you?"

"Yes, I'll call Jerry and Ron across the street," she said anxiously.

Pat and me just before going on a walk, 1977.

Pat at 6 ½ months.

Pat in the tree in his grandma's front yard, 1986.

Kevin, Pat, and Richard, foolin' around for their dad, 1984.

Richard, Kevin, me, and Pat on our front stoop, 1983. Kevin and Pat have their light sabers. *Star Wars* characters and superheroes the boys drew are hanging on the door.

Pat and Marie during their college years.

Pat doing a handstand on our roof, summer 1995.

Pat and me before the start of the ASU/UofA game, 1997.

Patrick, Richard, Pat, me, Mike, and my mom at Richard's high school graduation at the Rose Garden, 1999.

Pat, Kevin in the center, and Richard at the Arizona Cardinals/San Francisco 49ers game, October 2000.

Pat the evening of his rehearsal dinner, May 2, 2002. Pat gave people hayrides from their cars to the house.

Richard, Pat, and Kevin on Pat's wedding day, 2002.

Pat and his father, Patrick, the day of Pat's wedding, May 4, 2002.

"All right. Mom, I'm sorry to tell you over the phone, but I don't know when this will be on the news. I would hate for you to learn that way."

"I'm fine, Dannie. I'll call Jerry and Ron right now."

As I hung up the phone, Alex ran in from Peggy and Syd's.

"Dannie," he said, "Peggy reached the right department at United, but the person who answered said they have no Mike Spalding working there."

I looked at Alex, perplexed. "Mike has worked there for more than ten years . . . Oh, wait. Mike goes by Stephen at work. Have her ask for Stephen Spalding."

Alex turned and ran next door. As I stood in the doorway staring dully at the sky, I realized I would have to call work to let my principal know what happened. As I searched my list of faculty phone numbers, I thought about how supportive he had been since Pat and Kevin enlisted. I had worked with Don McCloskey for nearly two years. Before he entered education, he had been in the Air Force and served during the first Gulf War. When Pat and Kevin joined the Army, a friend and co-worker, Marsha Walker, already had a son in the Marines. Don's time in the military gave him great empathy for what we were going through. After Pat and Kevin were deployed to Iraq, Don would occasionally walk down to my classroom to chat, ask about them, and see how I was doing. I dialed Don's home number, but the answering machine picked up. Not wanting to leave a message, I decided to call Marsha and ask her to try to contact Don. It was painful to tell her about Pat's death. She was stunned and so saddened. She told me she would make certain Don was told.

Alex returned to tell me that Peggy talked to Mike; he was on his way. Mike has always been devoted to his nephews. The news of Pat and Kevin's decision to enlist troubled him deeply, and he worried about Richard in their absence. He had confided in me just days earlier that he was very distressed that he didn't get to say good-bye to the boys before they left for Afghanistan. He thought he would have time to call them, but then he learned they had already been deployed. I remember he said, "I'll just have to stop feeling bad about not talking to them. I'll have to put that out of my mind and think positive thoughts about them coming back and telling stories about what they saw and did." What must be going through Mike's mind now?

Meanwhile, Alex began intercepting phone calls from friends, family, reporters, and the military. He tried to keep them short. We wanted to keep the line open; Kevin might try to call from Afghanistan.

I heard a car come up the driveway. I looked out the opened door and saw my friend Sherri Greer. I had been holding myself together fairly well, but when I saw Sherri, I broke down in her arms. Sherri had been my assistant—an indispensable one—during my first year of teaching at Bret Harte. The following year, she ended up getting a different job at Leland High School, but we remained close. Once Sherri and I stopped crying, we went into the family room. Sherri stayed with me while I sat, exhausted and silent, waiting for Mike.

From the couch, I could hear the sound of Mike's truck coming up the driveway, and I saw the headlights as he pulled in behind Alex's car. I saw his shadowy form walk rapidly across the lawn, and I heard him as he stepped through the front door. Through leaden eyelids and swollen eyes, I watched him as he walked toward me, his arms open.

"Pat's dead, Mike," I cried quietly.

"I know," he said as he held me tight.

Mike held me quietly for a few minutes, then he sat down and I explained what happened. I told him that Pat was shot in the head and died in a field hospital an hour later. Mike clenched his jaw, and moisture clouded his green eyes. I told him we didn't know where Kevin was; we only knew he was safe. I told him Kevin was with Pat when he was killed. Mike stared solemnly at the floor. After a moment, he asked where Patrick was, and I told him he had gone to Los Angeles to tell Richard. Again, I related Richard's message to me earlier in the day. Mike looked at me soberly and said, "I hope he can get there in time. I hate to think of Rich learning this on the news."

I stared vacantly out the window, not wanting to think about it. Mike told me that he called our mom on his way to my house. She told him Patrick's mother called, and one of Patrick's brothers was picking her up to take her to my mother-in-law's house; Patrick had called his mother and told her what had happened. I was so relieved to know that Mom was not going to be alone in her house.

The phone had been ringing almost continuously for three or four hours. Each time it rang, I hoped it was Kevin. A call came in at about nine p.m. Alex walked to the step leading to the family room holding the ringing phone. He scanned the caller ID, then he looked at me, eyes filled with dread. "It's Richard."

"Oh, no!" I gasped. "I can't talk to him. He'll know something's wrong." I looked to Mike.

I could see the tension in Mike's jaw as he took the phone from Alex.

"Hello," Mike said, trying to sound as normal as possible.

"Hello," I heard Richard respond loudly. "Who's this? Is that you, Uncle Mike?"

Mike looked me in the eye and mouthed, "He's been drinking."

I watched Mike's expression, looking for a sign that would tell what Richard knew. Mike listened for a few seconds and shook his head to indicate Richard didn't know anything. I was so relieved. It concerned me that Richard had been drinking, but under the circumstances, it was probably good. I continued to listen to Mike's end of the conversation. I could tell Richard was puzzled as to why Mike was at my house and not at work. Mike told him he took the whole day off to repair shingles for me. Richard was aware that I had been having trouble with my roof during the spring rains, so he accepted that story, but he didn't understand why I wasn't home. Mike told him I had gone to the store, but Richard thought it was odd that I was at the store so late.

"Well," Mike said, "I've been slaving on the roof all day, and I'm hungry. Your mom didn't have any food in the house, so I think she went to Safeway. It's open twenty-four hours."

Richard didn't question that explanation. He and Mike talked a little longer, then Mike hung up. I could see he was devastated about lying to Richard, and I felt horrible for placing him in that position, but I didn't know what else to do. By this time, several of Pat's closest friends, Tony Doran and Jason Haase, arrived to give support. All of us sat vigil by the phone, waiting to hear from Kevin and hoping to learn that Patrick had gotten to Richard in time.

Richard's friend Michelle called after ten p.m. I told her gently that Pat had been killed. It took her long seconds to speak. She had never met Pat or Kevin, but she did get to speak to them on the phone before they were deployed. Michelle knew how close the three of them had always been, and I could sense her compassion and concern for Richard. She told me she would go to his apartment right away.

The phone rang again within minutes; it was Patrick. He said he'd been waiting at Richard's apartment when Richard and his roommate, Eric, had arrived a half hour earlier. He said he had rented a car, and they would soon leave for home. I spoke to Richard for a few seconds. He was in shock, and the pain in his voice devastated me. There was nothing I could do but remind him that I loved him. The phone was still in my hand when Michelle called to ask if it would be intruding for her to fly here the next day. I told her I welcomed her and that I believed Richard would benefit from her presence.

We were all relieved and grateful that Richard and Patrick were on their way home. Sherri sat quietly by my side on the couch while I clutched a framed picture of Pat and Marie to my chest. I stared dully out of the window. It was very dark, but the glow from the porch provided enough light that I could see Alex, Tony, Jason, Mike, and several other figures as they stood talking in the shadows of the yard. I couldn't hear what they were saying, but the hum of their voices put me into a trance. I shuddered when the phone, silent for more than an hour, started to ring again. I don't remember who answered it; I just remember someone called to me gently, "Dannie, it's Kevin."

My chest froze. I had to remind myself to breathe. I placed the photograph on the table and quickly got up. I could feel blood rushing to my arms and legs and my heart pounding. Trembling, I took the phone.

"Kevin!" I said, my voice shaking.

"Mom! Mom!" Kevin said, his voice breaking. "I'm so sorry."

Tears pooled in my eyes, then spilled down my cheeks as I heard the raw pain in his voice. "Kevin, it's not your fault," I said gently.

"Mom, I haven't left Pat's side since we got here to the hospital."

My whole being ached for Kevin, and my body wanted to convulse into sobs. It was clear his thoughts and emotions were in chaos; shock held him together and allowed him to speak. I willed myself not to break down. "I know, Kevin. I know you have been there for him. Who is there with you?"

"There are guys here with me, Mom. There are guys here with me. I am okay. I'm here with Till, Mom. I'm here with Till."

"I'm so grateful you're with Pat, Kevin," I said, my throat burning with anguish and worry. "When are you and Pat coming home?"

"I don't know, Mom. It's too dangerous to fly us out now."

I was seized with panic. "What do you mean, Kevin?" I wanted to scream and the tears poured faster.

"I don't know, Mom. That's what I've been told."

"Just get home as soon as you can," I said, my voice trembling. "I love you, Kevin."

"I love you too, Mom," he said, struggling for composure. "Are Rich and Dad all right?"

"Yes, Kevin. Dad flew to LA to tell Rich in person. They are on their way home." I looked over at my brother and saw the worry on his face. "Kevin, can you talk to Uncle Mike?"

"Yes, Mom—for just a minute," he said.

"Good-bye, Kevin." I was terrified to let him go.

"Good-bye, Mom. I'll see you soon."

I handed the phone to Mike and sat in a chair while Mike spoke with

Kevin. When the conversation ended, Mike placed the phone down and looked me straight in the eye and said firmly, "He'll be all right, Dannie."

I stood up, feeling emotionally and physically depleted. My head throbbed from loss of tears, and my eyes felt like swollen, burning slashes. I walked aimlessly down the hall to my bedroom and closed the door. I lay in bed conscious of the concerned and worried whispers of my brother and friends until, at some point, I fell into a tormented form of sleep.

The roosters crowed around four thirty a.m. I opened my dry eyes, and immediately my heart began to race. For an instant, I hoped I had been having a terrible nightmare, but reality quickly pushed away that hope. I got out of bed and stumbled to the bathroom to wash my face. I looked in the guest room to see if Richard had come home while I was asleep, but it was Mike who was under the covers. In the front of the house I found Sherri asleep on the living room couch; Tony and Jason were sleeping on the floor of the family room. Alex had gone home to be with his young family.

I quietly sat down on the chair. I heard the whine of an engine and looked out the window. A strange car pulled into the driveway. I walked outside and saw Patrick get out of the rental car. I could see Richard's face through the passenger window.

Now I look out at my front yard. Tears obscure the place where Patrick parked the rental car two months ago. In my mind's eye, I watch Richard slowly open the door and get out. His face is drawn, and his dark, almond-shaped eyes, so like his big brother's, are red and swollen. He looks tenderly down at me from his six-foot frame, holding his arms wide. In his hands are the journal Kevin had given him, a small double frame with pictures of his brothers, and the inscribed axe Pat presented him for being a best man at his wedding.

I slowly approach him as he envelops me in his arms and cries softly into my shoulder.

9

We'll be friends until forever, just you wait and see.

—WINNIE THE POOH, A. A. MILNE

I've been home from Washington barely a week, and I'm packing my bags to leave for Birmingham, Alabama, to visit my dad's youngest sister, Katie. Katie is only eleven years older than I am, so she's more like a sophisticated older sister than an aunt. Katie came to be with me as soon as she heard about Pat's death. Before she went home, she told me she wanted me to visit her and her family as soon as school got out, and she wrote me a check to cover the cost. She said it would be good for me to get away. It's difficult to find joy in anything with Pat gone, but I thought it would be healthy for me to be around people in a different setting.

That was before I learned about the fratricide. Now, as I pack my clothes, I'm feeling uneasy about leaving. I've been looking at the 15-6 report and have found many disturbing contradictions. I want to investigate further, but it'll have to wait until I get back from Alabama. Maybe a little break from the report will be good for me anyway.

As I go through my closet looking for a light summer dress, I find the pink one I wore to Pat's memorial service. The sight of it brings back a flood of memories. Feeling suddenly drained, I sit on the edge of my bed.

Gently rubbing the linen between my fingers, I recall the anxious days leading up to Kevin's return home with Pat's body.

Patrick had flown to Los Angeles and driven all the way back in just over ten hours, then returned the rental; he'd had no time to process what had happened. Now there was nothing to divert him from the reality of his loss. He looked totally exhausted, and his eyes looked despondent. He said he was going to go home to shower and rest before coming back with his girlfriend. I hugged him and thanked him again for telling Richard in person and driving him home. He hugged me back, but I could tell by the vacant look he gave me that he was consumed by his own thoughts.

Mike, Sherri, and Pat's friends Jason and Tony were still asleep in the house, so Richard and I sat on the front stoop and talked quietly. He was still holding the journal and pictures of his brothers; the axe rested against his leg. We sat silently for a short time. Richard's tired, bloodshot eyes stared out at the trees; his face was drawn and his eyelids were puffy.

"Mom," he said quietly, "I knew something happened. I knew it when I woke up yesterday. I knew something had happened to Pat or Kevin." His eyes were rimming with tears, and when he finally blinked, they spilled over.

"Is that why you called me yesterday?" I asked gently as I stroked his arm.

"Yes. Something wasn't right," he said, choking back sobs. "I was upset all day, then I called to talk to you, but you weren't home from work yet. Eric came home and saw that I was upset. I told him I had a bad feeling about Pat and Kevin. He tried to reassure me, but I was still worried. After a while he asked me if I wanted to go get a drink, so we went to a bar. I called you from the bar, and Uncle Mike answered." He turned to face me and asked earnestly, "Did Mike already know, Mom?"

"Yes," I said wiping my eyes. "We didn't want to tell you over the phone, so I asked Mike not to say anything. We wanted you to hear from your dad. We wanted him to be there with you. I'm sorry. Mike felt terrible about not telling you the truth."

"It's all right. I wouldn't have wanted to be told over the phone," he said, looking at me with his soft, sad eyes. "Mom, when Eric and I walked back to the apartment, Dad was standing outside." He looked down and his tears fell onto the cement. "The second I saw Dad, I knew. I just didn't know which one." Tears ran down my face and I leaned my head on his shoulder as I continued to stroke his arm.

"I could feel the anger building in me, Mom. I yelled, 'What the fuck are you doing here?' I wanted to run away. Dad and Eric somehow got me into the apartment, and Dad told me that it was Pat, it was Pat who was killed." He could barely get the words out. "I tore the apartment apart; Dad and Eric couldn't stop me. When I finally calmed down, I grabbed my journal, the pictures, and my axe, and we left." I leaned my head against Richard's shoulder until neither one of us had any more tears to cry.

It didn't take long for the phone to begin ringing. Fortunately, Sherri and Mike were able to answer it while I drove to school to drop off some books. I wanted to get there and leave before anyone could see me.

Not long after I returned home, Alex arrived. I asked if he had talked to Marie again. He said that he had; she was being very strong, and her parents and sister Christine were with her. He told me Christine was having a rough time. She was devastated for Marie, but in addition, Pat and Christine had developed a great respect and appreciation for one another. Pat had spoken very highly of Christine, and it saddened me to know how hard she was taking his death and to realize how difficult it would be for her in the months to come, trying to support her sister while caring for two little boys, Ryan and Adam. Three-year-old Ryan was Pat's first nephew. Pat enjoyed being an uncle and took pride in the fact that Ryan was so intelligent. Adam, barely a year old, was Pat's godson. Pat only got to see Adam a few times, but I remember him telling me with a big grin that he thought Adam looked a lot like Marie.

I tried several times to call Marie that morning, but I couldn't get through. Richard could see I was very anxious, and he asked if I wanted to go for a walk around the Pretty Road. "The Pretty Road," I said with a smile. "I would like that."

The "Pretty Road" is the endearing name Pat and Kevin had given Bertram Road when they were three and two. Richard was at least seven before he knew it as anything else. Bertram runs along the opposite side of Los Alamitos Creek, parallel to our road. It has a storybook quality—narrow, winding, and canopied by trees. It also has light traffic. When the boys were little, we would go for wagon rides on Bertram after dinner, or I might take them during the day if they became restless. About the time Richard was one year old, he was usually the only child in the wagon, for although Pat and Kevin might start out riding, they would eventually get out and run along the creek, climb on rotted logs, pick up leaves, or hang from trees.

The houses on Bertram are unique, rustic, and cozy. There is also Saint Anthony's Church, built in 1858; La Forêt, a French restaurant housed in a structure originally built in 1848; and the Hacienda Cemetery, which dates to the 1850s and since 1898 has been the resting place of thirteen-year-old Richard Bertram Barrett's left arm. He lost it in a hunting accident, and the law at the time required that the arm be given a proper burial.

Richard and I walked Bertram Road in relative silence for about a quarter of a mile, and then he asked if I remembered when Pat was eight or nine and had brought home a fish from the creek. Along with the tightness in my throat, tears of delight formed in my eyes.

I had been in the kitchen with Richard making cookies. We heard Pat, Kevin, and their neighbor friend, Ryan Kerr, coming up the driveway, yelping in satisfaction. They were taking turns carrying an old, rusty toolbox. Richard and I met them outside the door. Three sets of excited eyes looked up at me as Pat opened the box. Inside was a fish. I thought it was a trout, a little less than a foot in length. (Remember, this is a fish tale.) It flopped around, gasping for its last breaths of air. Pat bent over and picked up the squirming fish, holding it out to me. "Look, Mom," he said beaming with pride. "I caught him with my bare hands!"

"You caught him with your bare hands!" I shouted in amazement.

"Yes, Mom, he did," Kevin confirmed with a big grin.

"He didn't use a fishing pole, Dannie," Ryan said.

Richard looked at me eagerly. "Mom, you can cook it for Dad for dinner."

I clumsily took the poor, slippery fish from Pat and admired it, then put it back in the box. Richard knelt down next to the fish and gently touched it with his finger, watching it squirm. I let Pat know how awesome it was that he had caught the fish bare-handed, but I informed them that I couldn't cook the fish for Dad because there was too much mercury in the creek, and mercury is poisonous.

We all looked down at the fish as it stopped moving. I told the boys the fish was dead and they should probably bury it on the back hill. I told Pat he had quite a talent, but he shouldn't catch fish from our creek anymore because fish suffer if they are not in water, and since we can't eat the fish, we should let them swim. I also reminded them they shouldn't spend too much time in the creek water. They went out back and buried the fish. When they came in, they scrubbed their hands before sitting down to a plate of oatmeal cookies.

Now I looked up at Richard and smiled. "Yes, Rich, I remember." The rest of the way home, we expressed our concern for Kevin. Talking about what we thought he was going through was too painful for both of us; we just tried to concentrate on the fact that he was alive and would be coming home.

When we walked up the driveway, we could see that Patrick had returned, along with several of his brothers, their wives, and my mother-in-law, who brought my mom. As we passed by Syd and Peggy's house, Syd approached us with a solemn expression and handed me the newspaper. I looked at it, and a sick and unnerving feeling came over me. I recalled being in Kevin's room in Washington State, just before Pat and Kevin were deployed. I noticed Kevin had a picture of himself in his Ranger uniform on his bookshelf. I picked it up and told him I thought it was very good. A short time later, I asked Pat if he had a Ranger picture. He told me he wasn't too wild about his picture; he'd show it to me later. He never did. I could not have imagined I would see that picture for the first time on the front page of the paper with Pat's obituary.

As I walked lethargically into the house, Sherri handed me the phone. It was Marie. I went to the back room to talk to her without disruption. The last time I had spoken to her, I was hysterical. I needed her to know I was all right. I asked her how she was doing, and she said she was in shock. She couldn't believe Pat was gone. She told me she was grateful that her parents and sister were with her, but she felt like a zombie. I told her I understood that feeling, and that maybe feeling that way was good, at least for a while.

I asked her if she was comfortable telling me how she had gotten word of Pat's death. As Pat's next of kin, she was the first person notified. She said she had been ready to leave work at about five thirty. One of her co-workers asked her to follow him to the conference room. Something in his behavior made her believe something was wrong. When she walked into the room, there were three people in class A uniforms, the dress uniform. She knew from military briefings that if soldiers wearing class A uniforms came to inform family members of a soldier's condition, it meant the soldier was dead.

I couldn't imagine how surreal that situation must have been for her, how stunned she must have been. She said she called her parents immediately from work. They made arrangements to get to her as soon as they could. The military chaplain drove Marie home in her car, and the other officers drove in the government vehicle. Two of Marie's friends from work followed behind. Marie said when she called her brother-in-law Alex from her cell phone, he already had been informed by her parents. He had told Christine, who would fly to Washington with her mom and dad to be with Marie. Alex told Marie he was on his way to my house, but she warned him that I didn't know yet. She wanted him to get in touch with Mike first so he could be there with me, and that's when he called my mom. By the time I contacted Marie at her house, Alex was only a few miles away from me. The three officers at Marie's were trying to direct the female soldier to my home and locate Pat's father. Marie's friends found an address for Pat's dad on the computer, but it was out of date.

Marie had spent hours trying to make sure everyone was informed before word of Pat's death broke on the news. She was under such terrible stress. I marveled at her strength and composure, but I was grateful her parents and Christine got to her as quickly as they did. I asked if she had heard from Kevin. She said she had, but he hadn't been able to tell her much more than he had told us. I told her to call if she needed anything or just wanted to talk. I hung up, thinking how proud Pat would be of his wife.

For days, from early morning until late at night, my house and yard were crowded with people. Family, friends, co-workers, and neighbors brought support, food, flowers, and . . . toilet paper. I remember a friend calling me early on Saturday, the 24th of April, asking if there was anything we needed. I told her so many people were coming that we would need bathroom tissue. Obviously, she had let everyone she spoke to know I made this request—nearly every other person that came up our driveway carried a package or two of toilet paper.

This became greatly ironic when several hours later Richard came out of the bathroom to inform me that my septic tank had backed up into the bathtub. We had fifty guests paying respects and twenty packages of toilet paper, and we could not operate the toilet. Richard, Mike, and I walked dazedly past the guests in the house and yard to see if the septic tank had leaked outside. There was a putrid puddle forming outside my bedroom, and Mike motioned several curious people to keep away. He said he thought a pipe might be clogged with roots.

I looked up at the eucalyptus tree where Pat would often sit when he was young. The light shining through the leaves and shredded bark was so bright, my vision blurred and I diverted my eyes. After a few seconds, I looked back at the tree and teasingly implored, "Pat, what is it about the major events in your life that make my septic tank explode?" Tears ran down my face, and I chuckled out loud as if I were really talking to him. Richard's sad eyes brightened faintly, and he hugged me before we both walked back in the house.

I dialed the maintenance company I had called before the wedding rehearsal dinner nearly two years before, but I got no answer. Patrick suggested I call a friend in the construction business to see if he could recommend a service that worked on Saturdays. He suggested San Jose Plumbing. The woman who answered was very pleasant. I told her what had happened with the septic tank and explained there had been a death in the family and I had a lot of people at my house. She said she would speak to the owner to see if someone could come out. She asked for my address and phone number, and then she asked my name.

"Mary Tillman," I said hesitantly.

"Okay, I'll call you back Mrs. . . . oh . . . Tillman. Mrs. Tillman, I'm so sorry for your loss." Her voice trembled, and I was afraid she might cry. "I'll call you within five minutes."

Minutes later the phone rang.

"Mrs. Tillman, the owner will be out in less than forty-five minutes.

His name is Kevin Garza. I hope everything works out with the septic tank. Again, I'm sorry for your loss."

"I appreciate that, thank you. Good-bye."

My brother, Patrick, and Richard let people know someone was coming to look at the septic tank. In the meantime, Peggy and Syd kindly offered their bathroom for use by my guests. Within a half hour, Mr. Garza arrived. He validated Mike's suspicion; an overgrowth of roots had caused the pipe leading from the house to the septic tank to clog. He spent four hours and about that long the following day digging up my yard and repairing the pipe. He refused to take any money. Several weeks later, I estimated the cost of his work and sent him a check. Within days, he mailed the check back.

In the first days after Pat's death, my friend Judy McGrath flew in from Atlanta, and Richard's friend Michelle flew up from Los Angeles. Aunt Katie came from Birmingham. I was touched that she came out to be with us, and I was strengthened by her presence. I was grateful to have all my friends and family around us. At first, I was able to carry on conversations and function fairly well, but gradually the reality of Pat's death, my fears for Kevin, and my lack of sleep caused me to become increasingly anxious, until I psychologically withdrew. Months later, my friend Sherri told me I spoke to people and carried out tasks, but I wasn't really there. "Your eyes were gone," she told me.

I wandered around my house and yard and through groups of people. There are bits and pieces of conversations I remember, but I mostly recall being watchful of Richard. For the first forty-eight hours after learning of his brother's death, his face reflected confusion, shock, and loss. After that, it was clear Richard was fighting anger. Thankfully, many of his, Kevin's, and Pat's friends were at the house almost around the clock. Peggy and Syd brought over all their lawn chairs, and the young people sat around the yard telling stories about happy times, trying to distract Richard from his grief and fury over Pat's death and his concern for Kevin. Looking back, the one thing I regret about that time was that I didn't stop everyone from bringing alcohol. I understood that the drinking helped numb their pain, but it also prolonged it.

At night, when it got chilly, Richard and all the friends lit firewood in the barbecue and stood around it to stay warm. One night the wood didn't burn very well, so the guys squirted lighter fluid on it. They nearly set the big elm on fire as flames shot up, licking the overhanging leaves. My friend Judy overheard Richard say he was going to make a fire pit by digging a big hole in the yard so they could sit around it. Judy was afraid he might actually carry out his idea and kept a close watch on him for several days.

Because Pat's death was newsworthy, there was a constant stream of media people trying to talk with us. Peggy and Syd, my sister-in-law Joan Tillman, and Sherri did a remarkable job intercepting phone calls and keeping reporters who drove out from coming up our driveway. Sherri's husband, Jim Greer, is a deputy sheriff, and he had the sheriff's department send cars to the house to ensure our privacy. I must acknowledge the fact that members of the press behaved quite respectfully regarding our request not to be disturbed. However, I vaguely recall Patrick calling the police when a press helicopter continued to fly over our house.

I believe it was very late Sunday night, April 25, when we got a call from Kevin. He was in Germany. He told his father and me that he would be arriving in Dover, Delaware, sometime the following day. Everyone was reassured to know he was out of Afghanistan. The Army was arranging for Marie to fly from Seattle to Dover to meet Kevin and Pat's body.

When Marie called to tell me about the arrangements, she also indicated the memorial service would probably be May 3. My chest froze when I heard the date—the day before Marie and Pat's second anniversary. I wanted to say something to comfort her, but a quality in her tone of voice made me believe it was best to let it go. I told her Pat's dad,

Richard, and I had considered flying to Dover as well but decided it was more appropriate for her to go herself. Pat, Marie, and Kevin had made the decision that Pat and Kevin would enlist. The three of them had shared the previous two years of their lives together. They went through the excitement, boredom, frustration, anxiety, and monotony of military life. Kevin and Marie needed time alone together to absorb their loss. I learned later that the Army did not follow through with the flight for Marie. She was able to get to Dover only because a generous man anonymously offered the use of his plane.

Richard answered a call on the morning of April 26; it was Maria Shriver. She told Richard that she and her husband, Governor Arnold Schwarzenegger, had just read a newspaper article about Pat, and they wanted to give their condolences. Knowing her family history of coping with tragedy made Richard extra appreciative of her call. He told her that Pat had admired the public service of her family and respected Arnold Schwarzenegger for being a self-made man, someone who set goals for himself and accomplished them. Ms. Shriver told Richard he should tell her husband that himself, and she handed the phone to the governor.

Richard was thrilled to speak to him. It was the first time I had seen him smile in days. They talked for a short time, and then Richard asked Governor Schwarzenegger if he might be able to speak at Pat's service. When Richard told him the date, the governor said he would be visiting wounded troops that day at the military hospital in Germany—so he would not be able to attend. He then asked to speak to me.

The governor was very gracious, expressing disbelief about Pat's death and his concern for us. He told me he regretted his inability to speak at Pat's memorial, but he said Maria would be privileged to represent him. I told him her presence would be greatly appreciated and thanked him for the call. He gave the phone to his wife, who was kind and compassionate. She asked a lot of questions about Pat, and we talked for about fifteen minutes. She told me she would make arrangements to get to the service. I gave her Alex's phone number so she could learn the details. I also told her that she and Pat shared the same birthday, November 6.

I think it was that same day that I learned Arizona senator John McCain would be speaking at Pat's memorial. I didn't know how his presence was arranged, but it seemed fitting. He was the senator from Pat's "adopted" state, and he was someone Pat had admired growing up. Pat had read several books about McCain and his experience in a prisoner-of-war camp in Vietnam. He was amazed at the courage McCain had exhibited. I was pleased to know the senator was going to attend.

Kevin, accompanied by fellow Ranger and friend Russell Baer, arrived with Pat's body on April 26 at Dover Air Force Base. Marie was there to meet the plane. It saddened me that Marie had to make that journey alone, yet I believe it was something she wanted to do and had to, as Pat's wife. I was comforted knowing she would be there for Kevin and he for her: Kevin was not only her brother-in-law; he was a good friend.

Pat's body was taken immediately to Rockville, Maryland, where an autopsy was performed the following day. Kevin and Marie called to let us know they would be arriving home very late Wednesday night, April 28. Knowing Kevin and Marie were heading home with Pat gave everyone a bittersweet sense of relief. My sons' friends all spoke to Richard about doing something special for Kevin. They were devastated by Pat's death but grateful Kevin was coming home alive.

They decided to make two banners. One read "Every Day's Sunday, Baby," based on a baseball adage Pat was particularly fond of saying—or shouting, depending on the occasion. The banner was so huge that the guys enlisted the help of the fire department to hang it two miles down the road. The firemen generously put up floodlights so Kevin would be able to see it at night. The other banner read "NUB," Pat's nickname for Kevin from the time he was born. That one was hung across the approach to our driveway. We were uncertain how he would interpret the gesture. We knew we were taking the risk of possibly upsetting him, but we all hoped the banners would make him feel loved.

My house was filled with food and flowers. Many people had no appetite, but food was there for those who did. Although I appreciated the flowers and the sentiments behind them, their presence and scent had become oppressive, and my mom and I started placing them outside. Alone with my mom while arranging the flowers, I confided that I was worried about the older of my two younger brothers, Rich. He is two years younger than I am, and at the time of Pat's death, he had been homeless for more than fifteen years.

Rich doesn't cope with the stresses and bureaucracies of this world, but he is tough, resourceful, and resilient. He is also one of the most kind, generous, and unselfish people I have ever known. On Thanksgiving, 1961, when Rich had recently turned four and I six, my mom had us think of a wish while holding a wishbone. I squeezed my little finger around my end of the bone, closed my eyes, and wished for every material thing I had ever wanted. When it was time to pull, I tugged on my end until I heard a snap. I looked down to find I had "won." My mom knelt next to Rich and asked what he had wished for. He looked at her earnestly and said, "I wished for the biggest piece."

I immediately felt a rush of guilt, and I could almost feel my heart break. I knew at that moment that Rich was an innately better person than I was. However, his gentle nature has not prevented him from standing his ground when necessary. He has never suffered fools gladly, and he has been in a position to defend himself more than a few times in his life. Rich was a tremendous athlete. He had amazing coordination, strength, and endurance. Unfortunately, our family moved nearly every two years because of my dad's work, so he never had the opportunity to fit into a sports niche at the schools he attended.

When Rich got out of high school, he joined the Marines, and he excelled. After he was sent to Okinawa, Japan, however, something happened that changed his perception of the Marines and himself. After being discharged, he struggled for years to fit into the conventional world, living in Fremont, California, and San Francisco. He eventually moved south to San Diego and Los Angeles, where he has lived by his wits on the streets. For several years, he came home periodically on holidays, but after a time, he stopped coming home. We have stayed in touch by receiving his calls or sending mail to him at a post office box address.

In 2001, when Pat was playing for the Arizona Cardinals, Rich called to tell me he had been in the Veterans Administration Hospital due to an extremely severe case of cellulitis. He said he had been in the hospital nearly five weeks but was doing much better. I was astonished when he told me he'd been hospitalized that long; he must have been in very bad shape. I asked why he hadn't called, but he just brushed me off, saying he'd been in good hands at the hospital.

During the conversation, I told Rich that Pat had called early in the season to see if Rich would want a ticket to the Cardinals-Chargers game, which would be played in San Diego in several weeks. Rich was thrilled. I asked that he call me a few days before the game in case Pat had anything he needed to know.

Several days before the game, Rich called, and I told him that Pat said the ticket would be at the "will call" window and to bring identification. I also told him his nephew Richard and some of his friends would be there. Peggy and Syd, who had been visiting family in Los Angeles, also decided to go to San Diego to see the game. I told Rich that Pat said the seats should be together, so he could meet Richard inside the stadium. He hung up the phone, clearly happy to be going to the game.

As I recall, the Cardinals won that game 20–17, and Pat played very well. My son Richard called me a day or so later to tell me he had a great time with Uncle Rich. Initially, he said, Uncle Rich sat away from him and his friends, in unoccupied seats, fearing he would embarrass Richard because he was so obviously homeless. But Richard assured him they wanted his company, so Rich moved over to sit with everyone else. Richard said his uncle brought his own bread and meat to make sandwiches, but he eventually allowed Richard to buy him sausages and a beer. Richard said his uncle was very pleased with Pat's performance and cheered and yelled like he hadn't a care in the world.

Pat made sure all of his guests were on the list of people allowed through the gate to see the players before their buses left for the airport. Richard told me Rich seemed proud to be introduced as Pat's uncle and really enjoyed talking to Pat. When it was time for the players to leave, Pat excused himself to talk to some of the other players. He had forgotten to bring extra money for his uncle, so he gathered what he had and collected more from his teammates to give to Rich for being such a great uncle, a gesture that touched Rich. After seeing Pat off, Richard and his friends took Uncle Rich out on the town, and everyone enjoyed his company. But when it was time for the guys to get back to Los Angeles, Rich asked them to drop him off on a corner where he spent time. Richard's voice faltered when he told me how hard it was to leave Uncle Rich behind.

I hadn't heard from my brother for quite a long time. He had purchased a bus ticket to Florida and spent several months there, but he couldn't tolerate the humidity. He ended up calling me shortly after Pat and Kevin told us they were enlisting. When I told him, he was furious. He said the military was no place for two guys who had played professional sports, that there is too much jealousy in the military; he had experienced it himself. He warned that Pat and Kevin would be targets for every petty and resentful soldier and officer they ran into. He was angry with me for "allowing them" to enlist.

I told him that, in fact, Mike and I had tried to talk them out of enlisting, but they had their minds made up. I told him Mike had made a special trip to Arizona to talk to Kevin and that we had an intervention at my house. Marie's parents, Bindy and Paul; Patrick, Alex, Christine, and I met with Pat, Kevin, and Marie after the honeymoon, just prior to the enlistment. It was very painful to recount that story to Rich that day, but I did so in great detail because I believed he needed to hear it.

I explained that as we sat around my table that afternoon, it soon became clear that Pat, Kevin, and Marie were comfortable with their decision and had come to the meeting simply because they loved us and knew that we needed to discuss this more with them. I feared that we would not be able to change their minds. Marie's parents spoke first. Marie's mother made a point by telling Pat there was honor in staying home to care for his wife. Pat did not disagree with her, but I also knew he felt Marie did not need to be taken care of. He knew she was making a tremendous sacrifice by supporting his decision to enlist, because it would mean they would be apart for long periods of time. I believe he and Marie both felt that what they were forfeiting would be worth it, however; it was a contribution they were making together, and they would each grow from the experience.

As Bindy, Paul, and Patrick spoke, my mind started to wander, and their voices faded from my consciousness as I flashed on a memory more than twenty years old: I was driving down a road with my husband in the passenger seat. A squirrel suddenly darted in front of the car. I swerved to miss it, but a second squirrel was right behind him, and I struck that little squirrel. "You just hit Kevin," Patrick said sarcastically. My heart sank; I felt nauseous. I felt awful about hitting the squirrel and didn't understand why he would say such a bizarre thing. It must have been a nervous reaction. As I sat at the table, recalling that incident with great trepidation, I looked at Pat, then at Kevin, and I asked myself: "Which one of my squirrels is going to die?"

At that moment, I became aware that Paul was questioning Pat about the wisdom of giving up so much money from his lucrative football career. Looking back, I know he was simply appealing to Pat's sense of responsibility, but I became outraged. I stood up and yelled, "Why are you talking about money? The boys could be wounded or be killed!" I could see Paul felt terrible. He didn't mean for his remarks to hurt anyone. I looked from Kevin to Pat. "What if something happens to one of you? What about the damage that will cause the one left behind and everyone else who cares about you both?" I was shrieking and shaking.

Kevin's eyes got real wide and he said, "Mom! Get a hold of yourself!" I was clearly scaring him; he had never seen me like that before.

I turned to Pat: "You just got married!" Pat got tears in his eyes. He got up, walked over, and put his arms around me. I was crying into his chest as Marie's parents and Alex and Christine left. Patrick was stunned at my reaction. He stayed for an hour or so to give support, then left. Pat, Marie, and Kevin obviously felt bad that I was so upset, but they had made their decision; I would give them my support.

Rich listened to my recollection of the intervention, and I hoped he appreciated our efforts to talk Pat and Kevin out of enlisting. But it didn't change his fears that something would happen to them, and he continued to express those fears. I remember standing with the phone in my hand, paralyzed with dread and confusion, not knowing what to say or do. I was also thinking about how my son Richard had been afraid for his brothers. My brother was so upset that he ended the call abruptly, without saying good-bye. I understood his anxiety for Pat and Kevin; I was feeling it, too. In fact, I felt it more strongly now. But Rich had been in the military and knew more than I did.

Rich called several times after Pat and Kevin were deployed to Iraq. He seemed to have come to terms with the fact they were there; he indicated during one call that he had decided to think positively. After that, I didn't hear from him again, and I had no current post office box address. Just before Pat and Kevin were deployed to Afghanistan, I drove to San Diego and hung flyers in and around La Jolla because I knew he liked to spend time there. The flyers asked that he contact me. I wanted to be sure he had the latest information, but I didn't hear from him.

Now, as we placed fresh flower arrangements around my backyard and threw out the ones that were dying, I told Mom I had no way to tell Rich about Pat's death before he saw it in the newspaper. The image of him reading the news for the first time tore at my heart and weighed on me for days, so much so that I didn't want to talk about it to anyone, as I knew I would fall apart. But here with my mom, I needed to say out loud what she must have been thinking. We both just hoped he would call us once he read the news.

There were so many people coming and going that my friends Jim and Paulette Woolridge offered to lend me their camper so close friends or relatives could stay overnight. Several hours later, Jim returned with his huge recreational vehicle. Guests who had cars in the driveway scrambled to move them down to the main road. Navigating my driveway is tricky for the average car, but this RV was gigantic. Jim managed to get it up the portion that ran in front of Syd and Peggy's house, but he stopped at the entrance to my driveway because of the low-hanging power lines. Everyone in the yard milled around, trying to figure out a way Jim could get into my driveway and not block Peggy and Syd's. Meanwhile, I was contemplating how the heck he would get back out.

One of our guests was Ronnie Lott, who had played for the San Francisco 49ers, the Oakland Raiders, the New York Jets, and the Kansas City Chiefs. Pat had met him while he was in high school, and their paths had crossed many times since. Pat had great respect for him as a football player and as a person. He always called him Mr. Lott, and I can't bring myself to call him anything else. Mr. Lott and Richard determined they could get on the roof of the RV and lift the wires up with something long-handled as the vehicle passed underneath. Richard grabbed a rake and Mr. Lott grabbed a broom, then they climbed onto the roof of the camper. Jim slowly drove under the wires as Mr. Lott and Richard raised the power lines as high as they could. I stood in front of Peggy and Syd's, fearing they would fall or, worse, get electrocuted.

As I was standing there cringing, Paulette walked up the driveway. She had followed Jim, but because of all the cars, she had to park down the road and walk back to my house. She came up behind me and stared intently at the scene playing out in front of my house, focusing on the backs of the two figures on the RV's roof. Her expression turned quizzical, and then she said, "That looks like Ronnie Lott's ass." I turned to her and said, "That *is* Ronnie Lott's ass." I actually laughed out loud.

Just before Kevin was due to arrive home with Pat's body, my friend Marcelle Chapman took me to buy a new dress for the memorial. I had a black dress, one of my favorites, but I refused to wear it. Pat's life represented light; I didn't want to wear black.

Other than taking some books to my classroom and going for a walk with Richard, this shopping trip was the first time I had left my yard since Pat's death. We drove down the driveway and saw that American flags had been hung along both sides of Almaden Road. To my amazement, the flags flanked the road for more than a mile. They were beautiful, waving gently in the soft spring breeze. I was filled with warmth at the efforts of my neighbors. The flags were wonderful, and they were heartbreaking.

Once we got off Almaden Road and onto Almaden Expressway, I began to feel disoriented and nauseous. I suddenly didn't understand how people were going on about their lives; I could not grasp why the world was still turning. When Marcelle and I finally got to the store, we found simple pink linen dress.

Kevin, Marie, and Russell Baer arrived at the San Francisco airport accompanying Pat's body very late on the night of Wednesday, April 28. Russell left to be with his family in the East Bay, not far from San Francisco. A hearse met Kevin and Marie to transport them and Pat to Willow Glen Mortuary. Patrick, Richard, Mike, and I drove there at around eleven p.m. to meet them. I was so eager to see Kevin and Marie, yet I was filled with dread at the thought of seeing Pat's coffin. At the same time, I felt compelled to see his body one last time. During our conversation before he left Dover, Kevin said he was told by the mortuary affairs staff that Pat's body could be viewed Thursday morning. Kevin said he didn't want to view his brother's body but that if his father and I chose to do so, we could; Patrick told Kevin he definitely wanted to see Pat. In the car, Mike tried to dissuade me from viewing Pat's body. He believed it would be too traumatic for me and that I should remember him as I last saw him.

The parking lot of the mortuary was faintly lit. As we walked toward the building, I stayed several paces behind Patrick, Richard, and Mike, trying to gather myself. I could faintly see Kevin's silhouette under the archway leading to the front entrance. He stood tall in his dress uniform. Patrick, Richard, and Mike stopped to allow me to approach Kevin first. He looked at me through eyes glistening with tears reflecting pain, loss, and numbing sadness; yet the set of his jaw was strong and determined. I wrapped my arms around him and felt his tears fall on my cheek as he leaned down to hug me. "Pat is inside, Mom," he said softly in my ear. I cried quietly into his chest as he held me close. Slowly, I backed away and looked at his dignified yet somber face. I smiled at him as bravely as I could. I told him I loved him and was proud of him, and I thanked him for bringing Pat home. I looked on as he tightly embraced his father, then his uncle. Richard walked up to Kevin and looked at him unwaveringly. I wiped tears from my face as they firmly held each other.

The mortuary director approached us. Patrick asked if he could see Pat's body. The director told him he could view Pat in the morning, but Patrick insisted on seeing him right away. It was clear by the look on the man's face that he was apprehensive about obliging the request. Pat's body had just arrived, and he was not sure of its condition. But Patrick was so insistent, the mortician agreed to open the coffin. Kevin said that, like him, Marie had chosen not to view Pat, but that I had to do what was right for me. My brother looked at me uneasily. "Dannie," he said solemnly, "I really don't think you should see him, but if you are going to view him, so will I." I told Mike, Kevin, and Richard that if Pat was brave enough to risk his life and die, I had to have the courage to see him. I realized I could regret it, but as his mother, I felt I might regret it more if I didn't. Richard decided to view Pat as well.

The lights in the hallway of the mortuary were very bright. I wondered how the hall was so luminous when the circumstances were so somber. I walked down the hall next to Kevin as Marie walked out of a room that Patrick, Richard, and Mike had just entered. She looked very thin, and her face was extremely pale. The blue eyes that had always been so happy and vibrant looked cloudy and vacant. I hugged her gently and then moved away, smoothing her blond hair against her shoulder. She smiled at me weakly, and then she and Kevin directed me into the room where Pat's body had been placed. Marie seemed reassured to see us, but I also sensed agitation that I could not quite comprehend at the time. Looking back, she must have felt tremendous conflict, wanting to graciously share Pat with all those who loved him while wanting to protect him and spend time with him alone.

Patrick was already standing over the partially open casket when I walked into the dimly lit room. The mortuary director and his assistant stood uneasily on the opposite side. From where I was standing I could see the white lining of the casket, and I could vaguely make out the top portion of Pat's face. My head became light and my stomach sick. I walked quietly over to a chair next to Richard and sat facing the open door, terrified to look in the direction of Pat's body. Mike leaned over and whispered that it was all right if I wasn't able to view him.

At that moment I glimpsed Patrick reach into the coffin to touch Pat. I looked at the morticians and I saw the trepidation on their faces as Patrick tenderly lifted Pat's upper body. He held Pat for several seconds; then, as Richard approached, he gently laid him down. Richard stood over his brother, speaking gently to him, and then he leaned over and kissed his nose. Mike moved toward the coffin while I sat frozen in the chair, staring bleary-eyed out into the hallway. Kevin walked in the room, avoiding looking in the direction of Pat's body, and knelt down in front of me.

"Remember, Mom," he said, "that isn't Pat; he's already gone."

I looked tearfully at Kevin and mouthed, "I know."

Slowly, I stood up. Patrick, my brother, and Richard stepped back slightly with agonized, helpless looks on their faces. The morticians kept their heads bowed as I walked slowly toward the casket and looked down. My eyes were so clouded with tears that it took me a moment to see clearly; I had to remind myself to breathe. The lower half of the coffin was closed; Pat was only visible from the waist up. He was wearing a white T-shirt. The back of his head was wrapped in gauze and plastic and his face was distorted and bloated; yet there was something familiar about the mouth and eyebrows. His skin looked as though it had been covered with a layer of wax, and I noticed a small concave spot on his head that looked as though it had been patched. I saw that his hands were wrapped in white towels, and the only thing I truly recognized was his left forearm.

I laid my hand gently on his chest, and I said, "Hi, Pat." Through tears, I smiled at him, as if he could see me. I was startled at how absolutely cold and hollow he felt. Pat had been strong, athletic, and vibrant; now he looked small and vulnerable. It was painful to see his broken body, yet it made me appreciate even more how big and wonderful his spirit was. His body, once beautiful and strong, truly was only a casing containing the best of him: character, courage, fortitude, conviction, and strength—his essence. Kevin was right. That isn't Pat; he's already gone.

I realize I am sitting on the edge of my bed clutching my pink dress, having been lost in my thoughts. I notice the time and realize I must finish packing; my ride to the airport will be arriving in less than an hour. I wipe the tears from my eyes, look up at the dimples in my ceiling, smile weakly, and say, "Hi, Pat."

10

Walking through Birmingham International Airport, I see my aunts Katie and Lannie waving from the end of the corridor. Lannie has flown in from New York to spend the week with us. It's good to see them. The drive to Katie's from the airport is surprisingly short. She lives just blocks from downtown in a wonderful two-story brick house with a wraparound porch. Birmingham is a very hilly city with an abundance of lush trees. As Katie parks the car, I can't help but think how much Pat would have appreciated the eclectic and historic houses that line the narrow street.

Grabbing my suitcase, I follow my aunts up the front walk to the porch. The screen door opens, and Katie's husband, Tom, comes to greet us. The first time I met Tom was at Pat's wedding, yet I feel like I have known him a long time. He has a calm, relaxed presence, and I'm glad to see him. Katie leads me to the guest room where I'll be staying. I recognize the four-poster bed that had belonged to my grandmother, and I feel at home. Once I put my suitcases down, Katie and Lannie show me around the house. The rooms have high ceilings, crown molding, and richly colored walls accented with books, paintings, and framed family photographs. The furniture is a creative and tasteful blend of old and new, wooden and upholstered. Lannie and I follow Katie into Tom's office, an inviting room with walls the color of cinnabar. A framed black-and-white photograph of a handsome young man sits on one of the bookshelves. As I get closer, I can see he is wearing a World War II–era uniform and standing aboard a ship. The young man is Tom's father, who Katie tells me was killed when a Japanese fighter plane flew into his ship. Tom and his brothers were little boys at the time. I had no idea Tom's father had been killed in the war; the knowledge is oddly consoling.

Katie makes dinner, and the four of us sit around the dining room table and talk. I tell them what we learned at the 15-6 briefing at Fort Lewis, and I go over some of the discrepancies between that and what we previously had been told. They are appalled at the inconsistencies. Katie asks me about viewing Pat's body. I tell them I have no regrets; I needed to see him one last time. Fortunately, I'm not haunted by the image of his lifeless form. When I think of Pat, I only see him alive and vibrant. I believe that is a testament to how vital he was. Katie's eyes well with tears as Lannie and Tom ask about Pat's memorial service, and Katie wants to know about Kevin's reaction to the banners. She had been at the house when his friends were planning to make them, but she had to return home before Kevin arrived. As Katie serves coffee, I begin to recount Kevin's return and the days before Pat's memorial. I begin at the funeral home.

By the time Marie's parents picked her up at the mortuary, it was twelve thirty a.m. Patrick, Richard, Mike, and I drove with Kevin to my house. The whole drive, I was nervous about Kevin's reaction to the banners; I feared he might be uncomfortable being welcomed home when

Pat was never going to return. Others also were a bit worried about how he would interpret them. Before we could see the first banner, we could make out the floodlights in the distance. As we got closer, it was evident that Kevin thought there was something strange about the glaring lights. When the banner came into view, Mike, Richard, and I turned to look at Kevin. His dad watched from the rearview mirror. At first his brow furrowed in puzzlement, then he read the words "Every Day's Sunday, Baby," and he smiled weakly at the familiar baseball expression. "Thank you," he said, looking directly into Richard's teary eyes as we drove beneath the outstretched sheet.

"All your and Pat's buds did it," Rich said.

Kevin swallowed hard. "It's awesome."

We drove two miles down the road to the house. The moon was bright enough that we could faintly see the flags waving against the trees and a sign the Pelosis hung on their fence that read "We love you, Kevin." Kevin's eyes reflected how touched he was. He stared straight ahead as we approached our driveway and swallowed hard again when he saw the welcoming banner that read "NUB."

Slowly, we drove over the crest in the drive. Standing in the yard, illuminated by the porch light and the firelight from the burning barbecue, were fifteen to twenty friends of my sons, along with my mom, Judy, and Michelle. They waited silently and reverently for Kevin to get out of the car. As he walked toward them in his dress uniform, their faces showed numerous emotions: awe, admiration, respect, love, concern, and tremendous sadness. Guardedly, they surrounded him and said, "Welcome home, Nub." Kevin first hugged his grandmother and Judy, then each one of the friends. They gathered around the barbecue until nearly three a.m.

That night, I didn't sleep much. When I woke, I made a pot of coffee and laid out pastries and fruit that neighbors had brought over the day before. Quietly, I went outside and sat in the morning sun so I would not disturb anyone. Pat's visitation was going to be at one. I knew Marie had decided the casket would be closed and the visitation would be only for family and those closest to Pat, yet I found myself feeling anxious about there being a lot of people. People had surrounded me for days; maybe my brain was telling me I needed to be by myself. I sat listlessly for about an hour, and then Judy came out of the camper. I poured her a cup of coffee, and we talked until everyone else woke up and ate the pastries. We were all apprehensive about the day; very little was said as we got ready to go to the funeral home.

When Mike, Mom, and I arrived at the funeral chapel, a number of family members and friends were already there. I spoke to several people for a few minutes, and then Kevin and Marie walked me to the visitation area. The room was small, and I remember it being brightly lit from sunlight shining through frosted windows. There were six rows of pews on each side of the room. Pat's flag-draped coffin was placed in front of an unadorned white wall. We had asked that no flowers be sent to the mortuary, but one Japanese flower arrangement did arrive and rested on a pedestal at the head of the casket. I found it perfect in its simplicity.

I walked over and placed my hand on the flag covering the coffin, trying to grasp the reality that Pat's body was inside. Gradually, people started coming into the room. Some sat reflecting or praying in the pews; others stood quietly in their thoughts next to the coffin. More visitors came throughout the afternoon until late at night. There were many tears, but there was also a great deal of laughter. By early evening, Pat's friends were sitting on the floor in front of his coffin sharing stories about him, from lighthearted to very funny. Had Pat been there, he would have laughed the loudest. I can always imagine Pat's laugh when I hear something I know would amuse him.

Later on, Alex walked up to the coffin holding three-year-old Ryan in his arms. Ryan's brown eyes stared down on the strange, flag-covered box.

"Is Uncle Pat in there?" he whispered softly.

"Yes," Alex gently told him.

"Well, why doesn't he get out?"

Marie smiled at me with moist eyes and we said simultaneously, "Yeah! Why doesn't he just climb right out of there?" I was able to conjure the image of him doing that.

At the end of the night, Kevin, Richard, Alex, and Pat's dad brought in several cases of Guinness for those still at the funeral home to toast Pat. However, the funeral director told us we couldn't drink inside the premises. I was very upset by that. I wished we had brought Pat's coffin home to our front yard so we could have said our good-byes in the setting where Pat grew up, the setting he loved, and toast him properly. Instead, we gathered outside to toast him under the stars. I told myself his big spirit was unbound now; more of him was floating in the ether than in the confines of the coffin. Shortly after the toast, nearly everyone left. I remember standing next to the coffin, petrified to leave; I didn't want Pat to be alone. Suddenly, I was aware of Marie's pale, slender hand reaching out to stroke the casket. I knew then it was time for me to go.

Pat was cremated the following day, Friday, April 30, 2004.

On Saturday, I finally got a call from my brother Richard. He had tried to call several times, but the phone had been constantly busy, so the call went straight to the message machine, which was full. He had read the news in the paper on April 23. He said he walked around in a daze for hours. I felt horrible. I expected him to be angry, since he had been so upset when Pat and Kevin had enlisted, but it was too late for anger. Before we ended the call, he became more emotional. I told him I loved him, then I handed the phone to Kevin. They spoke for about ten minutes. At the end of the conversation, Kevin told me his uncle would call again soon.

That afternoon, Judy's husband, Neal, and her daughter, Christie, flew in from Atlanta. Judy and Neal used to live in San Jose, but they moved to Atlanta a few years ago. When Pat and Kevin were stationed at Fort Benning in Georgia, they often stayed with them during their leaves. Because Neal had been a Marine during the Vietnam War, Pat and Kevin felt a special bond with him. I was pleased and grateful that he was now here for Kevin. Judy picked up Neal and Christie at the airport, then came to the house for a while. Sometime in the late afternoon, they left to check in to a hotel, and when they returned, they presented us with a brand-new fire pit. Judy told me she was afraid Richard would eventually burn the elm tree down if he continued to burn wood in the barbecue, or he would dig that deep homemade fire pit in my front yard. That night, we burned our first fire in the new pit.

Our family and a number of friends sat around the flames, talking. I overheard someone cautiously ask Kevin what it was like to be in an ambush. I held my breath for a second, concerned about his reaction. He looked intently at everyone for a moment, and then very straightforwardly said, "It was frightening." I pulled up a chair and sat down as Kevin continued. Recalling the afternoon of Pat's death, Kevin said they were half expecting to get ambushed when they saw the nature of the canyon. He said everything seemed to be in slow motion. His M19 would not fire, and his rifle had jammed. He ended up firing his pistol. However, he said, he was aware of the ricocheting of bullets and was cautious because he didn't want to hurt any of his own men.

I worried about Kevin answering too many questions, but I realized it was probably good for him to talk. After a while, the topic changed. I was aware of the hum of conversation, but I wasn't really listening. Watching the flames, I started to think about how much Pat would love sitting by the fire when he got home, then I caught myself—Pat wasn't coming home.

The next night, Steve White, a young Navy SEAL Kevin and Pat had befriended in Iraq, came to the house. He was going to be speaking at Pat's memorial the next day. Kevin said they weren't really supposed to hang around with the SEALs—I guess it is like fraternizing with soldiers of a higher rank—but he and Pat would sneak away to spend time with them and swap stories. It was clear that Steve's presence was a comfort to Kevin, and as the night wore on, I could see his company made Richard feel better, too. Kevin was expecting Russell Baer, the young soldier who was with him when he flew home with Pat's body. He wanted to introduce us to him, but Russell never made it to the house.

I remember very little about the morning of May 3, 2004, other than that I helped get my mother dressed, and I couldn't find the earrings Marie had given me for my birthday. Pat Dando, whose daughter-in-law is one of Marie's best friends, was the vice mayor of San Jose. She arranged for two limousines to pick us up shortly before noon and take us to the memorial service. Kevin, Richard, and Michelle got into one car, and Patrick, Mike, Mom, and I got into the other. When the car got to the bottom of the driveway, I could see the flags billowing at the sides of the road. We drove about two hundred yards when I saw twenty-one motorcycle officers standing at attention along the white picket fence beneath the row of flags against the backdrop of the Casa Grande, a Civil War–era structure. It was an imposing and touching sight. I stared at the floor of the car and willed myself not to cry. Once we passed the police escort, the officers got on their motorcycles and escorted us to the Municipal Rose Garden. On the way, we stopped to pick up Marie. She got into the car with Kevin, Rich, and Michelle.

The large garden displays more than a hundred varieties of roses and has a natural grass stage surrounded by a cathedral of redwood trees. Pat, Kevin, Richard, and Marie had their high school graduations at the garden. When we arrived, I was shocked to see more than a thousand people already gathered. We were taken to a nearby home, away from the heat and the commotion, to wait for the service to begin. There, we were introduced to Ms. Maria Shriver; Senator John McCain; Lieutenant General Philip R. Kensinger Jr., head of the Army's Special

Operations Command; and a Colonel Chen. Ms. Shriver was kind and very down-to-earth. Senator McCain was gracious and respectful. Both of the officers appeared to be sincere and compassionate; it was a comfort to have them there.

Just before one o'clock, we were escorted to our seats in the front row, facing the grass stage. Enlarged photographs of Pat were set up on large easels. Many of the pictures I had never seen before. As I looked at them, I could hear bagpipes in the distance. Pat loved bagpipes. The sound of the instruments gradually got closer until the bagpipers were walking down the aisle toward the stage. I held back tears as they walked past us and out of sight.

There were many wonderful speakers that day, but I was in a haze and therefore could not absorb everything that was said. However, since ESPN-TV televised the memorial nationally, there was a tape of the event, and a friend transcribed the speeches for me. So now, sitting with Lannie, Katie, and Tom, I am able to relate the memorial in detail.

All of the presenters spoke of Pat's character so eloquently. Yet what I appreciated most were the stories about Pat, many of which I had never heard. Jim Rome, host of a nationally syndicated sports radio show, *The Jungle*, was the first speaker. I knew he had interviewed Pat several times when he played for the Cardinals, but I had no idea Mr. Rome had such an appreciation of who Pat was. His speech was quite moving.

There are no heroes in sports. Athletes today are often referred to as heroes or warriors, when in reality, they're neither . . . . Athletes are urged to sacrifice, to go the extra mile, to pay the price, all in the name of winning because winning isn't everything, it's the only thing. As it turns out, winning isn't everything, and winning isn't the only thing. But risking your life for a belief is. . . . Pat Tillman risked and ultimately lost his life because he wanted to make a difference. He felt it was his obligation and his responsibility to help improve the world in which he lived. Pat was not like the rest of us. Pat didn't see the world like the rest of us. When everybody else is asking "Why is life so hard?" Pat asked, "Why was life so easy?" . . .

Charles Barkley once said, "I'm no role model; raise your own damn kids." Believe it or not, he's right. It's not his job to raise our kids. . . . I've spent my entire career talking to and talking about athletes. But I have never spoken to my three-year-old son Jake about a specific athlete . . . and although he is not ready for this conversation, I decided quite some time ago the first athlete I would ever tell my son about would be Pat Tillman.

I can't wait to sit my son down and tell him how much I admired Pat, to tell him about that legendary Tillman intensity, his hunger, his desire. I can't wait to tell my son that it's not necessarily about being the fastest or the strongest or the most athletic because Pat was never any of those things. But nobody rated higher in those intangible qualities that you could develop: hunger, desire, courage, competitive spirit, integrity, honesty, selflessness, the things that make you a great athlete and a great man. . . .

Pat's the man we should all aspire to be, a man of honor, courage, patriotism, and loyalty. Money, material possessions, luxury cars, huge mansions—these things meant nothing to Pat. Integrity, relationships with family, friends, and teammates meant everything. . . . I admire that Pat married his high school sweetheart, Marie. . . . Pat had the maturity and the integrity to invest in deepening the relationship that was already so important to him. . . .

I can only assume that Pat and Kevin were mortified by the events of 9-11, like all of us. Like the rest of us, they were probably furious, devastated, saddened; they wanted a piece of someone, wanted to do something to defend this country, to protect our families. Ultimately, of course, the horror and the shock and the devastation of the day began to fade some for those who were not directly affected. Certainly none of us, nor the world in which we lived, would ever be the same after the terrorist attacks, but we had no choice but to forge ahead. We gradually regained our sense of routine and normalcy. The terrorist attacks were no longer front and center in our minds. But not for Pat and not for Kevin.

It seems they couldn't shake those horrific images; they couldn't push them out of their minds, they didn't want to forget, they couldn't just go back to work. To Kevin, it was a no-brainer; he was going to quit the minor leagues, he was going to give up his dream to become a major leaguer. He was going to enlist and give everything he had to become an Army Ranger. To Pat, football was the farthest thing from Pat's mind. Shortly after the attacks, he did an interview with NFL Films, where he said, and I quote, "I play football, and it just seems so, Goddamn, it is unimportant compared to everything that has taken place. I feel guilty even having the damn interview."

Pat continued, "My grandfather was at Pearl Harbor, a lot of my family has gone and fought in wars, and I really haven't done a damn thing. I think of this, this kind of sounds tacky, but I've always thought about Pearl Harbor, and the people and the boats and the bombs kind of coming down, and what they were going through," Pat went on, "their screaming and the passion they exuded and how they lost their lives. I think of stuff like that. I imagine I'll probably have a few other things to think about now, maybe a fireman running up those stairs."

Imagine Pat, a guy who starred on the field in college, gradu-ated in three and a half years with honors and set an Arizona Cardinal record, single-season record for tackles, despite being a seventh-round draft pick. Imagine him, of all people, thinking, "I haven't done a damn thing."

Of course, we all spent a few days talking about what we'd like to do to make it right. But Pat and Kevin made the ultimate commitment and sacrifice: They left behind the lives they had known and they went and they did something about it.

Let me take a few minutes to talk about Kevin. I had never met Kevin before about an hour ago, but I've heard all the stories about Kevin. Make no mistake—he's a Tillman through and through. There are a lot of great football stories flying around about Pat right now, but if you go to anyone in the Cleveland Indians organization, they will tell you Kevin is one of the hardest, toughest guys they have ever had. Kevin was playing in a rookie league game in Burlington, North Carolina, one time, scorching hot day, doubleheader. He's busting it all day long.

In his final at bat that day, Kevin steps out of the box and you could tell he wasn't just right. He was rubbing his leg. He steps back in, and he mashes, he hits one to the wall, but he could not get out of the box. The Indians assistant general manager, John Mirabelli said, "His leg just locked up, like a lead pipe. He then . . . Frankensteined it to first base, where he collapsed with cramps and severe dehydration." Mirabelli, the assistant GM, said somebody brought him the tape the following day and said, "You have to see this." Mirabelli said upon seeing that tape, "It was the most incredible thing I have ever seen."

Kevin may not have left millions of dollars on the table the way Pat did to enlist, but he is every bit the hero that his older brother is, every bit the ass-kicker that Pat was. And I guarantee big brother is looking down right now every bit as proud of Kevin as Kevin is of Pat.

. . . I can remember Pat coming to one of my *Jungle* tour stops in Arizona. Understand we've done thirty-two of these appearance or tour stops nationally over the past fifteen years in California, Ohio, Texas, Florida, New York, everywhere. Some of the best of the best have come out for these events—coaches, team owners, All-Stars, even Hall of Famers like George Brett and Nolan Ryan. But of all the athletes and celebrities who have attended, I have never looked as forward to meeting somebody as I did Pat Tillman. I told my wife, Janet, "We're going to Arizona; we're going to finally meet Tilly."

Janet, having heard Pat on the radio, was excited, as excited as I was. We were all fired up; we were going to finally meet Pat. Because Pat had that intangible "It," he had an aura, he had a presence. It's hard to explain, but you know it when you see it. It was rock and roll, he was a man's man and he did not disappoint, he lived up to all the hype that day. Pat freaking Tillman.

I'm proud to say I knew him, I'm proud to say I met him, and when his coach at Arizona State, Bruce Snyder, told me on my radio show last week, "Jim, Pat liked you. He liked coming on your radio show," that was as nice a compliment as I've ever received in this business. I'm going to miss Pat. I'm going to tell my son and my family about Pat. We're all going to tell our families about Pat. God bless Pat Tillman.

I sat in my seat in intense heat looking at Mr. Rome through a blur of tears. I had never felt such devastating sadness and intense joy at the same time. The stories he recounted about Pat brought him vividly to life. I could picture his face, see his body language, and hear his voice and thunderous, contagious laugh. I loved hearing the story about Kevin. Pat had flown to North Carolina to see that game. He saw his brother smash the ball to the fence and drag his leg to first base. I remember so well when Pat called to tell me about it. He said, "Kevin was fucking amazing!"

Maria Shriver walked to the podium next. First, she read from a letter from the governor, which noted he was visiting a military hospital in Germany, and the letter continued:

Pat had it all—intelligence, movie-star good looks, a loving wife, athletic prowess, fame, a lucrative and promising career. Who among us could walk away from riches and a job we love and put ourselves in harm's way out of a desire, a need to do something for our country? Pat did, and so he left us with a brilliant legacy. I've been told Pat admired me. Well, let me tell you, it's the other way around. I am humbled because the fact is that Pat's story, Pat's life, his journey—that's the real American dream, and he sacrificed it for us and for our country. That is my kind of hero.

Ms. Shriver then read from a letter she wrote.

Dear Pat,

I called your mom the other day to see how she was doing. Our conversation started off in a humorous way. She told me that you and I shared the same birthday and we were both in love with the same man. I thought you would want to know that she is holding up really well. We had a wonderful talk about you. . . . She told me how you always had a burning desire to give something back to your country. She told me that you and Kevin never had a moment's doubt about abandoning your brilliant careers for the ideal of service, to give something back.

Your mom told me there was another hero in this story as well—your wife, Marie. Your mom told me how amazing she has been throughout your marriage, how supportive and how selfless. ... [Your mom] wanted to make sure that people knew about you and the life you led. And, believe me, Pat, they do, we all do.

We know not just about the football and the service, but about the big heart and the kind soul that made you the person you were. We know that when you took the class "Orientation to the Exceptional Child" in college, it wasn't just an academic exercise. We know that you met and befriended a student with Down syndrome named Duff, a student whose life you touched and changed forever....

Pat, forty-three years ago, in his inaugural address, my uncle, President John F. Kennedy, who was speaking for his generation, a generation that had sacrificed and served, made a suggestion to all generations to come: "Ask not what your country can do for you, ask what you can do for your country." By your deeds, by the choices you made, Pat, you and so many other young Americans have lived those words. Pat, your family doesn't have to worry anymore. You are home, you are safe, and you will not be forgotten. You will live forever as an example and inspiration to all of us. As a mother and a wife, on behalf of Arnold and all Californians, in fact all Americans—thank you. And may God rest your soul.

I smiled through tears at Ms. Shriver after she finished speaking. Senator McCain's speech followed; it was compassionate and thoughtful. He started out by saying he never had met Pat, but he described him quite accurately.

By all accounts he was quite a man. ... He's remembered as a good son, brother, and husband; a loyal friend; an excellent student; an overachieving athlete; a decent, considerate person; a solid citizen in every respect. . . . But it was his uncommon choice of duty to his country over the profession he loved and the riches and the comfort of celebrity, and his humility, that make Pat Tillman's life such a welcome lesson in the true meaning of courage and honor. . . .

Pat Tillman understood his obligations, no better than his comrades in arms, perhaps, but better than many of his contemporaries. He must have known that such debts are not a burden, but their recompense earns us our happiness. So he volunteered to take his place in the ranks.

The senator closed his speech by saying "May God bless him. And may God bless us all." I remember thinking that the first three speakers had referenced God, yet Pat wasn't religious. However, that didn't prevent him from wanting to do the right thing or trying to make a better person of himself. I really don't know what Pat believed about our destination after death. I know Pat thought about it because he thought about everything. Yet, I doubt he dwelled on it; he was too busy living.

Steve White walked to the stage next. Kevin and Pat had a lot of respect for Steve, and they enjoyed their time with him and the other Navy SEALS they had met in Iraq. Steve looked so dignified in his Navy dress uniform. Several times in his tribute he was overcome with emotion and had to stop, and his voice broke in several places, but he was eloquent nonetheless. He started by telling a story about how Pat was offered a chance to get out of the Army early to go back to another team in the NFL and turned it down to complete his three-year commitment. Right after he made the decision to stay in, Pat "gets ordered to cut about an acre of grass by some nineteen-year-old kid" who outranked him. Steve then talked about serving with Pat and Kevin in Iraq.

I first met Kevin and Pat at chow hall right after the war started. . . . [We spent] a lot of times in the evenings out there enjoying what we could; those Arabian nights, they're pretty nice, a lot like California. And we'd talk about our past experiences, our friends back at home, our family, and then Pat and his conspiracy theories. Man, you could never get enough of those things. I couldn't get enough of his football stories, and on his part, he couldn't get enough of my SEAL stories, so we kind of evened it out the whole time; it was good.

We ended up leaving that place and moving into Baghdad for the duration there. And pretty much every night for the next three months if we weren't working, we were out drinking coffee and enjoying each other's company out there, getting to know each other. . . . The very first mission that we conducted over there we took a whole lot of fire coming in, and took some casualties right off the bat, and one of them happened to be a Ranger that we were working with. He happened to be the primary SAW gunner, which is a light machine gun carried by one man, and he was in Pat's platoon . . . and now Pat, who was the secondary gunner . . . for the duration, he was the number one guy, and he would go on every single mission from there. He was thirsty to be the best, he wanted to be the best SAW gunner, and he would thrive in getting every bit of knowledge that he possibly could from my guys, from his guys; he couldn't get enough. And take it from me, there is nothing better than having a bunch of squared-away Rangers on your side, and Pat definitely raised the bar for him and his guys, no doubt about it.

1976–dash–2004. That one little dash in there represents a lifetime. How do we spend our dash?

I got the news early on Friday morning about Pat's death. I'd been spending the day flying back home, and I watched the news on every layover, waiting for the word to break. Once I saw that it was out, I contemplated at that point calling Marie. I knew that there was going to be a lot going on and I didn't want to add to it. When my wife picked me up at the airport, she asked if I'd called. I gave her my reason, and she looked at me and said, "If the tables were turned right now, would he have called me?" That's the kind of man Pat was. I immediately picked up the phone.

I had the opportunity to go to Washington, D.C., now and then, and one of the most impressive sites there is the Tomb of the Unknown Soldier. On the side of that tomb an inscription reads 'Here rests an honored and gloried soldier known only but to God.' And as we gather here today, here rests Pat, an honorable and gloried sportsman and soldier known not only to God but also to the many lives that he touched. He was absolutely one of the most remarkable human beings I've ever met. Whether as a dutiful son, a loving husband, or a faithful teammate, Pat's unencumbered zeal for life will never be forgotten. . . .

I've had teammates who are passed and are now guardians over the men who are fighting right now. Pat's joined them now. So when that little voice in your head tells you not to do the easy things but the right things, it's Pat right in your ear, man, it's Pat.

The real test of a man is not when he plays the role that he wants for himself but when he plays the role destiny has for him. Pat has more than passed his test.

The Silver Star and the Purple Heart that Pat has earned will be given to Marie at a private ceremony. The Silver Star is one of this nation's highest awards; the Purple Heart is rewarded for wounds received in combat. If you're the victim of an ambush, there are very few things that you can do to increase your chances for survival, one of which is to get off that ambush point as fast as you can. One of the vehicles in Pat's convoy could not get off. He made the call; he dismounted his troops, taking the fight to the enemy uphill to seize the tactical high ground from the enemy. This gave his brothers in the downed vehicle time to move off that target. He directly saved their lives with that move. Pat sacrificed himself so that his brothers could live. Blessed are the peacemakers, for they shall be called the sons of God."

I, like everyone in the audience, was greatly affected listening to the young Naval officer speak. He was the first person to give us an account of Pat's death. All we had been told was that he was shot in the head getting out of a vehicle. I forced myself to stare straight ahead. I did not want to break down at Pat's service.

Darius Rucker, the lead singer for Hootie and the Blowfish, followed Steve to the stage and sang a wonderful a cappella version of "America the Beautiful." Then came Jake Plummer, who was Pat's teammate throughout college and during his four years with the Cardinals. They had become very good friends. I smiled when Jake walked out to make his remarks wearing a suit and, in honor of Pat, a pair of flip-flops. Jake, who was now the quarterback for the Denver Broncos, said he was speaking on behalf of the teammates from the Cardinals and other players around the country.

As a teammate I was with Pat at Arizona State. I saw him come in on his recruiting trip with the long hair, some beat-up jeans and sandals; he really didn't look like he cared to be there much. But when he signed, I was happy. I could see something in the guy. I knew he was going to be a special player. As a teammate, he led by example. He was all-out, every play, whether it was practice or the game. He had an intensity that you can't describe. . . .

That was an inspiration to everybody that played ball with

Pat; it was an inspiration to the fans that watched Pat. That's why he touched so many people, just by running down on kickoff cover and maybe getting the hand on the guy, and the PR guy for the Arizona Cardinals or Arizona State was a smart man, would say "Pat Tillman on the tackle" because he knew the crowd would go crazy—whether he made the tackle or not.

He was fearless on the field, reckless, tough. He sprained his ankle his last year with the Cardinals, sprained it very badly. During practice I looked up and saw Pat running around the field on Wednesday. Most people would be in the training room, taking a break, getting out of the hot sun, saying ah, it's all right, I'm going to ice this down. He was out there because he felt his duty was to be on the field to be there with his teammates.

He was very courageous, he was unyielding, crazy—if there's ever a crazier man I'll meet in my life I'll be hard-pressed that he'd be crazier than Pat—in a good way. He was unbreakable and very unbelievable at times.

Another circumstance on the field I remember was him getting the ball on a kickoff. He wasn't supposed to, but he happened to catch the ball. He almost took it to the house, and I mean take it to the house by scoring a touchdown. When he got tackled he jumped up and looked around like, "What's the big deal, this ain't that hard." And that was Pat. I was laughing as I went out to take the offense out there and laughed the whole way out, just the fact that that he almost broke it and wasn't even supposed to be returning the kick.

He was a very caring teammate. He spent a lot of hours helping people that were hurt. A friend of ours a lot of people may know, Chris Gedney, he suffered from [ulcerative] colitis, was out of football for a couple of years, and Pat was at his bedside, he would go visit occasionally because he knew that it mattered, he knew that Chris was up there by himself and it was just Pat being Pat. He cared about everybody that he played ball with and was friends with. . . .

Before he left to go back for his last mission in Afghanistan he called to see how I was doing. And if that doesn't show the compassion and care of somebody, to call and check on me when I should be calling him to check on him—that was Pat. . . .

He was thought-provoking, and loved to have a deep conversation with some Guinness, a cold Guinness, and he would make you think. You would walk away saying, "I've got to become more of a thinker" . . . because the man was always thinking about everything. He liked to challenge your intellect in that regard also. If you argued with him you would usually lose because he was right every time. . . . He was so unique in so many ways. . . .

I was in the store the other day, and I saw *People* magazine, and it had the cover of fifty most beautiful people in the world, or America, and there was a picture of Pat, and a memorial to him. And it was kind of ironic because I really looked and said, what is beauty? Is beauty a pretty face, a nice smile, flowing hair, nice skin? Not to me, it's not. To me beauty is living life to higher standards, stronger morals and ethics and believing in them, whether people tell you you're right or wrong. Beauty is not wasting a day. Beauty is noticing life's little intricacies and taking time out of your busy day to really enjoy those little intricacies. Beauty is being real, being genuine, being pure with no façade—what you see is what you get. Beauty is expanding your mind, always seeking knowledge, not being content, always going after something and challenging yourself. Beauty is red, white, and blue, with stars and stripes, and beauty is why we're here today. To me, Pat was one of the most beautiful people to have ever entered my life as well as [the lives of] many others. Today and forever, let's remember what he was, let it filter through our lives so that we may become more beautiful inside and honor Pat in that way.

The last thing I want to talk about may be the saddest of all, or maybe the most disappointing, to me. Because we all know Pat through his career, ran a marathon, did a triathlon, gave up football to go join the Rangers—he shocked us all. To me the saddest part is to not know what Pat had planned next. I was looking forward to seeing him come out of the Rangers and to see what he had on his plate, so I could sit back and laugh and smile and go, "Man, that guy is," like I said earlier, "crazy." The challenges he made for himself we will never know.

And I believe that to really honor Pat, we should all challenge ourselves. No more "I'm going to do this" or "I'm going to do that." Do it. As Pat would say, probably, "Get off your ass and do it." Why, you ask, should we honor him this way? Because that's what Pat did his whole life.

I was so impressed with Jake's eulogy. He captured his friend as the young man I knew.

Alex then came up to the stage. He walked in front of the podium and poured a pint of Guinness into a glass, left it full in front of the podium, and then stepped up to the microphone.

There have been some extremely eloquent and powerful words said today about Pat Tillman the war hero, Pat Tillman the football player, and Pat Tillman that public figure. You know what, they're awesome words, and they're very, very much appreciated. But . . . for those of us up at the front, his close family and friends . . . we've lost our Pat.

So there's part of me that wants to step back and give up . . . throw in the towel, chalk it up, whatever term you want to use, but . . . you all out here know what the answer is, and it's a simple answer: There's no way that Pat would ever accept us giving up on life. There's not a chance because Pat's glass wasn't half empty; it wasn't even half full. Pat's glass was filled to the rim. It was overflowing with life.

And you couldn't feel any better about who you were when you were with Pat; you couldn't feel any better about life when you were with Pat. And he made you feel so good about yourself in so many different ways. Pat was good at just about everything he did, and living his life was absolutely no exception. If there was a manual on how to live life, Pat should have written it.

Pat surrounded himself with vast relationships, both broad and deep. And for those of us privileged enough to know him, we knew that our relationship with him was special and those relationships with Pat were absolutely genuine. He was big, and I'm not talking about how ripped he was, I'm talking about how big his heart was. And that heart was huge, and he spent his life filling that heart with friends and family like all of us.

It was a commitment, an absolute commitment, to be Pat's friend; he demanded—he accepted absolutely nothing less than—one hundred percent from you. When Pat asked you how you were doing, he looked you in the eye and listened to your answer. . . . He was a friend, he was a confidant; he was a friend who absolutely listened to what you had to say. There was no gray area with Pat, none. You knew how he felt about you.

Actions speak louder than words. He's a war hero—didn't talk about it. He's a football player—didn't talk about it. But with his personal friends and family, he wasn't mushy, but you knew how he felt. . . .

He's affected those of us in the front but so many people here and around the world [as well]. I had a friend call me when he heard the tragic news and said, "Man, I spent just a few hours with that guy having a couple of beers and he changed the way I think about life, he made me want to be a better person." Now the key to this is, this was five or six years ago, this was before Pat was a war hero, before Pat was a football player, when he was just Pat. So he touched lots of people. . . .

And then there's Marie. His sweet Marie. The biggest place in that heart was for Marie. She owned it, and Pat knew . . . that she was a champion. . . . And make no mistake, Pat felt absolutely lucky to have her, he knew she completed him. Marie humbled Pat, and . . . as you watched them go through their lives together [it] was a thing of beauty. . . .

Pat had a wonderful sense of humor. We all thought so, and the person who thought he was the funniest was Pat. He thought he was hysterical, and he was, he absolutely was, and he loved his friends and his family because we laughed at his jokes. And as a running joke he'd elbow me and say, "See, I'm funny," and he was.

And he had an infectious and just booming laugh. I can't do it justice, but his head would roar back and his hands would go wide, knocking stuff over, and it would just be booming, his eyes would get all slanty, and he would use that laugh anytime anywhere, and damn the consequences.

If you were in a restaurant and the people were disturbed, he was looking at them going, "I don't know why you're not laughing, 'cause this is really funny." And the laugh came easily and often. . . . You couldn't help but laugh when you were with him. And you couldn't help but laugh at him. He had this Christmas sweater and pink slippers and a kimono, which he thought was cool. And he wore them together. . . . He had a wonderful sense of self-deprecation; that humor was amazing. Pat and my friend Todd are the godfathers for my son Adam. There's no god-mother . . . so Pat decided to come to the baptism dressed like the godmother; he came dressed as a woman. Now he changed [his clothes]. But that's Pat, making fun of himself. . . .

Pat was on a constant quest to improve himself. He was pleased with who he was, but he was always growing. . . . Dannie . . . described it best. She said that Pat was deliberate about mak-ing himself a better person, and he really was.

And Pat's the kind of guy who talked to everyone. If you went running with Pat and Kevin, you were talking to everyone. . . . They said hello to everybody. You went in to get coffee with Pat, he was saying hello to the baristas, introducing you, you'd sit and have your coffee, and on the way out, he would make sure to look them in the eye and tell them thank you. That was Pat. People don't do that. But Pat did. And you couldn't help it when you were with him to want to be like that, to say please, to say thank you.

. . . Pat never met a topic that he didn't want to discuss. He'd call them debates or discussions, and he would develop an opinion oppo-site of yours just for the sake of discussing. . . . If you said it was left, he said it was right, if you said it was black, he said it was white. And he made sure to be educated so that he wasn't half-cocked, at least most of the time. And a great evening for Pat was spent with his friends and family and Marie having a couple of beers or coffee . . . and discussing or maybe playing Trivial Pursuit and making sure that everybody on the team got their say.

. . . And Pat never told you what to do. But he certainly helped you find your way, even when you didn't know you were lost. And if he thought he should do something, he did it. "Ah, I'm going to do a marathon." Did it. Triathlon? Not just a tri-athlon, a half Ironman triathlon. Play in the NFL? "Sure, I'll be an All-Star." "I'm going to go join the Rangers." But . . . when he decided to do something, he made the commitment, he put the effort behind it and he did all that it took to complete it. It wasn't easy.

... He was well read. Here's a man who read voraciously and he read anything and everything that he found interesting. He read the *Economist*, he read the Bible, he read the Koran, he read *Mein Kampf*, he read *The Communist Manifesto*, he read Thoreau. And as he read, he would underline passages that he found interesting.... You would often get letters from him, very eloquent letters, but you would often get articles that he'd cut out with something highlighted [with] "Hey, let's discuss..."

He made you feel that he wanted what you had, not in a jealous way, no, in a way, because Pat was so confident and so secure and comfortable with who he was, [that] allowed him to be absolutely genuinely happy for you. And that's a gift.

... Pat Tillman was a war hero, Pat Tillman was a football star, and he was a larger-than-life person, he was absolutely all those things. But ... the best thing about Pat was his commitment to his family and friends....

So would Pat let us give up? Not a chance. Would he let us give up on life? No. In fact it's exactly the opposite. And whatever cliché you can think of, he'd want us to seize the day, go forward, seize the bull by the horns, whatever one you want to put in there, that's what Pat would want us to do. So the single best thing about Pat is that he made you feel alive.... He made you challenge things, he made you appreciate everything every day, he made you appreciate your family and friends and respect them, he made you laugh, he made you think and made you want to be a better person.

Pat made you feel alive. Pat made you feel alive when he was here, and it's on us, to keep that going, and then he's never really gone.

Alex then walked in front of the podium, picked up the glass of Guinness, toasted Pat, and introduced Richard. I was struck by how tired and sad Alex looked. He was being very strong, but the pain in his eyes was obvious. Over the last several years, Pat and Alex had spent a lot of time together. I knew Pat was important to Alex and that he was feeling a profound sense of loss.

Alex walked off, and Richard walked up to the microphone. I was stunned. I didn't realize he was going to speak. I had given him a poem I wanted to have read; my close friend Julie Filippini e-mailed it to me. Julie was out of the country and unable to attend the service. I expected Richard to give the poem to someone else to read. He was so grief-stricken and angry; I didn't think it was wise for him to be up there. Marie was also concerned for him as she took my hand and squeezed it, knowing I was anxious for him.

I didn't do a good job of teaching my sons not to swear. The fact is, I did a terrible job. All three of them talked like stevedores, no matter the audience. After he took a drink from a pint of Guinness, I knew "f" bombs were going to fly. Richard had difficulty keeping himself composed. He was brief—and unforgettable.

> I didn't write shit because I'm not a writer. I just want to say it was really amazing to be his little baby brother, to be his Pooh [he starts breaking up here]. But I still have my Nubbin. [looking at Kevin] What up, Nub?
>
> I'm not just going to sit up here and break down on you. But thank you for coming. Pat's a fucking champion and always will be. But just make no mistake, he'd want me to say this, he's not with God; he's fucking dead. He's not religious, so thanks for your thoughts, but he's fucking dead. Yeah, take care. . . .

He walked from the stage, then returned.

Sorry, Mom, I almost forgot. My mom wanted someone to read the poem [attributed to Mary Elizabeth Frye] and I'm ... not pawning that off on anyone, I'll do that.

Do not stand at my grave and weep.
I am not there, I do not sleep.
I am a thousand winds that blow,
I am the diamond glints on snow.
I am the sunlight on the ripened grain.
I am the gentle autumn rain.
When you awaken in the morning's hush,
I am the swift uplifting rush
Of quiet birds in circled flight.
I am the soft stars that shine at night.
Do not stand at my grave and cry.
I am not there: I did not die.

Although Richard got a lengthy and supportive applause, I know there were people in the audience who cringed at his words. But oddly, I thought they were fitting—they were from the heart. The following day, Richard received quite a lot of criticism in the press for what he said. However, Dan Bickley of the *Arizona Republic* described Richard's appearance in almost poetic terms with an understanding of his grief and his background.

In the midst of a ceremony dripping with flags, tears and special guests in smart suits, the little brother walked on stage.

He was wearing a plain white T-shirt and blue jeans. The resemblance was so striking that it looked as if he could've fallen off his older sibling.

Before Rich Tillman said a word, he took a deep pull from a pint of Guinness.

"I didn't write [squat] because I'm not a writer," he said.

Then he announced with only a trace of regret that, for all the heavenly overtones attached to this lovely memorial service, Pat didn't have a religious bone in his body. Thus, he couldn't be looking down with appreciation or disgust or any other form of expression we'd so eagerly like to imagine.

"He's . . . dead," Rich Tillman said.

And there he was. Through his little brother's cameo appearance, Pat Tillman appeared in full view, complete with the candor, the nonconformity and the love of dropping cuss words at the most inopportune time. Especially when they can soil an elaborate broadcast.

I had no idea until after the memorial that it was broadcast on television; Richard didn't, either. Though, had he known, he wouldn't have changed a word.

Darius Rucker sang Pat's favorite song, "Desperado." The song was so beautiful but so painful to hear. Pat's friend Chad Schwartz followed Mr. Rucker. As Chad spoke, I was struck by the fact that Pat had given a eulogy for Chad's mother, Karen, Pat's "second mom," just seven months ago. Karen was an intelligent, warm, and generous woman. Pat liked and admired her. It was hard watching him as he sat at the kitchen table agonizing over what he would say. Now it was difficult to watch Chad as he paid tribute to Pat. Coach Lyle Setencich, Pat's ASU linebacker coach, lightened the mood. Pat was extremely fond of Coach Setencich, who coached Alex at Cal Poly University before Pat and several years later coached Marie's younger brother Paul at Berkeley. Coach Setencich started by mentioning them and other players he coached. Then he singled out several players in the audience, as if for support, and said to them of Pat:

> You know that he was different, he was different. It would be almost mind-boggling to try to explain to people how he was. I need to tell you a couple of stories. He and I did not get off on a very good note. He was a safety his first year at Arizona State . . . and I'm the new linebacker coach. And some of the coaches didn't feel he could play in the secondary so they moved him into linebacker. And I was brand new; I'd never met him before.
>
> Pat comes walking into my office. He says, "Hey, are you the new linebacker dude?" I looked at him, I said, "Yeah, I'm the new linebacker dude." He said, "Well, I hope you know your shit because I want to be good." And I said, "Son, I know my shit." He said, "What do you think about my freakin' hair?" which is down to his waist . . .
>
> I said, "Well, Patrick . . . young Pat, I'm a farmer, born and raised on a farm, and I've hunted all my life. And I've . . . had Springer spaniels with short hair [that] could hunt like hell, and I've had long-haired Springer spaniels that couldn't hunt worth a damn. But you know, when I found one that could hunt, I didn't give a damn whether his hair was long or short, I just wanted it to hunt." He looked at me square in the face and says, "Coach, I can hunt." From that time on, I had a special relationship with Pat . . . I loved him. . . . He was something special.
>
> I want to tell you about this time he came into my office. We'd just hired a new recruiting coordinator named Robin Pflugrad. [Pat] walks down, cruises by, his hair swinging, he says, "Coach, who's the new recruiting dude down there?" I said, "Coach Pflugrad's his name." He said, "Can he recruit?" I said, "Well, I don't really know him, Patrick, but I don't think

Coach Snyder would have hired him if he didn't think he could do a good job for us."

"Well, I got a list I want to show him . . ." He comes up with this list, and I said, "Let me see it, Pat." He says, "This is what we need. We need a big tackle, a gorilla tackle, three hundred pounds, and then we need a rush defensive end who can come off the corner and raise holy hell with the quarterback. We've got two good running backs, but we need another guy . . . we need a couple more guys; that's what we've got to have. And if we do, we're going to win the championship, we'll be national champions."

I said, "Patrick, you run down there and give it to him because hell, I'll probably get a new contract, at least get another year to work." And he runs down there and says, "Hey, recruiting dude, what's your name? Fluwind? Flu . . . ? You ought to change your name," Patrick says. "I've got this list for you . . . " [Pat went through his list and they did recruit those five players.] And we went and won eleven games, undefeated. . . . That was Pat, you know, most times he was right.

. . . He had this charisma about him, he had something. I'm going crazy at a linebacker, Derek Smith—Derek's out there somewhere today [gestures toward the audience]—I'm going nuts, and Pat would just say, "Hey, Derek. Hey dude, just line up over there, it'll be all right." Then he'd come back and tell me, "Hey coach, you shouldn't get so pissed off, you know that? I know what you mean, but you talk so goddamn much," he says, "no one can understand what you're saying, so just calm down; we'll be fine." That's how he was . . . .

The thing I liked most about Pat . . . [was that] young Pat Tillman would look at all the football field a guy could look at and he could make all these plays, but he'd come into my office about ten, eleven o'clock every night because he knew I was in there; my wife was still teaching in California.

And we'd sit down, and we'd start talking about things, start talking about God. He wanted me to read a Book of Mormon with him, so I did. We talked about that for hours, we talked about Kosovo for hours, we talked about all the kids in the ghetto who couldn't read or write, all the poor people in the country. What was this country going to do about those things? What could he do about it? Four nights a week, every night, we talked about something. . . . It was amazing, sometimes till two or three in the morning. It was something special, hard to explain.

One of the things I want to leave you with: Pat chose to do what he wanted to do. He made his own decisions. I talked to him about it. He came back from Iraq. I said, "What's the deal, Pat?" He says, "They'll let me out to go back to the NFL. But Coach," he says, "I want ask you a question; I signed up for three years. If you signed up for three years, what would you do? Would you leave early?" I don't want to answer that. He said, "Coach, I made a three-year commitment, I'm going three years. I'm not leaving." And that's the way it was. God bless Pat Tillman.

For a moment I sat stunned. I had no idea Pat had the ability to walk away from the military after his first tour of duty. Yet, I knew he would never have left Kevin, nor would he have broken his commitment to the Army or the Rangers. I knew Pat felt close to Coach Setencich, but I didn't know he would talk to him as often as he did. I thought it was wonderful that Pat felt comfortable enough with his coach to talk about important issues in life, not just football. And it was touching to watch the coach speak so movingly about him.

Two more of Pat's childhood friends, Jeff Bernal and Ben Hill, spoke. Ben went to kindergarten with Pat, and Jeff had been Pat's friend since they were seven years old. Both were in such shock, yet they were so articulate and moving. Another of Pat's coaches then walked to the microphone. Coach Dave McGinnis was Pat's defensive coordinator when Pat was drafted to the Cardinals in 1998 as a seventh-round draft pick. He later became his head coach. Coach McGinnis is a man with tremendous presence. Pat found him to be an excellent motivator and a good human being. He also has one of the most memorable and powerful voices I have ever heard. The audience sat transfixed the moment he started talking.

Pat Tillman was all that you've heard today: Honor, integrity, dignity; those weren't just adjectives in Pat Tillman's life; they were his life. Pat Tillman was the embodiment of loyalty and commitment. I experienced those firsthand very early on with Pat Tillman.

When Larry Marmie and I went to work Pat out before we drafted him over there on the practice fields at Arizona State University, a fifteen-minute session turned into a forty-five-minute ordeal because he wouldn't let us leave. He said, "Coach, you know damn well I can do it better than that, so let's do it again."

When Pat had a chance at free agency for a lot more money [$9 million for five years from St. Louis while he was making $512,000 with the Cardinals], I can remember standing there in the weight room when he came back from his visit. I said, "Tilly, what is it?" He said, "I'm not going anywhere." In his words, "How could I leave the organization and the coaches who believed in me and gave me a chance? That wouldn't be fair."

Martin Luther King, in one of his addresses, said, "The true measure of a man is not where he stands in times of comfort and convenience, but where he stands in times of conflict." There was never a question where Pat Tillman stood.

And if you wanted his opinion, all you had to do was ask him, and if you didn't want his opinion and didn't ask him, he'd still give it to you. The character of a man is a very valuable thing because it's very personal, it's something that every human being can mold within themselves. But the dignity of a character and the man is the ability to make a decision and stand by it. Pat Tillman dignified the word "character." . . .

Pat appealed to everyone; everyone felt like Pat belonged to them. I can still see us up there in Flagstaff, coming off the field, and the people surrounding Number 40 for his autograph were the little kids, their grandmothers, the macho guy that wanted to be a linebacker, the young girl, the old girls. It's because Pat Tillman . . . was a man that embodied everything, he was a man of many facets; he had an unbridled enthusiasm, a tremendous confidence balanced by a very genuine humility.

Pat Tillman has left us all a tremendous gift; it's his spirit, that unbridled unstoppable spirit of Pat Tillman. It's ours now . . . he left it for us. The last words I ever said to Pat Tillman were "thank you," as he left our locker room. I know that we'll all leave here today saying thank you to Pat Tillman and to those young men and women that are protecting our rights and our way of life. God bless Pat Tillman, God bless America.

I could picture Pat saying his good-byes to his former teammates and his coaches. I could see the gentle and sincere expression on his face as he left people who were so important to him. Tears spilled onto my dress as the coach left the stage.

Pat's close friend Jeff Hechtle then stepped up and read a touching personal letter he wrote to Pat. Pat and Jeff were extremely close, and it was difficult for me to see how much pain Jeff was experiencing over losing his friend. I will never forget how Jeff supported us the long days after Pat's death leading up to the memorial. He was an anchor, and he was hurting as much as we were.

Following Jeff was Coach Larry Marmie. Pat had enormous affection for Coach Marmie. He had been Pat's position coach for two years on the Cardinals, and then his defensive coordinator for two years. Pat liked Coach Marmie from the start, but the feelings were not reciprocated at first. Coach didn't care for Pat's brash approach or his penchant for using four-letter words. However, as he got to know Pat better, he began to change his opinion of him, and they developed a strong bond. Once, after Pat died, he shared his respect for Pat's intellect with a friend by describing how Pat had memorized the entire playbook before his first training camp started and corrected the coach when he made a mistake: "For four years, I felt like I was playing checkers and Pat was playing chess," Coach said. I had to steel myself for the speech given by this very earnest person.

> Pat was all about family. . . . In my mind, Pat Tillman was the guy we all want to be like. Pat lived life on his terms, he walked away from the comfort and the material things that most of us desire, he sought out danger for what he deemed to be a greater good, Pat was true to his heart. . . .
>
> Here's somebody that embodied the very concept of a role model. Fiercely unique, a strong dislike for the easy way out. He was caring, he was thoughtful, and he was soft. Pat was soft in the heart. He was humble yet confident, reserved, but he was hard. You wanted this guy on your team, and it didn't have to be a football team. You wanted him on your team in anything you were doing.
>
> Some people wonder why Pat did what he did; there had to be some other reason other than he felt it was the right thing to do. But simply put, that was his motivation. This past weekend a lot of teams around the National Football League had minicamps.

We had one, in St. Louis, where I now work. Everywhere, I looked I saw Number 40; I saw him sitting in the meeting room, I saw him on the field, I saw him in the dining hall.

One of my favorite memories of Pat was in the summer in Tempe, Arizona. Could be anywhere from 100 to 120 [degrees]. And usually after we got done with our minicamp work then, Dave McGinnis and I had us this little jogging trail that we would run almost every day on Warner Road. And so many of those days we'd be somewhere into our run, and here came Pat down Warner Road, 105 [degrees], windows down, didn't have any air-conditioning—didn't want it in his jeep—windows down, long hair flying, he'd stick his head out the window, he'd say, "Pick it up Coach, pick it up, faster, pick the pace up, keep on going." I'll miss that.

It was fun coaching Pat, it was challenging coaching Pat, it was an honor to coach Pat. I learned a lot from him. Players are usually trying to earn the respect of their coach; I found myself trying to earn Pat's respect. "Greater love has no man than this, that he lay down his life for his friends." Pat's earned his crown of glory.

God bless all the men and women that serve our country in our armed forces, and all those that have in the past.

Coach Marmie's voice broke with emotion several times. I could feel the coach's pain, and I bent my head down several times for fear my looking at him would cause me to cry. It is so clear why Pat had such admiration for this strong yet gentle man.

During Leland High School's 1993–94 title-winning season, Terry Hardtke was head coach; Pat played both offense and defense. Pat had known Coach Hardtke for years; his son B.J. was one of Pat's friends growing up. Terry already had been to the house and to the visitation. One evening he sat with Judy and me inside the camper that was parked in my driveway, and we talked about Pat and his friends for several hours. I knew he was struggling with Pat's death, and he was worried about his son losing his friend. He began his comments at the memorial by telling a funny—and typical—story about Pat. This was a story that had been reported numerous times, but the coach wanted to set the record straight.

We were in a play-off game . . . and at the half we were leading fifty-five to nothing; there was a running clock going on to make it easier to get the game over with. As we went back on the field in the second half, I went up to Pat and I said, "Pat, you're done for the day. I don't want you to play any offense, and play no defense." And he looked at me, real quizzical look, and he said, "Okay."

And as I am getting prepared for the second-half kickoff, my offensive coordinator turns to me and says, "You know, Pat's back there ready to take the kickoff." And I looked in astonishment and saw him back there, and he got the kickoff and of course ran it back for a touchdown.

And as he came off the field, I looked at him and all I could do is this [indicating "come here" with his index finger], and he came up to me very confidently and said, "You mentioned nothing about special teams." You know, he was right, [and] so that we didn't have any more misinterpretation of words, we claimed his helmet and his shoulder pads. . . .

[Another story] has to do when he was a freshman in high school, and he tried out for the baseball team. As a freshman he wanted to play varsity baseball, and Pat was a catcher. He was an outstanding . . . probably one of the best ones in his age group, he was an outstanding baseball player, this undersize catcher guy. . . .

And the final decision came down that he was not going to make the varsity baseball team. And so he was cut from the varsity and was going to be on the frosh-soph team. And he was not happy with that. In fact, he quit baseball at that point in time. And I came to him and I said, "You know, I really wish you wouldn't do that because I think you will have a great opportunity and a great future in baseball."

He says, "No, coach, I'm going to get into the weight room tomorrow and I'm going to become a football player." And . . . in my wisdom, I said, "Pat, that's probably a bad decision because if you're going to play a college sport it's going to have to be baseball; it certainly won't be football." So you folks don't have to ever listen to me again.

Terry read brief, touching letters from his sons, and then asked us all to celebrate Pat's life as Pat would have if he were there. He walked quietly off the stage as Zach Walz approached to address the crowd.

Zach went to a nearby private high school, Saint Francis. He and Pat played football at the same time but never against each other. Pat first met Zach at a basketball game when they were high school seniors. Pat went to Arizona State and Zach to Dartmouth, and later they were both drafted by the Cardinals. Zach began his speech with reminiscences from high school.

Pat's star even then shined quite a bit brighter than most others. He was a free-spirited, fast, feisty kid with a Fabio haircut. A long blond mane draped over the top of his shoulder pads. If he wasn't laying bone-jarring hits on running backs, you might witness him doing front flips on his way into the end zone. . . . He terrorized his opponents week in and week out and swiftly earned the reputation as one of the state's top players. My friends and I naturally admired him. . . . Not only was he the best player in our section, but he seemed like a cool guy. He was modest, fun, and he had this enthralling presence about him that can only be described as real. . . .

I remember it like it was yesterday, the first time I walked into the Cardinal facility. I was fresh out of the snow in New Hampshire, a pale, frightened, and undersized former Ivy League linebacker, surely not the most imposing figure. I was in a new city in a new state, I had no friends. . . .

I walked into our first meeting in the main lobby. I glanced across the room and the first person I saw was Pat. I went over to him, we shook hands, and he said in classic Tillman fashion, "What's up, dude? It's good to see you again, man." I was surprised he remembered. I don't think I ever told him how much he eased my fears. . . .

The Cardinals assigned us as roommates that very first day, which would last for the next five years until the final day that both our careers ended simultaneously. Every training camp, every home game, every flight, every restaurant, every practice, every meeting, every away game, every ordinary non-football day, he was my closest friend, he was my teammate . . . and I consider myself one hell of a lucky person.

In almost all sports, rookies have certain responsibilities to their veteran teammates, certain weekly chores that must be fulfilled. As a linebacker, our job was to bring the veterans breakfast every morning of every practice day prior to our seven thirty a.m. meetings. I was already having a hard time waking up at six thirty to make it on time. Now I had ten angry veterans demanding I bring them food at the crack of dawn. Needless to say, it took a little coaxing for me to get acclimated.

One day after practice, only seven weeks into our rookie season, our veteran group of linebackers slowly circled around me. They were trying to conceal some rolls of tape in their hands. It wasn't too hard to figure out what they were up to. I blanked on breakfast duty for the first half of the season. As punishment, they walked me over to the end zone, and in just a shade under five minutes, I found myself firmly attached to the big yellow goalpost.

The entire team went inside to eat as I was stranded outside in the Arizona sun, embalmed with white training tape. To make matters worse, a few lingering reporters and cameramen caught wind of the ruckus and were able to capture the story for the following day's newspaper. At one point, I was feeling pretty confident that I was going to be left out there for the better half of the afternoon.

Then, I saw Pat leaving the locker room and walking out toward me on the field. Despite repeated threats that he too would be taped up or dunked in the cold pool for freeing me, he continued forward. And remember, we were rookies, the lowest member of the food chain; our foremost goal was to not piss anyone off and do as were told. Even after I pleaded with Pat, "Don't do it, please Pat, it's not worth it, man, really, it's not worth it, I'll be fine," he still untied me. We walked back inside and finished our lunch. And that was that, I was free. Pat, on the other hand, was prepared to accept his fate, but strangely, nothing else came of it.

Although it may seem like a relatively meaningless story to some, it was the countless number of these minor accounts of Pat that best reflect the character and principle by which he conducted his life. He never turned his back on anyone—not his friends, not his family, certainly not his country.

Pat wore his emotions on his sleeve. If something bothered him, you'd know about it. And if he had the opportunity to fix it, he would dive in headfirst without even a second consideration. He was a charismatic leader; he was a fierce competitor. He was firm in his beliefs and he commanded respect.

Yet he also was a loving son, husband, a brother, and friend to thousands. He had an intoxicating passion for life and an unquenchable thirst for personal, intellectual, and social improvement. Tilly always acted in the way he knew was right, and to him, it was always worth it.

I found this article in my closet a short time ago. It's entitled "Cardinal Linebackers Adopt Military Path," dated Sunday, December 13, 1998. After making it to the play-offs in 1998, in an act of solidarity, our coach bought us personally engraved silver-plated dog tags. I'm actually quoted in this article saying, "We do consider ourselves soldiers, and these tags are kind of something we can stay close to as we go out and battle these last three weeks." Other quotes: "It's something we talk about all the time. We consider ourselves soldiers and play through pain, adversity, and things like that." "Coach looks at us like soldiers who go out there and lay it on the line every time we're on the field in practice, games and in meetings."

Listen to these words: *soldiers, battle, lay it on the line, adversity.* What the hell do we know? Indeed, our intentions were noble, but this article, with these metaphors, how hollow they now ring, and how hollow similar comparisons will forever ring from this point forward.

When I saw Pat this last December in Los Gatos, somehow this story leaped into my memory. Immediately, I expressed to Pat there could be no greater honor for me as a proud friend than to be able to wear the dog tags of a true soldier. I begged Pat for the symbol of his ultimate commitment so that I could forever carry it close to my heart and wear it with the utmost pride. His name inscribed on two metal cards is an inspiration to us all and evokes a magnitude of patriotism that only he could stir up.

Two weeks later, Pat sent me his dog tags in the mail. Words can hardly describe what they mean to me. It is often very difficult to not feel a sense of worthlessness in the presence of Pat. I felt compelled to give something back to him as he and so many others continue to sacrifice so much more. But that was the last time I saw Pat.

And now the only thing I can give back is to wear his name with honor, and willingly provide unconditional and unwavering love and support for his wife, his family, and his fellow service-men and women. But the final promise, and no matter what the end shall bring, we will continue to turn the wheel of progress, that Pat insisted, for as he once said, "If we're not getting better, we're old news."

And although I'm holding these dog tags in my hand today, I assure you this: This is the farthest as they will ever be from their place around my neck. For as long as gravity pulls, they will hang down close to my heart, the place where Pat Tillman has perma-nently emblazoned his mark.

I look forward to the day when I can pass these dog tags on to my son, then he too can share what's it's like to walk tall with pride, knowing the man around his neck to which he humbly pays tribute made this world a better place to live.

Someday I can share with him stories about that man, my old friend Tilly, as Richard so eloquently put it, the biggest effing champion I've ever seen. Although Pat is not with us in body, somewhere down the road, our souls will cross paths again, and you can count on it buddy.

Zach's speech was incredibly impressive and moving. He was so articulate and poised. I recalled how he had called me after learning of Pat's death. He was so grief stricken and shocked he couldn't speak. He had to call another time. I felt so helpless. I didn't know how to comfort him. There just weren't any words. I had never heard about Pat cutting Zach down from the goalpost. It didn't surprise me, though. Pat was never afraid to stand up to people he thought were in the wrong. I remembered so well the evening in the Los Gatos bar, when Zach told Pat he would be honored to wear his dog tags. I saw the expression on Pat's face. He was so touched that his friend would want to support him. I could only imagine how touched he would be by Zach's words that day.

Paul Ugenti, Marie's younger brother, also spoke, as did his father. Pat's father was the last speaker. I commended him for speaking; I would never have been able to do that. He wore dark glasses, but you didn't have to see his eyes to recognize the pain reflected on his face. He lost his composure when he spoke about losing Pat but regained it by thanking the people of New Almaden and the Tempe-Phoenix area of Arizona, as well as the San Jose police and fire departments.

I miss my son; it's only been a week, and it ain't getting any better. . . . The last few days have not been very pleasant, but they would have been a lot worse if we'd have been bothered by things that I didn't want to do. There's a lot of folks that have been helpful to us. The San Jose police department kept us nice and quiet and secure and gave us our week to just stay with each other and deal with the friends of the family . . . same with the fire department. . . .

. . . I want to thank anybody involved in the military, especially the Rangers, there's at least one SEAL I'm aware of; outstanding human beings.

I don't know a lot about what happened to Pat, and a lot of the details I really don't care about. But it's important to me to know that the situation was bad . . . and Pat was unlucky, it's unfortunate, but Pat was doing his job. And I don't even know what the Ranger motto is, but I'll bet you a buck that he upheld it. And I'll find out what the stuff is later on, but I know enough to know that Pat was going at it the way he always went at it.

Following the speakers, three soldiers in military dress approached Marie, Pat's father, and me, and presented each of us with a flag. I will never forget looking into the beautiful olive-green eyes of the young soldier who stood before me. They were filled with sadness. I instinctively stroked his wrist as he placed the flag in my hands. The bagpipes once again had begun to play, and we were escorted out of the garden.

We were driven back to our little community of New Almaden. Friends and family members gathered at the Casa Grande, the historical structure down the road from the house that is surrounded by lawn and a variety of giant trees. The scent of eucalyptus soothed and comforted me. Friends had set up an abundant buffet, and tables were set up for people to eat and talk. I was so exhausted by the time we reached the reception that my memory is vague. But sometime during the evening, military personnel arrived and very hastily presented Marie, Patrick, and me each with Pat's Purple Heart, Silver Star, and an abridged Silver Star citation.

The evening after the memorial service, a small gathering of several of our closest friends and family members came to our house, along with Steve White and the young soldier with the olive-green eyes. His name was Russell Baer. Immediately I recalled the name. Pat and Kevin had each written to me about befriending a young man, about Richard's age, who wrote beautiful poems. I learned he had been about twenty to thirty meters behind Pat on the ridgeline, and he had helped Kevin escort Pat's body from Afghanistan to San Francisco.

After some light conversation and a meal, Pat's father asked Russell to tell us what happened the night Pat died. Russell was visibly uncomfortable with the question, but he proceeded to tell us what happened. He told us that once Pat got out of his vehicle he sought out Bryan O'Neal. Sergeant Matt Weeks indicated that several fire teams were to move up the ridge. Pat and O'Neal ran up the steep incline. Russell said an Afghan Militia Force soldier followed Pat and O'Neal toward the enemy that was firing on the second serial. Baer said the fire team to which he was attached was to the left of Pat and O'Neal. He said Pat, O'Neal, and the Afghan were taking fire, and Pat positioned O'Neal behind a rock to get him out of the line of fire. He said O'Neal was frightened. Pat calmed him down and told him where to orient his fire. He told O'Neal he had an idea and he was going to get some guidance from Sergeant Weeks. Pat ran across the ridgeline to ask Weeks if he was in a sound position and to see if he could take off his body armor and try to move toward the southern ridgeline. Weeks told him his position was fine and he could advance the enemy, but he was to leave his body armor on. Pat said okay and returned to O'Neal.

The enemy fire became more intense, and Pat and O'Neal were firing back. Pat got hit repeatedly in the legs and as he went down, he was shot in the head. Tears streamed down my face as I listened to the story. It was gut-wrenching to learn Pat had been seriously wounded before he was actually killed. I quietly got up and walked to my room.

After I finish talking about the memorial, Katie, Lannie, and Tom sit reverently for several minutes. They don't know what to say. I tell them I don't need for them to say anything. I thank them for listening, then I excuse myself and go upstairs. I lie down on my grandmother's four-poster bed as Russell's account of Pat's death plays in my mind. I learned from Kevin shortly after we were informed of the fratricide that Russell was told by his superiors to keep his mouth shut when he accompanied Kevin home with Pat's remains. Russell was placed in a horrible position. He knew Pat was likely killed by his own troops, but he didn't know exactly what happened, as Pat's position on the ridgeline was obscured to him. Being ordered not to tell us what he knew was bad enough, but his situation was complicated by the fact that at the memorial service, the Army presented a narrative that wasn't true. He was so distraught by the Army's deception and having to keep what he suspected from us that he didn't return to Fort Lewis as ordered, and he was threatened with a court martial. Now I wonder what parts of his version of Pat's death were true. Did rounds repeatedly strike Pat in the legs? Was his body hit? Did he suffer? Softly, I cry myself to sleep.

II

If a man does his best, what else is there?

—General George S. Patton

I wake up to Katie and Lannie talking in the kitchen. Quickly I take a shower and dress. Once downstairs, I find Tom reading the newspaper, Katie cooking eggs, and Lan pouring muesli.

"Good morning," all three say cheerily.

"How about some eggs and fruit?" Katie asks.

"That sounds great," I say, helping myself to coffee.

We carry our plates to the cozy breakfast nook that looks out onto the tree-lined side street.

"Did you sleep all right?" Tom asks.

"Yes. I slept fine."

"Katie was telling me how wonderful your friends are," Lannie says. "She said everyone she met at your house was so compassionate, even your principal and fellow teachers."

"I have very special friends, and the people I work with have been amazing through all of this."

"How is Carmen?" Katie asks. "She is a lovely young woman."

Carmen Navarro, my assistant at school, has worked with me for two years. At twenty-six years old, she is one of the most innately wise individuals I have ever known, and she is magical with children. I have always felt she has been supportive of me, but the last few months I would describe her as vigilant.

"Carmen is doing fine," I say. "I'm very lucky to have her in my life. I hope she'll still be working with me next year."

"Dannie, I read you went to a memorial for Pat in Arizona. What was that like?" Tom asks.

"There were two memorials in Tempe. One was private and one was public. Both were wonderful tributes, but it was extremely difficult to go back there," I tell him. "I have such vivid memories of Pat in Tempe. Except for the last year and a half, he had lived in Tempe since high school."

I begin to describe what it was like to go back to the city where we shared so many good times with Pat.

After arriving at Phoenix Sky Harbor Airport, I walked slowly on the moving sidewalk in a corridor that connects the Southwest terminal to the main complex. I had walked that corridor so many times coming to see Pat and Kevin during their years at ASU and when Pat played for the Cardinals. My stomach felt queasy as I looked out of the window at the familiar landscape. When I glanced over at Kevin and Richard, I knew they were feeling the same. Once outside we waited for the shuttle that would take us to the hotel. Maybe it was the heat, but standing on the sidewalk across from the terminal, I felt like I was in a grainy haze. I always had associated Arizona with fun and excitement, but not now that Pat is gone. We boarded a shuttle for the drive to the Tempe Mission Palms Hotel. This place holds many great memories for me, but one in particular stands out.

It was in August 1994, when Pat began his first practice for Arizona

State University. Once his phone was connected in his dorm, he called home about every other day; he was terribly homesick. After two weeks, he called to tell me he really needed his bike. I knew he would need it; his dorm was much farther from the campus than we had expected. I told him we would try to get it to him in the next week or so. Patrick told me he couldn't get away from work, so we decided I would drive the bike to Arizona. But Patrick didn't want me to drive alone, and Kevin and Richard both had their own football practice, so he suggested that I ask my brother to go. Mike said he could leave the upcoming Friday after he got off the late shift; we were going to surprise Pat.

I let Pat believe the Arizona trip was tentative, and I assured him that if we couldn't drive there, we would ship the bike to him. "Well, I sure hope you come," he said.

The night we were to leave, Patrick put bike racks on the car, and Mike and I left for Tempe as soon as we could. After we passed the Gilroy garlic plant, Mike's throat started to hurt. He believed it was some kind of allergic reaction from the heavy garlic fumes in the air. He felt so poorly that we stayed the night in a hotel and left the following morning. We got into Tempe around six p.m. on Saturday and checked into the Tempe Mission Palms Hotel, which is down the street from Sun Devil Stadium. I started to call Pat, but my brother stopped me.

"Don't tell him we're here—let's *really* surprise him," Mike said. "Let's call and tell him we couldn't make it. The Greyhound shipping station is across the street from the stadium. Tell him you've shipped the bike and he needs to pick it up there. We can be there when he shows up."

"Oh, he's going to be so disappointed. I hate to do that to him," I said.

"Dannie, it will be worth it."

I picked up the phone and called Pat. "Hello," he said.

"Hi, Pat."

"Mom, hi. Are you here?" he asked anxiously.

"No, we couldn't make it. We shipped the bike to you. It's at the Greyhound station. You need to get it tonight."

"Mom, the Greyhound station is closed now," he said. "I really wish you could have come."

I felt terrible playing this game with him. I could tell he was so disappointed.

"Pat, I arranged for the bus station to stay open so you can pick up the bike. They're waiting for you."

"But Mom, I'd rather keep talking to you."

I looked pleadingly at Mike. "Don't tell him," he mouthed.

"I know, Pat. I want to talk to you, too. Go get the bike and call me as soon as you get back to the dorm."

It's a long walk from the dorm to the bus station, and Pat told me he would call back in about an hour.

"Mike, I can't believe I did that. He is so sad."

"Well, he won't be when he sees you," Mike said.

Mike and I had a drink at the hotel lounge, then drove to the nearby bus station. We parked, got out, and talked until I could see Pat walking toward us in the distance. We both quickly ducked behind the wall surrounding the parking lot. As Pat got closer, I could hear him whistling. When he walked by the wall we were crouched behind, Mike jumped up and said, "Hey, punk! You looking for a bike?"

Pat was startled and reflexively jumped into a defensive position. I stood up. Instantly, a huge smile formed on his face.

"Mom! Uncle Mike! You're here!"

The three of us started laughing. Mike grabbed Pat and gave him a big hug, then I walked over and hugged him.

"This is awesome! I can't believe you're here," he said with a giant grin.

"How about some dinner?" Mike asked.

"Sure! We're staying at the Mission Palms. Do you want to stay with us?"

"That would be great," he said. "Let me call my roommate, Brian, and let him know I won't be coming back tonight."

We ate dinner at Bandersnatch Brew Pub just down the street. Inside, the walls were brick and the lighting was dim. It had a very cozy atmosphere. We ate burgers, drank beer and Coke, and joked about the place being named after the fictional monster in Lewis Carroll's poems "Jabberwocky" and "The Hunting of the Snark." After too many beers, we all see our own Bandersnatch.

After dinner, we went back to the hotel and talked for hours. Pat spoke about how much he missed Marie and that he couldn't wait for her first visit. He also missed Kevin and Richard. We had three bedrooms in our house when the boys were growing up. They would take turns being roommates. The last three years, Pat had his own room and his brothers shared. He told me he missed lying in bed listening to Richard, our family comedian, tell jokes to Kevin and hearing the two of them just goof around. Pat said he would be in hysterics, too. We laughed about how the boys had a communal clothing bin; even though Richard was four years younger than Pat and three years younger than Kevin, they shared clothes, including underwear and socks. The bins also served as a holding area for clothes left behind by their friends, and the boys had no qualms about incorporating them into their wardrobe until their rightful owners claimed them.

Pat discussed how excited he was for Kevin's upcoming football season and told us he would miss playing on the same team with him. He said he was looking forward to his dad and Richard coming to Arizona to see his first college game. After driving so far that day, I should have been exhausted, but it was so great to see Pat that I didn't even feel sleepy.

The next day, the team had its first night practice in the stadium under the lights, and Pat was pretty excited. Mike asked if we could watch, but Pat said he didn't think spectators were allowed, so we told him we would take him to dinner after practice. The night was beautiful, the temperature comfortable, and there was a wonderful breeze. Mike and I were going to kill time walking around Mill Avenue, but when we saw the lights of the stadium and other people going in, we decided to discreetly go in and watch. The stadium was so impressive, and we were excited to be there to see Pat practice. The dry lightning that began to light up the desert sky gave us an even greater thrill. We sat in the stadium opposite to where Pat was practicing so we would not embarrass him by being there, but he spotted us. Instead of ignoring us, however, he smiled and waved wildly. We waved back with pride.

Mike and I stayed in Tempe for several days. The day Pat's classes began, we walked him to his first class. We were going to say good-bye then, but Pat asked us to stay until his class was over so we could all go to lunch. It was clear he didn't want us to leave. We agreed to wait. After lunch, Pat was extremely sad to see us go. I reminded him that his dad and Rich would be coming to his first game in a few weeks. As we were getting into the car, Pat handed me a note. With moist eyes, he told me to read it later. We hugged him and, with heavy hearts, drove away. I hung out the car window and waved until I could no longer see him. Once we got about ten miles out of town, I opened the letter and started to read it aloud.

Mom & Mike,

I would have just come out and said this, but I know my eyes would have swelled and I would not have been able to talk. I would like to tell you that I am very glad you came to see me. I don't think you realize how much it means to me. This whole thing is a lot harder to deal with than I ever expected. It makes me feel like a wuss every time I begin to cry. However, I can do nothing to change it. I'm sure I will be fine pretty soon. My moods right now change constantly from Ok to sad to really sad. Your being here really helped though. It is comforting to know someone cares.

I will call quite a bit and if either of you are bored please call, I will enjoy the company. . . .

My voice started to falter, so I put the letter down.
"It's okay, Dannie. We can finish it another time."

That memory faded as the airport shuttle pulled into the hotel parking lot. We checked into our rooms, then met up with Patrick, Marie and her family, and several of Pat's friends. We all went across the parking lot to one of Pat's favorite bars, Rúla Búla, for drinks before we got ready for the private memorial that evening, but sitting in the bar felt empty. Without Pat it was not the same for any of us. We had time before the memorial, so we walked down to the ad hoc tribute to Pat that was outside the stadium. We passed Bandersnatch and saw it was boarded up. All of us were saddened. We had shared many meals with Pat there. "When did it close?" Rich asked. "April 22," Marie said drily. We later learned it had shut down in October 2003.

The private memorial service organized by the university was quite touching. Professors, coaches, players, and others who knew Pat were there, and the speeches were eloquent. Sports newscaster Jude LaCava presented a video on the jumbo screen of three interviews with Pat I had never seen. Clips of his plays were shown, accompanied by touching yet haunting music. Seeing Pat speak on the big screen was joyous and heartbreaking at the same time. After the memorial, we spoke with many guests. One of Pat's professors brought

Duff McDougall, a classmate Pat had befriended. I spoke with Duff, and he told me Pat was a special person and a good friend to him.

The public memorial was the next day, May 8. Speakers included Arizona governor Janet Napolitano and Arizona State University president Michael Crow, along with coaches and teammates.

I remember smiling when Derrick Smith, who had played with Pat at ASU and was then playing for the Washington Redskins, recounted speaking to Pat on the field when the Cardinals played in Landover in 2001. Derrick asked Pat how he was doing. Pat told him he was fine, but his legs were a bit weary because he had spent hours the day before walking the National Mall, visiting all the memorials and looking at monuments. While listening to the speakers, I glanced over to the left corner of the field. My throat constricted. I could see Pat, ten years ago, smiling broadly and waving his arms at Mike and me as we sat in the stands watching his practice. I remember how excited he was to be playing, how hard he had worked to get to that point, and how hard he continued to work through college and the pros.

It was in the spring of his seventh-grade year that Pat decided he wanted to play football instead of soccer. Many of his close friends had played in the Police Athletic League (PAL), and he wanted to also. His dad and I were a bit nervous about injuries, but we agreed to it. He had a lot to learn, but he loved the camaraderie and contact. One weekend in early fall, Patrick went to San Diego for a legal seminar, and I took Richard and Kevin to Kevin's soccer tournament in Fairfield, three hours north of San Jose. Pat stayed with his good friend Chad Schwartz because he had a football game. We drove to Fairfield on Friday right after school.

At about midnight, I received a call at the hotel from Chad's mother, Karen, a nurse, that Pat had broken his ankle at practice. She told me it was a minor break and not to worry. I felt terrible for Pat. I knew he probably wouldn't be able to play for the rest of the season, and he would be upset. I told Karen I would be at their house in a few hours, but she discouraged me from driving. She said I should wait until morning. I took her advice and got some rest. At around six thirty a.m., I left Kevin in the care of his coach and his wife and took Richard with me to get Pat.

Richard and I walked into Karen's house to find Pat lying on the couch in a full leg cast. Even though he was heavily drugged, it was clear he was in great pain. Tears filled my eyes and a knot formed in my throat as I looked at him. I turned my gaze to Karen. Seeing my pained and confused expression, she sympathetically explained that one of the big tackles had fallen on Pat's leg during a play, and he actually had two serious breaks in his right tibia. She apologized for not telling me on the phone how bad his breaks were, but she was afraid she wouldn't be able to keep me from driving home in the middle of the night if I knew the truth. She worried that I would have an accident, and there was nothing I could do anyway. I was sick that I hadn't been with Pat when his leg was set. I knelt next to him, and through his pain he gave me a weak smile. "Hi, Mom," he said. The knot in my throat got bigger as I tried to hold back tears.

There was no way I could get Pat to our house in our Volkswagen Rabbit; he couldn't bend his leg. Karen told me her husband would drive him home in their van. Richard and I went ahead to prepare a place for him. We made a bed on the couch so he wouldn't be isolated in his room. Richard, who was nine, had recently had a cast removed from his arm, which he'd broken in a skateboard accident earlier in the year. He was feeling his brother's pain. As Pat rested on the couch, his leg throbbing and his stomach sick from codeine, Richard sat on a stool next to him, tears rolling down his face, rubbing Pat's arm and trying to make him feel better.

Days later, I learned from various people present that when Pat was injured, he had lain on the field for a very long time, as the ambulance took an unusually long time to get to him. A friend, Art Herbig, was watching another team practice at an adjacent field. His own son had just recovered from a pretty serious back injury, and he was keeping an eye on his practice when he learned Pat had been hurt. He told me he hustled over to Pat, who was lying on a mat in terrible pain, his leg obviously broken. Art bent over to give comfort. Pat looked up at him with glassy eyes and told him he was all right, then asked, "Mr. Herbig, how is Artie's back doing?"

It took more than four months for Pat's leg to heal enough to be out of the cast. He had lost a lot of weight, and his leg had lost a great deal of muscle. He was very anxious to get himself in condition to play football in high school the following fall.

He started running with Kevin's soccer team, the Outlaws, to get back in shape. It was late December, and Kevin's team still had several tournaments left in the season. Kevin's soccer coach asked Pat if he would be interested in playing on the team in order to get into condition, as well as help the team, which was short a player due to an injury. Because of Pat's November birthday, he was eligible to play in two different age divisions. Pat agreed to play for the remainder of the season. Kevin was delighted.

Pat practiced with the team for several weeks and decided his leg was strong enough that he could participate in the Fresno tournament. Kevin was a right wing, and Pat was made a forward. Every time Kevin got the ball, he would look for his brother and pass it to him when he was open. Each time Pat struck the ball with his still-fragile leg, I cringed. In the final game, time was running out, and we were down points. Kevin was running downfield and picked up the ball on a perfectly placed pass. He dribbled it around several players, then passed it to an open man. That player kicked the ball hard over to Pat, and I feared Pat would hurt his leg as he struck it for the shot on goal. However, the ball came in high.

Pat could tell the ball might go out of bounds if he waited for it to hit the ground, so he ran at full speed and punched the traveling ball with his crotch. The ball soared into the goal. I don't remember if that was the final play or even if we won the game. I just remember the look of extreme satisfaction on Pat's face when he scored. After five long months, he was thrilled to be a contributing member of a team once again. That night, my brother called to find out how the tournament went. Richard answered the phone and excitedly said, "Uncle Mike, Pat scored a goal with his nuts!"

By the time Pat started high school football practice in the summer of 1990, his leg was stronger than ever. Although he was considered small for a football player, he was determined to do well. One of his junior varsity, and later varsity, coaches, Don Swanson, told me he remembers the first time he saw Pat when he was playing on the frosh-soph team; he described him as a midget playing corner. That year was a learning year for Pat, as he had played so little football. He developed skills, learned plays, and took a great interest in conditioning. He worked out in the school weight room, and he, his brothers, and their friends would lift weights in our family room while they talked about life.

By the end of the season, Pat seemed satisfied with his play, but he mentioned to his dad and me that his buddy, Jeff Bernal, told him he was a terrible blocker. That was something he said he would have to work on. He wanted to play on the varsity team his sophomore year, but there was a rule that players had to be fifteen by the start of the season; Pat wouldn't be fifteen until November. He had to accept the fact that he would be playing junior varsity the following year.

Pat's quality of play improved a great deal by the time he started to play varsity his junior year. All of his teammates played solidly and looked forward to their senior season. Over the course of the spring, Kevin, a sophomore, decided he would go out for football, too. During the summer double-day practices, when they practiced twice a day, they had a terrific time. By the time school started, they'd been doing more with each other and with each other's friends than they had since early middle school. They worked out together, ran together, and stayed up late and talked together. In the mornings, Pat would drive Kevin to school in our old, copper-colored Rabbit. Of course, they always seemed to leave the house with very little time to spare. If they didn't find a parking space in a matter of minutes, they would be late. A friend of mine who lived near the school told me several times she saw Pat angle the nose of his car into a tight parking space on the street. The front of his car would be close behind the bumper of the car parked in front of him, while the back stuck out into the street. He and Kevin would jump out of the car, grab their backpacks from the back seat, lift the rear end of the car into the parking space, then run like hell to class.

Through the hard work and tenacity of the players and the coaches, the 1993–1994 season turned out to be exceptional. Leland High School won the Central Coast Section Division I championship. Pat earned Co-player of the Year honors for the Central Coast Section. He played hard and performed well. In one memorable game, he caught a punted ball and ran it back for a touchdown, only to have the play called back for a penalty. It was punted to him again, he scored again, and there was another penalty against Leland. A third punt, another catch, another touchdown; this time it counted, and the Leland crowd went wild. At the end of the season, Pat was expecting to be actively recruited. As it turned out, while he got a lot of encouraging letters, there were not many recruiting offers. The college recruiting process was very distasteful to Pat. It involved turning down universities that wanted him and being rejected by those he wanted to attend.

As good a player as he was in high school, there wasn't much interest in him by most colleges because he was considered small at 5 feet 11 inches tall and 195 pounds. Coaches didn't believe he could transfer his talent to the college level because he would be competing against much bigger players. When Pat interviewed with Coach Bruce Snyder at Arizona State, the coach asked him what he thought of the recruiting business, and Pat, characteristically honest, said, "It sucks. Nobody tells the truth."

Sometime shortly after Pat accepted the last scholarship ASU had to offer, Coach Snyder talked to Pat about the possibility of redshirting, which restricts players from playing their freshman year in order to extend eligibility. Pat didn't want to stay in college for five years just to play football. In the conversation with the coach, Pat told him, "I'm not redshirting. I've got things to do with my life. You can do whatever you want with me, but in four years, I'm gone."

His freshman year, Pat played on special teams, units that are on the field during kickoffs, free kicks, punts, and extra point attempts. In his first ASU game, Pat made his first college special teams tackle in front of the stands where his dad and Richard were sitting.

We would go to Pat's games whenever possible. Phoenix is about a ten-hour drive from San Jose and about a two-hour flight. Pat's sophomore year, 1995–96, he rotated in as linebacker. That year, Richard and I flew to Arizona for the UCLA game. We were so excited to be going. Unbeknownst to us, the time of the game had been changed because it was being televised, and it started earlier than our schedule indicated.

We got into a cab and told the driver to take us to Sun Devil Stadium. The driver turned around and said, "The game's almost over." He said he had been listening to it on the radio, and ASU was losing by a wide margin. Richard and I looked at each other and our jaws dropped. We asked the driver to turn on the radio again, and just at that moment, the announcer said, "Pat Tillman on the tackle." Rich and I were thrilled, and we pressured the driver to get us to the game quickly. We arrived at the stadium and hustled out of the cab. We heard thunderous noise coming from the field. Our tickets were at will-call, but the window was closed, so we ran straight to the gates. The stadium personnel weren't going to let us in, but I told them we had the game time wrong and we had just flown in. I pleaded,

"My son is playing." The two employees looked at each other, shrugged, and opened the gate. We walked into the stadium, and the crowd was going wild. The whole game had turned around. Rich and I slid into an aisle and stood in front of some empty seats. Everyone was on their feet screaming, yelling, and waving. We got to see ASU beat UCLA 37–33. Because the game turned around once we landed in Tempe, with more than some amusement, Rich and I took credit for the victory.

That same year the ASU Sun Devils played the Nebraska Cornhuskers in Lincoln. Patrick and my brother went to that game. They enjoyed seeing the city of Lincoln and watching the game in historic Memorial Stadium, often called the Sea of Red because of the devoted fans clad in Cornhusker colors. ASU got clobbered; the final score was 77–28.

The following year, ASU played Nebraska on September 21 in Tempe. The whole town was excited about the game, but no one had forgotten the butt-kicking the Devils got the year before. It was a new season, however, and now both teams were nationally ranked in the top twenty, Arizona State at seventeenth and Nebraska first. The season was young, and neither team had a loss. Patrick, Richard, and I arrived in Tempe early in the morning. We met up with Kevin, who had received a baseball scholarship to Arizona State and joined Pat in the fall of 1996. We could feel the tension and excitement. Huge banners had been hung all over town to pump up and support the team. By midafternoon, we started to notice how many Cornhusker supporters were walking on Mill Avenue and on Fifth Street, in front of the stadium. A Sea of Red was forming in Tempe.

We anxiously passed the last few hours before the game people-watching around the stadium. Richard proudly sat with Kevin in an area reserved for the ASU baseball team, while Patrick and I sat midway up in the stands looking over the thirty-yard line. It was thrilling to see the stands so packed with fans, although clearly, the Nebraska fans outnumbered ours. When the Cornhuskers entered the field, it appeared their players outnumbered ours as well. I joked with Patrick that their side of the field looked like an illustration from *The Cat in the Hat*. Every time I looked out at the Nebraska side, I saw more players coming out of their tunnel. I didn't think teams could bring so many players to away games, but evidently the conference rules for the Big 12 were different from ours in the Pac 10.

After the first quarter, ASU was winning 9–0. In the second quarter, Pat got a safety after tackling the quarterback, Scott Frost, in the end zone after Frost fumbled the ball on a miscued play. I jumped up like a maniac cheering for him. Everyone was excited that the Sun Devils were playing so well and keeping the Huskers from scoring. By halftime we were ahead 17–0. The ASU fans were excited, but this was Nebraska; anything could happen. When the final whistle blew, ASU had beaten the number-one-ranked team in the country 19–0: one touchdown, two field goals, and three safeties. Coach Snyder said he had never been in a game where three safeties were scored.

There was absolute, delightful pandemonium. Patrick ran from the stands to see if he could find Pat before he went into the tunnel. I sat mesmerized by the scene before me. Everyone seemed to be moving in slow motion, exulted expressions on the faces of the Arizona fans. They flooded the field to congratulate players, and a mass of them took down one of the goalposts and carried it out of the stadium. The following day, the *Arizona Republic* said it was recovered somewhere on Mill Avenue, more than four blocks away.

Arizona State went undefeated in the regular season, ensuring its Rose Bowl berth by beating Cal Berkeley 35–7 on November 9 in front of a record crowd of 74,963 fans. Again, the fans went wild. Kevin, in his excitement, still had the presence of mind to grab a handful of turf from the field. He later purposefully arranged the remnant below the front-page newspaper photo of the field after the win, framed it, then presented it to Pat just before he left for Pasadena in Southern California to play in the Rose Bowl against Ohio State.

I was born in Columbus, Ohio. My father, his brother, and his sisters went to Ohio State. My uncle's wife had been Woody Hayes's secretary until the coach's dismissal in 1978, and members of my mother's family continued to be huge fans. Everyone was so excited that Pat would be playing the Buckeyes in Pasadena; they all said they were switching their loyalty for the upcoming game. Kevin, Richard, and their friends went to Pasadena early to share as much Rose Bowl mania with Pat as possible. Patrick, Mike, and I got there just before the Rose Parade. The crowds were overwhelming, but the display was magnificent.

Once in the Rose Bowl, all I could think about was how proud my dad would be that Pat was playing his alma mater in the prestigious bowl game. ASU was coming in ranked number two in the nation, and OSU was ranked number four. If the Sun Devils won the game, they could be national champions. Both teams played exceptionally well, and fans on both sides were treated to a thrilling game. With just over a minute left, the Devils were ahead 17–14. Pat was playing so hard and so well I was beside myself with excitement for him. In the last seconds, the Buckeyes scored the winning touchdown. I looked painfully and hesitantly up at the scoreboard at the final score, 20–17. Pat took the loss better than the rest of us; his team played well, he had played well, and it was a fantastic experience.

Altogether, 1996–97 was a remarkably successful year for Pat, in football as well as in academics. He was named the All-Pac-10 Academic Player of the Year for his solid grade-point average, and he won two other academic awards. On the football field he had the most interceptions, fumble recoveries, and pass deflections of anyone on the team. He also won the Defensive Player of the Year Award, which was renamed in his honor. Only one other player, Scott Von der Ahe, had more tackles than Pat did that year.

Pat's last college game his senior year was played at the Sun Bowl in El Paso. ASU defeated Iowa 17–0. Pat had a great season. He was named the top defensive player in the Pac 10 and ASU's most valuable player. He was a second-team All-American, and he was picked to play in the East-West Shrine Game. He had more tackles than anyone on the team, a team-high forty-seven unassisted tackles, three interceptions, and four sacks. He won All-Pac-10 honors again along with four other academic awards.

As hard as Pat worked on the football field, he may have worked harder in the classroom. Pat spent a great deal of time studying and preparing for classes. He went to summer school for two summers to ensure he had sufficient credits and to keep from losing sight of his priorities. He graduated summa cum laude in three and a half years with a 3.86 grade point average.

For all the excitement in Pat's life, he always craved and indulged a need for solitude. At home he found it by climbing the eucalyptus tree in our backyard and sitting high in its branches, where he could think. At Arizona State, it was a two-hundred-foot-high light standard at Sun Devil Stadium, which he would climb all the way to the top. He would sit on the platform taking in the Arizona landscape, alone with his thoughts.

Pat's goal his senior year was to get drafted by a professional football team—not for the money, but because he absolutely loved to play, and he wanted the challenge of playing at that level. In February 1998, the NFL combine was held at Notre Dame University in Indianapolis. This is a major event for college players, where the best players in the country are invited to work out for the coaches of all the NFL teams. Being invited to the combine pretty much assures a player of being drafted by a professional team. The combine is a prelude to the football draft in April.

Pat did not get invited to the combine. I knew he was disappointed, but he didn't talk about it too much. He did indicate that his best chance for the draft was the pro workout at Arizona State about two to four weeks before the NFL draft, when coaches from several NFL teams came to ASU to see the seniors work out. Two of those coaches were the defensive coordinator for the Arizona Cardinals, Dave McGinnis, and his defensive backs coach, Larry Marmie. The team's general manager, Bob Ferguson, who, I've been told, loved to see Pat play, was also there. There were a couple of offensive players who would be drafted for sure, and the two coaches also wanted to see Pat work out. Pat had been playing linebacker in college, but he was considered too small for that position in the pros. The coaches worked him out as a safety. Pat told me the two positions were very different, as were the skills required. He said he worked really hard, but he wasn't sure he did well enough.

The NFL draft took place April 18 and 19, televised live from Madison Square Garden in New York. The draft is designed to balance talent to make the sport more competitive. Each team gets one pick per round, based on where they finished in the last season. The teams who finished last get to pick first. The wait is nerve-racking for the players. In the 1998 draft, rounds one through three took place the first day, and rounds four through seven the second day. I remember watching portions of the draft with Pat at Marie's parents' house. Pat was in good humor about the whole thing. He really wanted to play on a team, but he knew he was considered too small. He also knew there were coaches who had learned not to underestimate him. While watching the draft, Pat received a call from someone on the Oakland Raiders indicating that team was going to pick him in the seventh round. We all waited.

In the seventh round, before Oakland picked, Pat was drafted by the Cardinals. He was number 226 out of 241. I thought to myself, "There are a lot of dumb coaches out there." At least there were a few smart enough to see what Pat had to offer.

That was Pat's first hurdle. His next challenge, in his mind, was making the starting lineup. He succeeded in earning his starting position, and he played very well. The Cardinals went to the playoffs that year. Pat encountered some frustrations and disappointments with regard to his play at times, but he continued to strive to be a team player and work hard on his skills. In 2000, he broke the franchise record for tackles with 224.

Pat had played football in Arizona for eight years, and the admiration of the fans was plainly evident in the speeches at his memorial. As the final speaker concluded, twenty-seven doves were released, representing the twenty-seven years of Pat's life. A single white feather drifted to the ground, landing at my feet. Patrick picked up the feather and handed it to me. I held it tenderly in my hand.

"Dannie, how wonderful Pat has had so many tributes," Lannie says when I finish telling them about the memorial.

"I know. They have been wonderful and we appreciate them. Pat would be so honored. But sadly, when the tributes are over, we are back to feeling hollow."

"Well, I understand that," Katie says. "Someday, though, those tributes will bring you happiness."

"Maybe," I say, trying to be polite. I pick up my breakfast dishes and take them to the kitchen.

For five days, Katie, Tom, and Lannie have kept me very busy. They have taken me to the Birmingham Civil Rights Institute, Sixteenth Street Baptist Church, and Kelly Ingram Park, all located in the Civil Rights District. We have seen a play, gone on a hike, taken leisurely walks in the neighborhood, and sat talking and drinking Chardonnay beneath the fans of their cozy front porch. I have enjoyed getting to know my cousins—all of whom are at least sixteen years younger than me, the youngest being a month younger than Kevin—and meeting their small children. Several nights ago, I sat up with Lannie until one or two in the morning talking about our families, our childhoods, our friends, and about life and death.

Now Lannie has to return to New York. I'm also scheduled to return home, but Alex informs me there is a function in Decatur, Alabama, at which Pat will be honored. I decide to stay. Katie and Tom tell me they would like to accompany me. We meet Patrick and Alex in Decatur, where we are treated to a catfish dinner in a rustic local eatery where large, sweating pitchers of cold sweet tea are placed on the table and you can serve yourself soft ice cream. We then go to nearby Huntsville, where we are given an interesting tour of the NASA center. In the evening, we are taken to a lovely reception, where we meet the many people who organized the tribute to Pat. The following day we are given a tour of the historic district of Decatur before attending a July Fourth celebration, where Pat is presented with the Audie Murphy Patriotism Award. Sitting on the stage looking out at the people in the audience, I feel the same vulnerability I felt at Pat's memorial service. I try to cloak my sadness and discomfort behind a genial smile. It is an honor for Pat to be so graciously recognized, but I don't want the award. I want Pat back.

Katie, Tom, and I drive back to their house. The next day, standing in front of the terminal of the Birmingham airport, I thank them for showing me a wonderful time. I hug them both, then wave good-bye as I walk through the terminal doors.

12

Action is the antidote to despair.

—JOAN BAEZ

I have been home for nearly a week. I'm still living out of the suitcase I took with me to Birmingham, and I'm trying to organize some of the letters, cards, and other tributes people have sent to me since Pat's death. I look through a stack of cards and come across one from Pat's agent, Frank Bauer. I sit looking at the card, reminded of a phone conversation I had with Mr. Bauer shortly after Pat's death.

He told me he had never met anyone even remotely like Pat, then he went on to tell me how he was also the agent of Mike Martz, head coach of the St. Louis Rams. In 2000, the Rams had just won the Super Bowl after a remarkable 1999 season. Frank asked Pat to interview with the Rams because they were interested in recruiting him. Pat didn't really want to leave the Cardinals, but he agreed to meet with the Rams' coaches, mostly as a favor to his agent. Mr. Bauer told me, "Mike Martz loved Pat."

He told me the team president, John Shaw, tried hard to get Pat to make the move. He made an offer of $9.6 million for five years, with $2.6 million up front. Mr. Bauer told me Pat said, "'No. Number one, the Cardinals gave me a shot; Bob Ferguson [the general manager] drafted me in the seventh round. I love Coach Mac; I love Phoenix, I've played there, everybody knows me, I love the area; I don't want to leave.'" Pat was making $512,000 with the Cardinals. Mr. Bauer said to him, "Pat, you're killing me!"

The story was characteristically Pat. He was such a loyal person. He always wanted to do right by the people who mattered to him. I remember people trying to get him to rethink his position on accepting the offer from the Rams, but he wouldn't budge. Not only did he feel he owed it to his coaches and those who believed in him to stay, he also liked the idea of being part of a team in transition. It wasn't appealing or challenging to him to be part of an already victorious team. He loved being a Sun Devil in the years when the team was transformed from mediocrity to a powerhouse. He hoped he could be part of the same thing with the Cardinals.

I smile recalling what a unique man Pat was, then become angry thinking about the contradictions in the stories and documents with regard to his death. I get on the computer and begin to look up all I can find on friendly fire deaths, and I enter Pat's name to see if anyone with knowledge of what happened to Pat has posted anything. After several hours, I become very frustrated and angry. I type into the computer, "What happened to my son?" I'm so distraught; I expect an answer. When none comes, I begin to cry.

School started two weeks ago. Kevin calls as I'm leaving for work to tell me Marie is having trouble getting Pat's autopsy from the Army. He tells me he is going to talk to the casualty assistance liaison himself and see what he can do. He then tells me he has talked to the medic who got to Pat's body first. The medic told him Pat was gone when he got to him. There was no attempt to save him. Hesitantly, he informs me the medic said Pat's bulletproof Kevlar vest was riddled with green markings; American ammunition is green-tipped. This further confirms that Pat was hit by his own men. He told Kevin Pat's uniform and equipment had been burned because they were a biohazard, and that one of the soldiers who burned the vest mentioned the green tips. I can tell Kevin is very disturbed knowing Pat was hit so many times.

I try not to make it worse for him by getting upset, but when I get off the phone, I find myself feeling tremendous sadness and outrage. I think to myself, "How could any of the soldiers not realize Pat was killed by his own men when his vest was full of U.S. rounds?" I leave for work, but I can't get the disturbing question out of my mind. I'm also angry that the Army hasn't provided Marie with Pat's autopsy report.

At lunchtime I call Senator John McCain. I have made several calls to him in the past few months about concerns we have. When he comes on the line, I ask him if we are being unrealistic to expect Pat's autopsy after five months. He tells me we should have it by now and indicates he will make sure it's sent to us. When I tell him I have many questions about the 15-6 report, he tells me to formulate a list for the Army, and he will get it to the proper people.

When I get home, I make dinner, grade a few papers, then sit at the computer and try to find any information I can to help us determine what happened to Pat. I look up smoke grenades. It has always baffled me that Sergeant Greg Baker and his soldiers claim they never saw the smoke when other soldiers indicate they did. I remember the smoke quite well from seeing it used at Pat and Kevin's boot camp graduation. It is thick and moves like liquid. I don't see how anyone could mistake it for flying dirt. I read that the average soldier can throw a grenade about thirty to thirty-five meters, and it ignites within three seconds. The documents indicate that Lieutenant Colonel Jeffrey Bailey found the grenade canister near the road just in front of where the vehicle would have passed. This makes me wonder if Pat was far closer than we have been told. I also discover that white smoke is produced for 105 to 150 seconds. Why didn't they see it?

The next day school is busy and I'm somewhat distracted, but I keep forming questions in my head to send to McCain. I'm also anxious about the autopsy. I wonder if calling McCain is enough. Maybe I should call the office of the secretary of the Army. Trying to contact people, especially with the time difference, is frustrating. I try to make my calls to the East Coast in the morning before I go to work. It's often difficult to catch anyone during my break or lunchtime.

As soon as I get home, I see an envelope from FedEx. The envelope was sent from Rockville, Maryland; it's Pat's autopsy report. I sit at my kitchen table staring at the envelope that contains the coroner's findings. The cover letter tells me not to look at it alone, but I prefer to read it by myself. Slowly, I remove the cover letter and begin to read the document. The first time I read through, I process nothing. The second time I'm struck by information that disturbs me. I go back and read the top of the first page.

Final Autopsy Examination Report
Name: Tillman, Patrick D.
Autopsy No. xxxx-xxx
SSN: xxx-xx-xxxx
Date of Birth: 6 NOV 1976
Rank: CPL, US
Date of Death 22 APR 2004
Place of Death: Afghanistan
Date of Autopsy: 27 APR 2004
Place of Autopsy: Port Mortuary
Date of Report: 22 JUL 2004

I read where it indicates Pat's autopsy was performed on April 27, 2004, then see where the date of the report is July 22, 2004. I wonder why it took so long for the coroner to complete and sign the document.

The second page presents a description of the gunshot wounds. I don't understand the information other than to recognize much of Pat's head was gone. I move on to the next page. Pat was five foot eleven—seventy-one inches tall—but the autopsy states he was seventy-three inches. I can't understand, considering the nature of his head wounds, why he would measure taller.

The autopsy states that Pat was wearing a gold wedding band, yet his ring was platinum, having a dull, silver appearance. I'm also struck by the fact that no distinguishing features have been documented. Pat had a scar under his right arm, the result of rotator cuff surgery; a torn bicep from a football injury; a broken little finger on his left hand; and residual scarring on his lungs from having had valley fever in college. None of these features are mentioned. I then come to a section of the document that says "Medical Interventions." It reads: "A $3\frac{3}{4} \times 3\frac{1}{2}$-inch area on the left upper chest is consistent with an attempt at defibrillation."

"Defibrillation!" I say out loud. Why would Pat be defibrillated? The medic told Kevin that he made no attempt to save Pat on the scene. He said Pat was clearly gone. Pat had been wrapped in a poncho and deemed KIA, killed in action. He must have been dead nearly two hours before he arrived at the field hospital. "Why would anyone defibrillate a body with no head?"

I don't want to alarm Marie, but I feel I must call her. I'm certain she received the autopsy report as well, as I told McCain to have it sent to both of us; however, I'm not certain she would have read it yet. When Marie answers the phone, I attempt to make small talk, but she cuts me off. She has read the report and feels as I do; something is wrong.

"That isn't Pat," she says.

The next morning before I leave for work, I place a call to Commander Craig Mallak, Armed Forces medical examiner at Rockville, Maryland. Commander Mallak explains that he didn't perform Pat's autopsy; a Dr. James Caruso did. He says Dr. Caruso is currently in Iraq, but he tells me he is quite familiar with Pat's case. I ask Dr. Mallak why Pat would measure two inches taller when he was missing so much of his head. He tells me that the measurements aren't very exact. He says he may have been measured with his toes pointed. The explanation sounds ridiculous, but I just go on to the next concern. I tell him Pat's wedding band was platinum, yet the report says the ring was gold. Mallak tells me the ring was described from a photograph and that the lighting in the room made the ring appear gold in the photograph.

"Why aren't descriptions written down while looking at the body? It makes no sense to describe details from a photograph."

"Yes, ma'am," he says. "We can send you a cropped photo of your son's hand if you like, or I can send you a photo of the ring itself after it was removed."

"Sir, my daughter-in-law has Pat's ring. What concerns me is that we might have the autopsy of the wrong man."

I ask him why none of Pat's distinguishing features were documented. I go over them with him carefully. He tells me the torn muscle was not noted because they don't do internal examinations. He disregards me when I explain that Pat's injury was plainly visible. Mallak says there were no signs of active fungal infection of the lungs, although he admitted Pat's lungs were not looked at microscopically. Looking at the pictures, he finds there is no indication of a rotator cuff scar or a broken finger. My frustration is mounting, and I feel as though I want to cry.

"Why would Pat have been defibrillated?" I ask. "He essentially had no head, and he had been dead at least two hours before getting to the field hospital."

"Ma'am," he says self-righteously, "we normally don't fault someone for trying to save someone's life."

I want to scream. "I'm not faulting anyone, sir. I just wonder why there was an attempt to save his life when he was so clearly gone."

The commander explains that the shape of the abrasion on Pat's chest was interpreted as a mark from a defibrillator. He says the abrasion could have been from prolonged CPR or other medical treatment. It is as if he isn't hearing a word I'm saying. I can see I'm getting nowhere, and I don't want to get so upset that I alienate him, but I ask him one more question.

"Commander, why is Pat's autopsy dated July 22, nearly three months after the autopsy was performed?"

"Ma'am, Dr. Caruso and I didn't believe the information we read on the casualty report. Enemy rounds don't cause the type of wounds your son had. Dr. Caruso refused to sign the autopsy report."

"Thank you, Commander," I say, stunned, as I hang up the phone.

I have been researching information on fratricides and trying to get information on Pat's death since I returned home from Alabama. The information I just learned from Dr. Mallak makes me more fearful and suspicious that Pat may have been killed intentionally. I say very little about my suspicions to anyone other than my closest friends and family because I know people won't understand. I have tried getting information from the computer using Pat's name, but I always get ultra left-wing, often irrational sites with far-fetched conspiracy theories. I have no interest in reading them. I type in the words "military lies," and a list of sites comes up. I click on an article titled "Lies Upon Lies Upon Lies: US Military in Crisis," by Brian Cloughley, dated June 13, 2004, more than three months ago, right about the time we were being briefed at Fort Lewis. I scan the article and find it is quite interesting, but it doesn't have anything I'm looking for. Then, just when I'm ready to click off, I read:

> Here is the official US Army citation concerning the award of posthumous and hysterically-publicized bravery decoration to an American soldier who was killed in Afghanistan on April 22.

Oh, my God! I can't believe what I'm reading.

"Through the firing [soldier X's] voice was heard issuing fire
commands to take the fight to the enemy on the dominating high
ground. . . . Only after his team engaged the well-armed enemy
did it appear their fires diminished. As a result of his leadership
and his team's efforts, the platoon trail section was able to maneuver through the ambush to positions of safety without a single
casualty."

But here is what really happened, according to a reliable
source, an Afghan, who was reported by CBS News on May 29 as
saying that "two groups of soldiers had drifted some distance
apart during the operation in the remote Spera district of Khost
province. 'Suddenly the sound of a mine explosion was heard
somewhere between the two groups and the Americans in one
group started firing,' the official said, citing an account given to
him by an Afghan fighter who was part of that group. . . . 'Nobody
knew what it was . . . or what was going on, or if enemy forces
were firing. The situation was very confusing,' the official said.
'As the result of this firing, that American was killed and three
Afghan soldiers were injured. It was a misunderstanding and
afterwards they realized that it was a mine that had exploded and
there were no enemy forces.' "

There was an ambush with enemy forces, I say to myself. The information I'm reading is shocking and frustrating. I had read an Associated Press
account of Pat's death just after the fratricide information was released
that said there was no enemy and no ambush. The article stated there was
an explosion that caused confusion, and the two units of soldiers started
firing on each other. However, that is not true. Kevin was involved in the
ambush, and he and fellow soldiers saw enemy on the high ground, above

the canyon walls. I think, "If that wasn't the enemy, who was it?" I'm perplexed by the article's reference to three injured Afghans. "Three Afghans weren't injured. Where is this information coming from?"

In other words, there was a monster stuff-up. And this sort of thing is far from unknown in battle: tragic disasters occur frequently. But what is astonishing and unforgivable is the deliberate, systematic, official, Bush-government-approved lying about what happened at the time.

It is evil and dishonorable that the account of the death of this young man was a Pentagon machine fabrication. The gallantry citation was a downright lie, forged for public relations' [sic] purposes because soldier X had a national image.

The article goes on to discuss how Lieutenant General Philip R. Kensinger lied to the media in the press conference about what happened to soldier X, whom I realize is Pat. When the members of the press tried to get answers, he refused to take questions. The author calls Kensinger "a moral coward." Since we have learned about the fratricide, I have wondered if Kensinger knew the true circumstances of Pat's death when he came to the memorial service. It upsets and angers me that he might have known the truth and let a false narrative be read. I have got to find out more about the author of this article.

I discover Brian Cloughley is a writer/journalist living in New Zealand. He enlisted in the British Army in 1958 and served in both the British and Australian armies. I read on from his Web site.

He was later commissioned, spent nine years as an artillery officer on regimental duty, mainly as a Forward Observer[1] and

---

1 Soldier responsible for directing artillery fire and close air support onto enemy positions.

saw active service in Borneo with 42 Commando, Royal Marines; 1st Battalion Sarawak Rangers; and 4th Battalion of the Royal Australian Regiment.

He also served as an intelligence officer in Cyprus at the end of colonial rule, on attachment with the Jordan Desert Police Force, as Reconnaissance and Survey Officer in a nuclear missile regiment in Germany, and officer commanding the Australian Psychological Operations Unit in Vietnam. . . .

He has been involved in analysis of South Asian affairs since late 1970s. In 1985 he visited Pakistan at the invitation of President Zia, and travelled extensively in Balochistan. In 1996–1997 he was consultant to the OECD[2] on the relationship between defence expenditure and international aid in South Asia and had government-level discussions in Bangladesh, India, Pakistan and Sri Lanka.

When I finish reading his biography, I learn his e-mail information is provided, and I'm able to locate a phone number for him. It is clear Mr. Cloughley has had extensive experience with the military, and he continues to work in Pakistan and surrounding regions. He has very solid credentials. I need to know where he got his information about what happened to Pat. I quickly type an e-mail and send it to him.

Mr. Cloughley

I'm Pat Tillman's mother. I read your article, "Lies Upon Lies Upon Lies: U.S. military in Crisis." I would very much like to speak to you. The circumstances surrounding Pat's death are very suspicious. The army has not given us a straight story either. . . .

---

2 Organisation for Economic Co-operation and Development

Thank you.
Sincerely,
Mary L. Tillman

After sending the e-mail, I also place a call to him. I have no idea what time it is in New Zealand; I just hope I'm not calling at three in the morning. The call goes directly to an answering machine, and I leave a message for him to contact me.

The following day Mr. Cloughley writes:

Dear Mrs. Tillman,

Thank you so much for writing to me. I offer my deepest sympathy on the loss of your son, I know you will always remember . . . no matter the circumstances of his death . . . that he was a fine person and behaved honorably.

I'm sorry but I can't add anything to the official statements and press reports about the cause of his death. If I knew anything at all, I would of course tell you at once. And if I do hear anything, you will be the first to know.

At the moment I am in Britain, attending a conference, then I travel to Pakistan for a week, then go home to New Zealand.

He continues by telling me he will be in touch when he returns home. He says in the meantime he will ask his "discreet" sources if they know anything about the manner in which Pat died.

Later that night, I call Mike and tell him about the article and the e-mail I received from Mr. Cloughley. Mike is very interested because he also thinks something suspicious surrounds Pat's death. He is also haunted by the autopsy report. It is a concern to both of us that local Afghans keep reporting to U.S. and foreign press that there was no enemy in the area when Pat was killed, yet there are witnesses who state enemy were firing on the unit. I wonder if it's possible the ambush was staged; I wonder if Pat was killed on purpose. Mike and I discuss the timing of Pat's death. April was the worst month for recorded casualties in the war; a tragically unsuccessful attempt had been made to capture Fallujah, one of the most peaceful areas of the country after the fall of Saddam; and the Abu Ghraib prisoner abuse scandal was being made public. Mike and I have believed for weeks that the military and the administration lied about the circumstances of Pat's death to rally patriotism and deflect public outrage over the breaking news from Iraq. Now we wonder if his death was deliberate.

Mike tells me he has read a book called *Bush on the Couch*, by Dr. Justin A. Frank. He tells me Dr. Frank is a psychiatrist who lives and works in Georgetown. He has done a lot of research on the president and has observed him from afar. The book states that Bush doesn't admire or respect the soldiers; on the contrary, he resents them. They are true warriors; Bush can only pretend. Mike brings the book to my house, and I read all night. In the morning before leaving for work, I call information and get Dr. Frank's number at George Washington University Medical School. I leave a message telling him my name and that my son was killed in Afghanistan in April. I let him know I want to speak to him and that I will be home by four p.m. Pacific time, then I leave my number. When I return home from work, I have a message from Dr. Frank. He tells me he knows who I am, and he will stay in his office until I return home to call him. Immediately, I dial the number, and he answers right away. I waste no time getting to the point.

"Hello, Dr. Frank. I'm Mary Tillman. I don't want to waste your time. I'm calling to ask you a question. Do you think it's possible that this administration orchestrated my son's death?"

"Sad to say, yes."

I'm positively stunned by his response. I thought he would gently tell me that he doesn't believe the administration is very honorable, but it would never do something so heinous as to have a soldier killed. "You believe they killed him?" I ask numbly.

"I think it's possible. Mrs. Tillman, I'm a psychiatrist. It would be unethical and irresponsible for me to tell a grieving mother to pursue such a thing if I didn't think it was possible."

Over the weekend the whole family goes to Arizona. The Cardinals are retiring Pat's number on Sunday, September 19. Mike and I fly to Arizona together, and we talk about what Dr. Frank told me. Mike encourages me to pursue answers. He has a very strong sense something is wrong. Mike and I share our suspicions with Richard, who also believes we need to get more information. Kevin and Marie are not in a frame of mind to discuss this topic. Kevin is especially apprehensive talking about this as anything but an accident.

While in Arizona, I check my home messages. There's one from Margaret Cloughley, Mr. Cloughley's wife. She received the phone message I had sent days before and wanted to let me know her husband was in Pakistan. I explain to her that he already responded to an e-mail I sent at the same time I left the phone message. She is very gracious and concerned. She says she feels terrible about what happened to Pat, and she supports us in our search for answers and hopes her husband can be of help when he returns.

On October 2, I receive a long e-mail from Mr. Cloughley.

Dear Mrs. Tillman,

I have now returned home to New Zealand. During my travels in the past month I talked with several people about your son.

There is no doubt his death was the result of what we former soldiers used to call a "patrol clash." I was close to one (but not directly involved) in Borneo many years ago, and experienced the shock that any soldier feels when things go terribly wrong and involve the death of men who are killed in error by their own comrades. But in [those] days (almost forty years ago) the natural reaction was to admit and to explain what went wrong. Things are different now.

The words "friendly fire" disgust me. It is a typical PR weasel phrase used to try to disguise the unpalatable fact that horrible accidents happen. And in this case the tragedy was made worse by lies told at the highest level to make it appear that your son died in circumstances that were later detected as being falsely described and notified.

. . . If you wish the case to be given Maximum publicity, then I suggest we approach a major newspaper. I happen to know the managing editor of the Washington Post (Steve Coll: we were in Pakistan together 10 years ago when he was a reporter and I was the Australian defense attaché) and would be prepared to ask him to have the story covered in a tasteful fashion.

I send Mr. Cloughley a summary of what we have been able to piece together about Pat's death. Again, he encourages me to contact Steve Coll. He tells me he tried e-mailing him but didn't receive a response. I indicate to him that I will try to get in touch with him as well.

During my lunch break at school, I call the *Washington Post* and ask for Steve Coll. After a few minutes of conversation, Mr. Coll confides that his Pentagon reporter was very suspicious about the way Pat's death was reported by the Army. He is interested in talking to me in person and viewing the 15-6 report. I tell him that, coincidentally, I will be in D.C. to meet a friend in several weeks. I let him know I can go to the paper to talk to him. After ending the conversation, I call Senator McCain. I tell him I will be writing questions and e-mailing them to him. I also let him know there are anomalies in the autopsy report, but I want to speak to Dr. Caruso when he returns from Iraq before I do anything.

As soon as I get home from work, I sit down at my computer, overwhelmed with all the questions I have about Pat's death and its aftermath. I go to my room and grab Pat's brown T-shirt and wrap it around my neck. I sit back down at the computer, and the questions come rapidly and sequentially.

1. Why would a unit hold up for two days in a village in a hostile area to repair a Humvee, allowing the enemy to prepare for an ambush? Why does the vehicle have greater priority than the mission? Why bring a jinga truck through a dangerously narrow canyon where an ambush is likely to take place?

2. Why the insistence from Florida to bring the vehicle to Tit rather than abandon or destroy it? Why are orders coming from Florida period?

3. Why were the terms "dawn" and "dusk" used when orders were given to move out to Manah? Why was military time not used?

4. Why the hysterical reaction from Baker and his men? Aren't Rangers trained to assess a situation before shooting?

5. Aren't Rangers trained to go back and help sections of their troops when they're in trouble?

6. Weren't Baker and his men prepared to watch for the first serial, as Rangers come back to help their troops?

7. The driver of Baker's vehicle stated he recognized the Afghan as a friendly "within a split second" of coming out of the canyon. He also saw friendlies on the ridgeline and U.S. vehicles down the road. Why didn't the others see these things?

8. Why didn't the driver do more to stop the shooting?

9. Why didn't the driver physically yank Baker off the vehicle or do something to let him know he was allowing his men to shoot at friendlies?

10. There was a cessation of fire after the AMF was killed. What caused that cessation of fire? Bailey suggested at one point they were reloading. Don't they look around when they're reloading?

11. Baker and his men say they had tunnel vision. If so, they had to have seen what they were shooting. Why didn't they recognize them as friendlies? Baker and his men also state they saw nothing. Which is it? Why didn't they see the smoke?

12. Why did Baker and his men shoot CPL Tillman in the head three times and riddle his body with rounds?

13. Why did Baker and his men drive down the road shooting at buildings? Isn't that illegal?

14. Why were CPL Tillman's clothes burned?

15. Why were young soldiers under orders to keep quiet?

16. Why were men asked to share the blame?

17. Why did it take five weeks to tell the family CPL Tillman was killed by his own men? Why was the family not given a copy of the 15-6 investigation prior to the meeting rather than when we were walking out the door?

18. Why was there no attempt to take accurate measurements?

19. Why were there sketches of vehicles rather than photos of real vehicles?

20. Why wasn't a person situated near the rocks in the photos so scale could be determined? Why were there no tough follow-up questions posed to the soldiers?

21. Why was CPL Tillman's death so embellished by the military?

22. Why did LGEN Kensinger not take questions at the press conference regarding the fratricide?

23. Why didn't the military clear up the untrue and nebulous stories that

were released after fratricide was determined to have caused CPL Tillman's death?

24. Why was CPL Tillman's death called an accident?

25. Why has it been stated there is no fault?

26. Why did the Army try to convince Marie to have a military funeral?

A week before leaving for Washington D.C., I read a column in the *San Jose Mercury News* about a woman named Dolores Kesterson, who lives in nearby Santa Clara. Her son Erik had been a Marine for eight years. In 2000, he earned the Navy and Marine Corps medal for heroism after pulling seven fellow Marines from a flaming helicopter after it crashed. Erik was living a civilian life when September 11th compelled him to re-enlist, this time in the Army. On November 15, 2003, Erik was killed when a chopper, flying in the wrong airspace, hit his Black Hawk helicopter. He was twenty-nine. Dolores was invited to Fort Lewis in June, along with other families of fallen soldiers, to meet with President Bush. The column indicates she was shocked by his behavior toward her. I call information and get her number. After several tries, I'm finally able to reach her, and we arrange to meet for coffee the next day.

Dolores is a strong, down-to-earth woman with a sharp sense of humor and a quick wit. Her large blue eyes reveal sadness as she takes out a copy of the letter she wrote to George Bush when she went to Fort Lewis. She describes how her purse was taken from her and searched.

She believes the letter was shown to the president before he met with her. She waited in a small cubicle until an aide announced, "The president will now see you." Dolores said [the president] "came marching in and got right in my face ... eyeball to eyeball, and said, 'I'm George

Bush, president of the United States, and I understand you have something to say to me in private.'" She felt like he was attempting to intimidate her. She would not be threatened, however. She made it clear to him that she believes the U.S. presence in Iraq is illegal. She shortly changed the subject to her son, telling the president that he was a young man with a zest for life and a wonderful sense of humor whose favorite saying was "Life is good."

The president looked at her blankly and said, "How do you know his life would have been good?"

Dolores was stunned by the insensitivity of his remark, and she shot back, "Life is life, good or bad, nobody wants to die." Dolores says, "Bush has no conscience about the death and destruction he has caused."

What Dolores has told me about her meeting with Bush is shameful, yet I'm not really shocked. The president does not appear to have any empathy. Anytime he tries to convey it, he comes across as insincere or callous. Dolores and I talk for about an hour, sharing stories about Pat and Erik. I let her know I will contact her when I return from Washington.

During my break the following day, I call Dr. Frank to let him know I will be going to D.C. and I'll be staying in Georgetown. I ask if he would be able to meet with me so I can show him the autopsy report. He says he would be happy to look at any documents I have.

Just days before I leave for my trip, I get a call from Dr. Caruso. He gives me the same information Dr. Mallak gave me. But he indicates that both he and Dr. Mallak were angry that Pat came back without his uniform or equipment. He tells me that all fallen soldiers are to be returned stateside with their uniforms. He mentions that the uniforms of wounded soldiers are usually destroyed. He, like Mallak, doesn't understand why I'm unwilling to accept the idea that someone tried to defibrillate Pat. He tells me I should have Marie request the field hospital report to find out what procedures were done there.

As soon as I get off the phone, I call Marie and Kevin and tell them what Dr. Caruso advised. Marie says she will call her casualty assistance liaison and make the request. I tell her I believe someone wants it to appear that there was an attempt at resuscitation because then there would be a reason to destroy the uniform. Uniforms of wounded soldiers can be destroyed. "I think they wanted it to appear Pat came in alive so they would have a reason to remove his uniform and destroy it. They needed to destroy the evidence of fratricide," I tell her.

I arrive in Georgetown on Sunday, October 17. I meet my friend Greg Martin for dinner, and we walk along M Street and talk about his trip to Canada. The next day we both meet Dr. Frank for lunch. I show him the 15-6 documents and the autopsy report. He agrees that many of the soldiers' statements are confounding and says he doesn't think the autopsy was very thorough. He believes I'm doing the right thing by requesting answers.

On Tuesday, Greg and I have lunch with Maura and Sheila Mandt before Maura and I leave to see Steve Coll at the *Post*. Maura is in the media business, and she suggested she come with me in the event I need some help. Once we arrive at the paper, we are taken to an area outside Steve Coll's office, where we wait for a few minutes. Mr. Coll comes out and introduces himself and his Pentagon correspondent, Josh White. We follow both of them through a maze of reporter cubicles to a meeting room where we sit around a large conference table.

I don't want to waste their time with small talk. I take out all the documents and place them on the table, then I draw a map of the canyon and label Magarah, Tit, and Manah. I outline the sequence of events and indicate movements on the map. I then outline all the anomalies and discuss my suspicions. I tell them what we find disturbing about the autopsy report. Steve is quite a quick study. It doesn't take him long to understand the situation. Josh White tells me he was present at both news conferences, the one that broke the news of Pat's death and the one that revealed his death was a fratricide. He says there was something suspicious about both of them. It was clear the Army was holding back.

I tell Steve and Josh that I would like them to do a story presenting Pat's true actions and the irregularities in the documents. I make it clear that I'm not convinced Pat's death was an accident and that my family feels the soldiers in the vehicle who killed Pat and the AMF soldier and wounded Uthlaut and Lane should have faced more serious consequences. We suspect they weren't dealt with more severely because a court-martial would implicate individuals of higher rank. I let them know that no one in our family wants to be quoted in the story. I explain that Pat's persona puts us in an awkward position, and we are not comfortable being in the public eye. Steve calls his secretary in to make photocopies of the documents.

Shortly after I get back to San Jose, I learn that Senator McCain gave my questions to the acting secretary of the Army, Les Brownlee. He asked the US Army Special Operations Command to address the conduct of the earlier investigation, the handling of evidence, and the delayed reporting of the true nature of Pat's death and report back to him. Lieutenant General Philip R. Kensinger assigned Brigadier General Gary Jones to conduct another 15-6 investigation into Pat's death.

I also learn from Kevin that he met an officer who did a previous investigation, which started within hours of Pat's death. The officer Captain Richard Scott became Kevin's Company Commander when Kevin asked for a reassignment when the unit came back from Afghanistan. One day, Kevin spoke to Scott regarding his unhappiness with the Army's handling of his brother's death. Scott attempted to help Kevin by talking to him and trying to clarify some of the inconsistencies in the investigation. Scott seemed to allude that he had recommended harsher punishment for some of the soldiers involved in the shooting and he had similar concerns about the ambiguity of the orders given. The regiment took over Scott's investigation and told him they were handing it over to an officer of higher rank. Kevin says Captain

Scott was shocked to learn the soldiers were not more harshly punished. Kevin and I discuss the fact that he will have to make sure Brigadier General Jones knows about Captain Scott's investigation.

I stay in touch with Steve Coll, keeping him updated with any information we get. He wants to go to Afghanistan to visit the site where Pat died and talk to local Afghans about what took place that day. I want to travel to Afghanistan with him, but Kevin doesn't approve. He is adamant that it's too dangerous for anyone to go over there. I don't want to worry him, so I let Steve know I can't go.

The first week of December, I receive a letter from a *Los Angeles Times* reporter, David Zucchino, which is addressed to Pat's father and me. The letter indicates that he has been in Afghanistan and has spoken to locals in and around Manah who say there was no enemy and no ambush. Mr. Zucchino says he is informing us as a courtesy that he will be writing the story within the week. I try to call Steve right away to let him know the reporter intends to write the story, but I can't reach him. The whole purpose of asking Steve to write the story is to get the story of Pat's death right—to get to the truth. If this reporter writes his piece without looking at documents or interviewing soldiers, he is going to skew the facts even more.

I place a call to Zucchino and tell him his story isn't that newsworthy. I let him know that the Associated Press printed a story in June about the fact there was no ambush. I explain that my son Kevin was there, and there were people shooting at the serial from the top of the canyon. He seems surprised when I tell him Kevin was part of the platoon. I can't believe he has never heard Kevin was there. I tell him I really don't think it's a good idea for him to write a story without the benefit of soldier statements. I suggest he will embarrass himself if the writes the story.

During the conversation, I give him information off the record, telling him he can use it to track down other facts. By the end of the conversation, Zucchino tells me he won't write the story without looking into the facts further. I find out he also called Patrick, who told him the same thing I did: that he needs to get more information before he writes a piece.

That evening I get a call from Steve and I tell him about the reporter. Steve says he'll have to rush his story. He doesn't believe the reporter will hold up his article. On December 5, part one of Steve's story on Pat comes out in the *Washington Post*. The piece is comprehensive, powerful, and distressing. It angers me on many levels that the Army lied about Pat's death, but what upsets me most is that Pat was removed from the context of his death and turned into a caricature. Steve did an amazing job presenting the events of April 22 and establishing Pat's true and honorable actions that fateful day.

On Monday, December 6, part two is published, and it is equally compelling and poignant. However, David Zucchino's story is printed that same morning in the *LA Times*. I'm absolutely furious—not only did he write facts that were not carefully checked, he also quoted information I gave him off the record. Patrick called to tell me Zucchino quoted him inappropriately as well. To be publicly quoted against your wishes is unsettling and a serious violation of journalistic ethics. I call Mr. Zucchino and tell him to never contact me again.

In March 2005, Brigadier General Jones briefs my family on the findings of his investigation. Kevin and Marie are briefed at Fort Lewis, and Patrick, Mike, and I are briefed at Moffett Field; however, Patrick is briefed at a different time.

My casualty assistance liaison picks up Mike and me at my house and takes us to the airfield. Brigadier General Jones greets us just inside the door. He is a tall, well-built man with a confident and friendly demeanor. He walks us down several halls to a meeting room. We are seated around a conference table with various military personnel, one of whom is a JAG officer—a judge advocate general, a legal officer—Lieutenant Colonel Michael Hargis. General Jones stands behind a podium and begins his presentation. He indicates right away that light conditions were very poor that evening. I politely interrupt him and tell him that Colonel Bailey told us he walked the site where Pat was killed approximately twenty-four hours after the incident, and he told us the light conditions were good. He told us he didn't understand how Baker and his men could not see the friendlies. Jones tells us that Bailey didn't walk the site at that time; he says Bailey was there in the morning hours.

"Are you saying Bailey lied to us about that?"

"No, ma'am," he says, then continues with his presentation.

He tells us that the farthest distance the Afghan was from Baker's vehicle was seventy-five meters. He indicates that Pat was around sixty-five meters away. However, based on soldiers' statements and looking at the photographs, Mike says the distance between Pat and Baker's vehicle would have been around 35 meters.

I question Jones about how the men in the vehicle could have not seen the Afghan, Pat, and the other friendlies at such close distances. I remind him that Bailey had originally told us Pat and the AMF soldier were nearly 150 to 200 meters away.

"I find it suspicious now that the distances are shrinking and the light conditions are deteriorating. How is it the driver, Sayre, was able to identify the AMF soldier and the friendlies?" Mike asks. "And why didn't he do more to stop the shooting?"

"There wasn't time for him to stop the shooting. They shot up that ridgeline in a matter of four seconds."

"What! Four seconds?" Mike and I yell at once.

"It took longer than four seconds for Pat to pull the pin and throw the smoke grenade," Mike says.

"You're telling us the men in that vehicle shot up the ridgeline in a matter of four seconds? From the time they left the canyon until they stopped past the village?" I ask.

"Yes, ma'am."

"Well, Colonel Bailey told us Baker was out of the vehicle when he shot the Afghan. He also told us there were several lulls in fire. In fact, O'Neal states in his testimony the vehicle stopped firing, then they got in a better position to shoot before they opened up again," I say in frustration.

"No one got out of the vehicle. That early information is incorrect, and O'Neal is the least reliable witness because he was so traumatized," Jones says.

"You won't believe O'Neal, but you'll believe the guys who were shooting at him!"

Jones stares at me before moving on to his next point. He tells us that the Army is very sorry for the fact we weren't told about the circumstances of Pat's death sooner, but there was misunderstanding about the protocol. He says the Army is going to begin telling families right away when fratricide is suspected.

I ask the general if he knows why Pat's uniform, MOLLE[3], and other equipment were burned, and he tells me his things were a biohazard.

"Well, Pat's body was a biohazard; why didn't they leave the uniform on the body to go back to Dover? Commander Mallak, the medical examiner, told me that all uniforms and equipment must be returned with the body."

"That's a new policy, ma'am. Not everyone is familiar with it."

"Pat's death was a suspected fratricide," Mike says. "Shouldn't his things have been preserved as evidence? Isn't that common sense?"

The meeting is becoming frustrating, and I feel we are not getting any answers. General Jones tells us we won't get a copy of the thousand-plus-page report for several weeks, but I'm given a binder with his summary. Mike and I thank him and leave.

---

3 MOdular Lightweight Load-carrying Equipment

I sit up all night reading and rereading Jones's summary. I also go over the 15-6 again. At about seven a.m., I call my casualty assistance liaison and ask her if I can meet with the general again today. She says she will find out and call back. Fifteen minutes later, she calls back and tells me General Jones has agreed to see me again.

I walk into the familiar room and sit down at the table. The same personnel are seated there.

Jones greets me and gets up to stand behind his podium.

"Could you please not do that? Could you please just sit here at the table and talk to me?"

The general looks over at his JAG for a second, then sits down in a chair across from me.

I tell him I have gone through his summary binder, and I found a few things I want to talk about. I tell him there is a protocol already in place about telling families about suspected fratricide. I tell him that there is also a protocol in the books about preserving the uniforms and equipment of fallen soldiers, which has been in place since before the new edict. I tell him I don't understand why so many soldiers and officers were unaware of procedure.

General Jones listens to me but doesn't respond. I tell him that in looking at the statements in the 15-6 report, I'm sickened by the remarks of some of the soldiers in the vehicle. One of the soldiers is asked if he positively identified his target, and the soldier said, "No." He wanted to be in a firefight. I ask the general how he got away with saying something like that. The general agrees the remark is horrible, but he doesn't indicate anything will come of it.

I ask him if he looked into the orders that were given from Salerno, splitting the troops and moving in daylight. He tells me that even though splitting troops and moving in daylight is not policy, it had been done before. Again, I feel I'm getting nowhere. I tell General Jones he will be hearing from me after I have a chance to go through the whole report. I thank him and leave. Three weeks pass before we each finally get our copies of the report. The report fills six binders, although the fifth binder is classified and unavailable to us. Going through this report is daunting. I welcome taking a break from it today to visit Pat. Today Pat has been gone a year.

I drive to Santa Cruz to the Crow's Nest, where Pat proposed to Marie. Sitting on the deck, I stare out at the water. Five months ago, on Pat's birthday, we chartered a little Popeye-type boat and scattered Pat's glittering ashes just past the lighthouse. I tell Pat that he would have loved the run that was held in his honor last weekend. Six thousand people showed up to participate in the first annual Pat's Run, organized by the Pat Tillman Foundation.[4] It was a wonderful celebration of his life and his infectious spirit.

Throughout early spring, media people have been calling everyone in the family, offering to do stories or investigative pieces. For a time we were interested in *60 Minutes* or *Dateline* doing an investigative piece, but ultimately both programs decide not to do anything because no family member will consent to be interviewed on camera. We had a family agreement that any story should be about Pat, not us. Josh White comes to the house and examines the Jones report once the documents arrive. He writes several solid pieces about his findings in the *Washington Post*, which draw attention to the lies told in Pat's situation.

One day he receives a phone call from the mother of a soldier killed just weeks after Pat. She is searching for someone to help her find answers. Josh calls me and asks if I will speak to her. He tells me her name is Peggy Buryj (pronounced "Booty"). I call her right away. Peggy tells me her son Jesse was killed May 4, 2004. She and her husband were first told Jesse was killed when a truck hit his vehicle. Three

---

4 The Pat Tillman Foundation seeks to carry forward Pat's legacy by inspiring and supporting young people striving to promote positive change in themselves and the world around them.

months later, they learned he was shot. Days ago she finally received
Jesse's autopsy report, after nearly a year, and it revealed he was shot in
the back. The Army is saying Polish allies killed him, but she doesn't
know what to believe. I tell Peggy I have no formula in trying to get
answers. Peggy is tough, smart, and resilient. I encourage her to keep
fighting.

Looking through my incoming e-mail, I notice I received two messages from my casualty assistance liaison. I see Marie got them as well.
One has an attachment of a psychological evaluation Pat had in December 2002. The other has the field hospital report attached. I had asked
Marie, as Pat's next of kin, to request both months ago. I remembered
that Pat had talked about having more psychological evaluations than
anyone he knew, and I wanted to see if I could learn why the evaluations
were given. I had wanted the field hospital report to help determine
why Pat had the strange abrasions on his chest. Since we know the
medic didn't attempt to defibrillate Pat, we think someone in the field
hospital did.

I first open the two-page field hospital document. I feel trepidation
as I begin to scan the pages. The report is filled out in typical doctor
scrawl. The first page is dated April 22, 2004. I scan the page. There are
notes written across the first sheet.

Gun/shrapnel to head
No BP [blood pressure] or pulse obtainable
Large calvarial defect: exposed grey matter
No cardiac tones

I notice the second page looks as though it is dated April 25, 2004.
The page is hole punched over the day, but I can clearly see that the last
number is a 5, and not a 2, suggesting the date of death as April 25, 2004.
The second page reads:

Surgery

Pt [patient] died of wounds no vs [vital signs] obtainable [through] resuscitation

Disposition-mortuary services

The document makes it look as though Pat died on the 25th. I turn back to the first page and read what the doctor wrote:

1.   CPR performed
2.   Trans to ICU for cont. CPR

What? If this were Pat, why would the doctor write that he was given CPR? Why would you transfer a man who had been dead for hours to intensive care for continued CPR? What kind of surgery would you perform on a man who had no brain and no skull, who was transported as a KIA (killed in action)?

I then open the psychological evaluation attachment, which is difficult to read. The psychologist's handwriting is so small that I use a magnifying glass to try to make out what it says. There are only a few lines I can read. One statement indicates that Pat is a "moderate risk." Others say he "doesn't respect authority" and "Cockiness will get him in trouble, will square off with authority," "arrogant."

I'm outraged as I read this assessment of Pat. I put the document aside, and I start to feel sick. Why would a psychologist write such things? Pat may have had some authority issues as a teenager, but not the man I knew before he died. I immediately am reminded of a lovely letter Pat's platoon leader, Lieutenant David Uthlaut, sent to Patrick and me last Christmas. He described Pat as down-to-earth and someone who was unusual in his consideration of others. He told a story about Pat's relationship with younger Rangers, particularly Bryan O'Neal, the soldier whose life Pat saved.

"Whenever a new soldier comes into the platoon," Uthlaut wrote, "the more senior soldiers generally take to 'initiating' them in some fashion, and make them prove themselves worthy of being in the Rangers. Pat saw his role very differently. When Private O'Neal came into the platoon and got assigned to Pat's fire team, Pat did not force him to prove himself; instead, he made it his primary mission to prepare this young and inexperienced soldier for the upcoming deployment. Every time I walked by the squad room, Pat was instructing; he was either showing O'Neal battle drills with a whiteboard and marker, showing him how to properly tie down his equipment, or giving him general advice on how to survive. By showing that he was not only knowledgeable, but that he also genuinely cared for the soldier under his charge, Pat embodied the qualities of a true leader. He will forever have my respect, not because he turned down NFL contracts to serve his country, but because he was an exceptional soldier and a talented leader."

I was very touched by Lieutenant Uthlaut's letter, and after I received it, I called him, and we had a nice conversation. He's an honorable man, and it is obvious he carries a sad and heavy burden because of what happened. I am sure he would be as dumbfounded as I am by the psychologist's evaluation of Pat.

A few days later, walking along Almaden Road, I watch the flags flutter in the slight breeze. The neighborhood put the flags up for the first anniversary of Pat's death. I cried when I drove down the driveway and saw them once again flanking the road.

Today is Memorial Day. I wonder if the flags will come down or if they will be left until after the Fourth of July. As I walk up the driveway, three hens and a rooster scurry past me. Walking across my yard, I notice a paper has been left on the ledge of my Dutch door. It is a printout of a column written by Robert Scheer titled *A Cover-Up as Shameful as Tillman's Death*. My neighbor Annie must have left it for me. I sit in a lawn chair in the warm sun and read. Mr. Scheer, a nationally syndicated columnist, clearly has been following Pat's story, and he very pointedly blames the administration for covering up Pat's death. I'm impressed with the courage it took to write the piece.

The next day I place a call to Robert Scheer at USC, where he teaches, to thank him for writing the column. He doesn't answer, so I leave a message asking that he call me. When he returns my call, his voice sounds uneasy. He tells me he was a bit afraid to call me. He thought I might have been unhappy with the piece. I laugh that he would take pot shots at the administration, but he was afraid of a phone call from me. Before we ended the conversation, Mr. Scheer asks if he might be able to come see the report. I tell him he can come anytime. He asks if the upcoming Saturday is all right, and I say yes. He then asks if he can bring his wife, the deputy editor of the *San Francisco Chronicle*. I tell him that it would be fine.

Early afternoon on Saturday, Robert Scheer and Narda Zacchino drive up my driveway.

13

Truth is beautiful, without doubt; but so are lies.

—RALPH WALDO EMERSON

M r. Scheer and Ms. Zacchino appear taken aback by leafing through the five thick binders, more than two thousand pages of material, spread out on my dining room table. I explain that I have been reading and analyzing them for more than two months. The content of the binders is confusing and infuriating; there is so much material that each time I open one, I find information I missed on previous examinations. Just as in the previous 15-6 report, the pages are splotched with redactions, thick black lines where indelible marker has been used to conceal words, sentences, and entire paragraphs; reading them is painfully time-consuming and frustrating. The redacted information includes places, missions, equipment, and names—essentially, most of the information that might allow my family and me to make sense of what happened to Pat. We were told the redactions of people's names are necessary to protect the privacy of individuals. Even my name is redacted in a section discussing the questions I had submitted to Senator McCain. Fortunately, through interviews with soldiers in Pat's platoon and information I gathered from other sources, I have been able to fill in some of the concealed information.

As my guests seat themselves at the table, Ms. Zacchino tells me she knows some of the details of Pat's last mission; two months ago, she was a Pulitzer Prize juror and had read Steve Coll's *Washington Post* series; she said she was riveted by the stories and heartsick at the senselessness of Pat's death. I explain that Steve Coll had the daunting task of writing those articles after an investigation relying on an initial report that was about a hundred pages. For the next four and a half hours, I brief Mr. Scheer and Ms. Zacchino on what I have learned from studying the Jones report, starting at the beginning of the mission.

The battalion deployed to Afghanistan on short notice as part of what the Army calls a "surge," a mission of short duration, intended in this case to disrupt the network of Jalaluddin Haqqani, commander of the Taliban forces and one of Osama bin Laden's most trusted associates in Afghanistan. The Rangers spent ten days patrolling the Pakistan border but found little evidence of Haqqani's fighters, so the chain of command, operating from the Tactical Operations Center (TOC) in Salerno, decided to move A Company to a new "area of operations." The commanders pulled out all the forces except for Uthlaut's platoon, which they directed to clear one last village, Manah, five miles north of the Pakistan border. The platoon was stopped at an Afghan Militia Force checkpoint along the Afghanistan-Pakistan border on April 21, when Captain William Saunders and his executive officer, Captain Kirby Dennis, were called back to the TOC by Colonel Jeffrey Bailey to help plan the next operation. The aircraft coming to pick them up was going to bring a fuel pump to repair the disabled Humvee, and then the platoon would finish its mission.

Saunders testified that he and other soldiers had been on the canyon road several times, and there had been no signs of the enemy in the area.

The next day, Saunders had a meeting at another base with the Afghan Militia Force commander to discuss their next mission, and he returned to Salerno around noon. Dennis gave him an update on what was happening with Uthlaut's platoon and the disabled vehicle; it could not be repaired, so they had towed it as far as Magarah before they could not tow it farther. Dennis told Saunders about hiring the local jinga truck to haul it. I explain to Mr. Scheer and Ms. Zacchino that I do not know the identity of the TOC commander as the name is redacted, but in his testimony, he referred to the disabled vehicle as a "hangar queen" because of its poor condition. He also said he didn't want to have the jinga truck tow it all the way back to Salerno because "it's just embarrassing," yet this commander did not give orders to leave the vehicle behind or to destroy it.

Saunders testified that it was important to get Manah cleared by the next day "so we would not get ourselves too far behind setting ourselves up for our next series of operations." All communications between the base and Uthlaut, who was seeking guidance about what to do with the vehicle, were by e-mail or satellite phone with Captain Dennis.

A decision was made at the command center to end the delay and have Uthlaut split his platoon to get half his soldiers to Manah and the others to take the disabled vehicle to the wrecker on the highway. A sense of urgency was imposed on the platoon leader, requiring him to split his troops in order to accomplish both tasks quickly.

Captain Saunders had to have known the potential for an ambush going through the canyon. Even though there had been no sign of the enemy when he was there, the fact that U.S. troops were stuck in Magarah for six hours certainly could allow time for the enemy to plan an attack. Saunders stated in his testimony that he thought the troops were going to split before entering the canyon, however in Uthlaut's communications with Captain Dennis, it's clear the two sections were going to take different routes before entering the deep and narrow pass. Not only did Uthlaut make the routes clear to the TOC, but the forward observer transmitted the route in his request for air support.

When Serial Two entered the canyon, several soldiers remarked that it would be a "perfect place for an ambush": a narrow gorge with no easy escape. It was obvious to many of the Rangers that spending hours in Magarah, situated in the heart of an area known to be controlled by the Taliban, made them vulnerable. Numerous villagers overheard Rangers discuss the planned routes of the two serials, as well as negotiations with the jinga truck driver as to where the troops would be heading. One of the soldiers was obviously angry when he testified. He had been given a note written by the village doctor, who said he needed to talk to someone with the unit about "something bad" that was going to happen. The soldier told his superior, but that individual told the soldier to keep his mouth shut. In his testimony, the higher-ranking soldier said that troops get all kinds of warnings, and they can't follow up on all of them.

There is confusion as to why the platoon set out during daylight. On an earlier deployment in Afghanistan in the fall of 2003, a member of A Company, Jay Blessing, had been killed by a roadside bomb while traveling in a daylight convoy near the Pakistan border. After that incident, the battalion commander, Colonel Bailey, had established a policy banning all daytime troop movement. It is suspicious to me that Colonel Bailey made a point of telling us on the visit to our house that Uthlaut misheard the order to get "boots on the ground by dawn" and instead heard "boots on the ground by dusk." In the report, it is well documented that the order was to get "boots on the ground by dark." It certainly seems that Bailey's explanation was an attempt to make Uthlaut appear at fault for daylight movement. Not only is there an attempt to fault Uthlaut for the fact the platoon set out for Manah before dark, there is also an attempt to portray the ambush as a far more intense engagement than it actually was in order to excuse the actions of a vehicle of overzealous soldiers.

Although the attack began with a series of mortar or RPG (rocket-propelled grenade) rounds that came close to hitting the lead vehicles of Serial Two, within minutes the assault was over, most of the few attackers were in the process of fleeing, and only sporadic and extremely ineffective fire from small arms followed. Significantly, no vehicles or personnel had a single nick from the ambush, and there was no shrapnel damage. There is not one statement from any witness that more than three enemy "figures" ever were observed. Most of the confusion was not created by enemy fire but by the overwhelming and outsized reaction of the Rangers themselves, whose volume of fire was so great that it created the impression on those not directly engaged that it was a major firefight. I was surprised that Colonel Craig Nixon (who had not been there) also told General Jones that the intensity of the firefight was similar to the opening scenes of D-day in the film *Saving Private Ryan.* A comment that was absurd, as there was no carnage during the ambush; no one suffered so much as a scratch. It's hard to take any of Nixon's testimony seriously. The chain of command and the investigators seem to be concealing or minimizing the loss of discipline and fire control under the manufactured premise of an intense firefight.

When the vehicle with Sergeant Baker and his men exited the canyon into the open area and began firing wildly onto the ridgeline, they were not taking fire from anywhere; Sergeant Baker testified that the AMF soldier was firing over his head, not at him, but Baker killed him anyway. Several of the soldiers remarked that they weren't taking fire or that they didn't know if they were taking fire. In their own words: "We were excited," "I wanted to stay in the firefight," "I wish I had taken a split second to identify my target." Their actions were not due to a fog of war, but a lust to fight. They were shooting so wildly they almost fired on the vehicle directly behind them. Sergeant Steven Walter, who was in charge of that vehicle and who saw the Americans on the ridge, testified about the behavior of Sergeant Baker and his men:

"[Sergeant Baker] obviously, didn't [have] control of his element . . . I'm watching from behind him and I'm seeing there are big guns on his vehicle and they're not even engaging targets, they're just shooting, pretty much sporadically at what they think are enemy, but they're really not . . . which is really doing nothing but wasting ammo. The fact that his .50-caliber gunner went Winchester in about a 400- to 500-meter stretch of road is pretty ridiculous in my eyes; as a leader I can't believe that he allowed that to happen.

"The second thing is the fact that even though he couldn't communicate with the rest of the convoy and get situational awareness, he still allowed everyone in his vehicle to shoot wherever. He didn't have communication with Serial One to my knowledge; I was on the same net, I did not hear them talking. He did not have communication with his platoon sergeant in the rear. So if that was me, I would have shot if I had a target to engage, but not if I would have just gotten out of the kill zone . . . I think he was negligent in his duties for not controlling his squad, sir, that's his job."

The soldiers in the vehicle said they did not "positively identify" their targets, but their neglect went far beyond that. The driver, Sergeant Kellett Sayre, said he saw friendlies on the ridgeline before Sergeant Baker shot the AMF, and several soldiers stated they saw waving hands. One soldier told General Jones it looked like the hands were trying to signal, "Hey, it's us." Even if you assume the soldiers believed the hands were those of an enemy soldier, to shoot at someone trying to surrender is a war crime. The vehicle then drove down the road as the occupants fired on structures occupied by women and children. Baker and his men clearly violated Rules of Engagement: "Deadly force may be used only when fired upon, hostile intent exists (if weapons are present, are they being aimed?), elements, mobs and or rioters threaten human life, sensitive equipment, and open free passage of relief supplies." The ROE at the time of the incident was "positive target ID is required prior to engagement." Soldiers also broke the Geneva Convention, which essentially says it is forbidden to shoot at structures possibly occupied by defenseless civilians, or to kill or wound an enemy (in this case a presumed enemy) who surrenders or who can no longer fight.

After the ambush, Saunders testified that he left the TOC for the scene where Pat and the AMF were killed, and "we got the whole team down there" in the middle of the night in order to determine what happened. While explaining the actions of the AMF soldiers, he made a very unusual statement: "When they [the AMF soldiers] heard the trail serial make contact, my understanding was that all the AMF soldiers stayed with the vehicles minus one guy. And that one guy dismounted and moved with Corporal Tillman. When he positioned himself on the ridgeline, he was to be south of Corporal Tillman. So the first thing that the GMV [Baker's vehicle] saw when it [sic] looked up the hill was an AMF soldier in the prone with an AK-47 shooting across the road."

I explain that I'm disturbed by the wording "was to be" when Saunders describes the position of the AMF. That phrasing is not often used in error. I tell Mr. Scheer and Ms. Zacchino that the remark implies that the position of the AMF soldier was planned. I explain that I have done some research and that it was highly unusual for AMF soldiers to get into fighting situations with U.S. troops in 2004; many of the soldiers testified to that. It disturbs me to speculate about the motives and actions of a man who is dead and who can't defend himself, especially when it appears he was trying to assist in the firefight, but that it was the AMF who drew the fire. I can't rule out anything under the circumstances. I also point out that Saunders states the AMF was in the prone position as a means of explaining why Baker couldn't identify his tiger-striped uniform. However, the AMF couldn't have been in a prone position facing downhill—he was shot eight times in the chest.

I explain that the most painful sections of the Jones report for me to read are those describing what happened to Pat and the graphic descriptions of his remains. I try to distance myself from my emotions and read the testimonies as if they are about someone else. But reading how First Sergeant Fuller found a section of Pat's brain and pieces of his skull is horrific: "As soon as the sun came up, I went to the place where Tillman died, and I took what was left of his head and put it in an ammo can, in a Ziploc bag; and I took it back to . . . the CSH [combat support hospital] . . . I wanted it to be with the body." I note that those remains never arrived in Rockville, Maryland, to be analyzed as evidence.

Testimonies reveal that Pat's uniform, MOLLE, and RBA[1] were burned rather than sent with his body to the medical examiner's office. The uniform, in cases of suspected fratricide, is considered evidence and is to be returned with the soldier's body. Green-tipped U.S. rounds were identified on Pat's RBA within at least two hours—grounds to deem Pat's death a potential fratricide. First Sergeant Fuller stated, ". . . there was no doubt in my mind that we shot him." Yet, the Cross Functional Team (CFT) commander who ordered the mission stated he knew the uniform and equipment were being destroyed but, "At the time, it didn't seem alarming to any of us because we didn't know it was a fratricide concern . . . [And] at this point he'd already been zipped up and put on ice literally . . . And there was no reason for any of us to haul around his uniform and that."

This commander was crude and insensitive. I also believe he might be the man ultimately responsible for disregarding Uthlaut's vehement objections to splitting the troops. Captain Saunders's testimony in the 15-6 report states he told the Cross Functional Team commander of Uthlaut's objections to splitting the troops, but the commander ordered them split anyway. In the current report, Saunders states that he must have misunderstood the order the commander gave him and

---

[1] Ranger Body Armor

that he himself must take the blame for giving Uthlaut his final order. When General Jones asked the CFT commander, "Who made the decision that the platoon should be split?" He answered: "The platoon leader, sir," making it appear as though he had no idea Uthlaut had protested the order. He said that he, Saunders, and Dennis together developed the plan to get the vehicle picked up and the mission completed. He states that he told Saunders to get the Humvee and the wrecker linked up, get the Humvee dropped off, and have the platoon finish the clearing operations in Manah; splitting the platoon was not discussed.

The commander was asked: "Did you ever tell Saunders to have the element split?" Answer: "No. I did not." He claims he did not know the platoon had been split until a couple of days after the fratricide, at a platoon meeting called an AAR (after action review), and that he would have questioned that move. He claims he had no idea about the communications between Uthlaut and Captain Dennis. Yet, Captain Dennis and First Sergeant Fuller both stated that at the TOC they observed Saunders talking to the CFT commander to tell him Uthlaut's concerns. Captain Dennis, the executive officer communicating with Uthlaut, testified that the split was originally Uthlaut's idea, although he offered it only as an option—and the least desirable one—if he was forced to hand off the disabled vehicle to the wrecker and get to Manah at the same time. As we know, "once it was chosen, he argued against it," Dennis said, adding that there was a discussion between the CFT commander and Saunders, which Saunders initiated about whether to split. Dennis said he was not present at the discussion but relayed the ensuing decision to split to Uthlaut. Dennis said he had a "gut feeling" that Saunders did not agree with the decision, but it was maybe something that was ordered." Usually in those circumstances, he said, the commander would defer to the platoon leader on the ground, especially one so firmly opposed to an order. I tell Mr. Scheer and Ms. Zacchino that Lieutenant Uthlaut, First Captain of his class at West Point, is a bright, highly capable young man; it was arrogant to ignore his concerns. Dennis said he regretted that he didn't argue Uthlaut's point more vigorously in the TOC because he agreed the split was a bad idea.

First Sergeant Fuller testified: "I remember Captain Saunders walking over to me saying, 'They don't want to split the platoon. They want to keep them together.' And I said, 'I don't think they should. I think they should keep them together.' And he says, 'I'm going to go talk to [the CFT commander] again.' Captain Saunders didn't think they should split. I didn't either. Saunders went to talk to [the CFT commander] about it." Colonel Bailey also indicated in his testimony that he believed the CFT commander gave the order to split the platoon, but that he may not have known exactly when the platoon left.

The commander testified that after the AAR meeting, it was clear the soldiers believed he ordered the split. "So I grabbed Satch [Saunders] afterwards and said, 'What the hell is going on here? And he told me, 'I thought you told me do it.' And I said, 'Satch, we worked on this plan together, and that was never my'—I mean, that was kind of the whole . . . disconnect that happened . . .'"

Saunders testified to General Jones that the decision "was ultimately my decision to split them into two sections. I had based that on having the discussion with the Battalion XO or the Battalion S3 at the time, who was the CFT commander. . . . He told me . . . words to the effect 'Hey, we can't have one vehicle stopping entirely [inaudible].' I know he said that. My understanding after that was that he said to split the platoon. He may or may not have said that. That might have been the way I understood it . . . I know he said we cannot have one Ranger platoon stopped for one vehicle . . . I think he said we need to look to split the platoon or something to that effect. He did not direct me to split the platoon; that was ultimately my decision." Saunders then said that he thought it would be all right to split the troops because each unit had a big gun, the .50 caliber in Serial One and the MK-19 in Serial Two. The MK-19 was Kevin's weapon, which it turned out immediately had jammed and would not fire. Saunders said each section had satellite radio and could communicate with Salerno. But Uthlaut's warnings that there would be no communication in the canyon were realized and contributed to the fratricide.

Uthlaut testified that the plan was for his platoon to bivouac outside Manah the night of April 22 and clear it the next day, so he did not understand why the entire platoon could not stay together, drop off the disabled vehicle, then set up camp together and clear Manah the next morning.

Uthlaut was asked: "Who told you [that] you had to have boots on the ground before dark . . . ?" He answered: "Sir, those were my questions to them. I said, 'So the only reason you want me to split my platoon is to have boots on the ground in the sector before dark?' . . . and the response I got back was 'Yes.'"

Uthlaut also did not see the need for urgency, especially with the safety of his men at risk. First Sergeant Fuller also thought the split unwise. He and others testified that there was no intelligence about the enemy or anything else to justify the urgency: "it's just a timeline, and we feel like we have to stick with it, and that's what drives this kind of stuff."

I tell Mr. Scheer and Ms. Zacchino that my family and I are very grateful that the investigation was done. General Jones revealed crucial information, but his report raises more questions than it comes close to answering, and appropriate consequences have not been meted out to soldiers or officers for negligent or possibly criminal actions. The first volume of the six volumes of the report begins with a briefing book, which contains a nearly incomprehensible explanation by General Jones about the confusion in the Tactical Operations Center over who ordered the split. It includes an explanation of how Saunders was offered immunity, and goes on for four pages, single-spaced. Jones says that he concluded that the CFT commander did not give the order to split and did not know about it prior to the after action review meeting. I read a portion of his statement:

1. "A critical piece of information to my original conclusion was Saunders' *current* belief in what [the Cross Functional team commander] told him on 22 April 2004 in the TOC. In his testimony in November 2004 and in his recent 23 February 2005 sworn statement, Saunders appeared to say that *currently* he is 'almost positive' that [CFT commander] told him to split the platoon. However, Saunders subsequently and repeatedly sought to clarify this portion of his statements, calling my legal adviser, [Lieutenant Colonel Michael] Hargis, several times. While Saunders was 'almost positive' on 22 April 2004 that [CFT commander] told him to split the platoon, he is positive now that [CFT commander] did not tell him to split the platoon. Saunders is also positive that he did not readdress the issue of splitting the platoon with [CFT commander] although he admits that he did tell [REDACTED] that he was going to do so.

2. "The clarification came after Saunders had been read his rights for false official statement and false swearing. This clarification came after [REDACTED] talked to [REDACTED] about his statement. [REDACTED] had been told that [REDACTED] had said he, Saunders, was 'almost positive' that [CFT commander] told him to split the platoon. [REDACTED] approaching a witness under these circumstances is not to be condoned. However, because Saunders corrected some language in his sworn statement. I believe that Saunders' recent clarifications are sincere and not the result of witness tampering by [CFT commander]."

Jones also stated that even though Captain Dennis saw Saunders approach the CFT commander in the TOC with the intention of conveying Uthlaut's objections to the split, he found it "plausible" that Saunders never did bring it up because "he was unwilling to question his superior regarding the order . . ." Jones concluded that, "The decision to split the platoon was, in my view, based upon a miscommunication of intent between Saunders and [CFT commander]."

I don't know what to believe, but I do know from talking to various soldiers and from reading the documents that everyone present at the TOC knew Uthlaut was aggressively opposed to splitting the troops. I find it highly unlikely that the CFT commander was not aware of Uthlaut's position. My family and I remain perplexed as to why no one in the chain of command took Uthlaut's protest seriously.

One of the most shameful and distasteful statements in all of the volumes comes from the officer placed in charge of the previous 15-6 investigation, whose name is redacted. In his testimony, he voiced criticism of our family, and Kevin in particular: ". . . nobody is satisfied with the answers in that family that they've been given. And it continuously, I mean it [is] just continuous through the last six months. I mean, personally, in my opinion, when this is done, sir, there is [sic] going to be more questions." Asked why he thought the family is not satisfied, this officer replied that he "found out" from a sergeant before Pat's "repatriation" ceremony, a ritual of sending a soldier's body home, that: " '[Kevin] Tillman doesn't want a chaplain involved in [Pat's] repatriation ceremony.' I'm like, 'Excuse me?' He goes, 'No, he doesn't want, they don't want a . . . chaplain to preside over it.' And I'm like, 'Why is that?' He goes, 'Well, evidently he and his brother are atheists. That's the way they were raised.' I'm like, 'Well, you can tell Mr. Tillman that this ceremony ain't about him, it's about everybody in the Joint Task Force beading [sic] farewell to his brother, so there will be a chaplain and there will be prayers.' "

He continued to tell Jones, "The underline [sic] . . . discussion of the whole thing or the view is, those that are Christians can come to term [sic] with faith and the fact there is an afterlife, heaven, or what-not. It is, I believe, it's being a Christian that it's easier to deal with that. Not being atheist, I'm not really sure what they believe or how they can get their head around death. So, in my personal opinion, sir, that is why I don't think they'll ever be satisfied. I mean, they were raised atheists, the father, I believe the mother is. I know Pat's wife, it's come out that she's—they . . . all are atheists. So I don't know if that's important but that's kind of the struggles that they're dealing with. And they do not want a chaplain even close to them, talking to them about Christianity and heaven or whatnot." Jones then called for a break in the testimony.

The officer's comments are extremely offensive. The religious beliefs of Pat and our family have nothing to do with Pat's death. I can't help wondering if this man's prejudice had any influence over how he conducted his investigation, or how serious he was about finding the truth.

Unfortunately, the same thought occurs when I read the comments of General Jones during the testimony of First Sergeant Fuller, who laments having to go through these investigations and answer questions.

Fuller says, "The bottom line is: It was our fault. It was the individuals' fault on the ground, and we know that . . . Can you say it was Baker? Partly. Can you say it was the PL [platoon leader]? Partly. Ours [in the TOC] for making him move? Yeah . . . I know we want to find out what happened here, but I've to ask for some [inaudible] for some of my privates who have had to say this over and over. And when they come and see me, wanting to go see this counselor again because . . . it's bothering them again . . . I mean he [Baker] was the team leader, and they were his guys . . . I just hate to see my guys do this over and over."

Jones, in apparent sympathy, says, "I appreciate your candor there,

Top ["Top" is an Army colloquialism commonly used when addressing those holding the rank of first sergeant]. We don't like doing these things any more than anyone else does. Bottom line is the secretary of the Army is [inaudible] the system . . . and we're just following through on questions that [McCain] asked us to look at. We're just going to look at the facts, and we're only going to report the facts. That's all there is to it. I share your concern and having to readdress this with kids that just have been traumatized over stuff like this that don't need it. . . . "

"Stuff like this" is how they regard the death of Pat in circumstances riddled with problematic questions, contradictions, and unmistakable instances of intentional deceit? *Stuff like this?*

There are so many disturbing statements in the files that it is impossible to list them all. Saunders testified that the chain of command at the platoon meeting after Pat's death told the soldiers not to talk about the incident because "we didn't want guys calling home" to spread rumors. More likely it was to try to keep a lid on the information in order to withhold from us or the American public the truth of how Pat died.

There are more questionable files feeding our suspicions that the military wanted to cover up the truth of his death. For example, there is an e-mail about a press release announcing Pat's Silver Star award that has in the subject line: "CPL Tillman SS game plan." Game plan? There was testimony from top officers that they knew within days after Pat died that he was shot by fellow soldiers, but no one told the family. One officer whose name is redacted talks about how, as the incident started to break in the news, the investigation came up and "It went to the 2-star [general] level and the 2-star took it right to the 4-star level. Basically we, you know, came to USASOC[2] when basically all, you know, everything opened up and now all of a sudden, okay, it's sort of like, 'Here is

---

2 US Army Special Operations Command

the steak dinner, but we're giving it to you on this, you know, garbage can cover.' You know, 'You got it. You work it.'"

Mr. Scheer and Ms. Zacchino seem stunned and disturbed by all this information. They both find the most compelling and damning document in the entire report to be the testimony of Captain Richard Scott, the officer who was assigned to investigate within hours of Pat's death.

14

Truth lives in the midst of deception.

—FRIEDRICH VON SCHILLER

Kevin first met Captain Richard Scott before Pat's death while at the 2nd Battalion, 75th Regiment at Fort Lewis in Washington. Kevin left A Company after he learned Pat was killed in a fratricide situation. He no longer could work side by side with the soldiers who had killed his brother. The first time he remembers meeting Scott in an official capacity was when he was transferred from A Company to Headquarters and Headquarters Company (HHC) to become part of a sniper section. Captain Scott was the Company Commander of HHC.

Shortly after transferring to HHC, Kevin went to an army school called the Special Operations Target Interdiction Course (SOTIC) at Fort Bragg, North Carolina. He didn't recall spending significant time with Scott until he returned from SOTIC around late October or early November. At this point, our family had learned the secretary of the Army had appointed General Jones to further investigate Pat's death. Kevin went to Captain Scott on numerous occasions to vent his frustrations over the massive contradictions of information we had received and to get some advice as to how to address his dissatisfaction with

General Jones when the time arrived for his testimony. As Kevin addressed some of the concerns about the disparities and conflicting information he received from the soldiers from his former platoon and from the most recent command briefing. Scott attempted to clarify some of the facts to dispel the confusion, contradictions, and inconsistencies regarding the investigation. After talking to Scott, Kevin was convinced that he felt the soldiers and officers involved in the investigation did not receive the appropriate level of punishment. It was at this point that Kevin realized that Scott was the initial 15-6 Investigating Officer assigned to ascertain the facts surrounding Pat's death.

I find it hard to believe that LTC Bailey would place Kevin under Scott's command under the circumstances. As Kevin's Company Commander, Scott would have some obligation to his soldiers and their welfare.

Kevin was shocked.

He had no idea that Captain Scott had investigated Pat's death. He thought Major David Hodne had completed the investigation on which the 15-6 report was based. No one ever mentioned there had been an earlier investigation. Based on Scott's testimony, Lieutenant Colonel Jeffrey Bailey appointed him to look into the circumstances of Pat's death less than twenty-four hours after it happened. Lieutenant Colonel Bailey had walked the area where Pat was killed, and based on what he observed, it was his belief that Pat's death had been caused by members of his own platoon. He felt it was necessary for Scott to begin his interviews right away.

According to Scott's testimony, he had never done an investigation of this magnitude. His background was not in investigations; he was a Company Commander at the time of the incident. He told Kevin he is an Infantry Officer by profession and not a Criminal Investigator. He was not school trained on forensics, investigating crime scenes, or collecting evidence. However, within hours of conducting interviews from key witnesses involved in the shooting, Scott quickly realized that Pat was most likely killed by friendly fire, rounds from his own platoon. Within eight to ten days Scott had completed his investigation without any assistance and informed his chain of command that he had concluded that Pat's death was the result of fratricide, and that there was potential for negligence on the part of soldiers on the ground and leaders at the TOC. After his report was sent to Regimental Headquarters, his superiors decided to conduct a second investigation at the regimental level, this time by a LTC and a JAG officer. Scott assumed it was because the findings and recommenations in his investigation revealed more serious implications. Scott let Kevin look over a copy of his report. After reading the report, paying close attention to the recommendations, he walked away from Scott's office furious.

Several days after the discussion with Captain Scott, Kevin was called to give his testimony to General Jones. At that time, he informed General Jones that Captain Scott was the initial 15-6 Investigating Officer and recommended that General Jones call Captain Scott to testify. Kevin believed the facts were not "reflected accurately" in the regimental-level report. The report and the punishments seemed "diluted." Scott had concluded that there was potential for "gross negligence" and possible "criminal intent," and recommended the involvement of the Criminal Investigation Division. Captain Scott's report stated that soldiers in the lead vehicle were shooting at their own men who were located on the berm just east of a local village. Scott also stated that based on eyewitness testimony, the soldiers located on the berm were waving their hands and arms in an attempt to signal a cease fire. However, the soldiers in the lead vehicle continued to shoot at the village, which was occupied by local villagers. It was apparent that the soldiers in the lead vehicle were firing without being fired upon. Scott's report revealed that the radio telephone operator (RTO) and platoon leader were wounded as a result of rounds fired from the lead vehicle. The lead vehicle was commanded by Sergeant Baker: information Lieutenant Colonel Bailey had given us as fact when he came to our house a year ago, May 2004, yet the regimental report is vague and inconclusive.

Kevin asked, "Why did [he] say that . . . it's inconclusive? Referring to the regimental investigator, It just doesn't make sense . . . why would

[he] say that? Did . . . he just not agree with [Scott's] findings, or . . . did he have someone's foot on his head to water it down?"

Before Kevin finished his interview with General Jones, he was adamant that the general call Captain Scott as a witness. We don't know if Jones was aware of the first investigation, or if he had intended to call Scott as a witness, but after Kevin's testimony, he had no choice.

Mr. Scheer and Ms. Zacchino ask questions while trying to digest the information I have shared with them. Both tell me they want to do whatever they can to help my family get to the truth. After an hour or so, I walk them to their car and watch them back down the driveway as they solemnly wave good-bye.

Back in the house, I sit down at the table, exhausted from going over the details in the documents sprawled out in front of me. I stare out the window, thinking about how difficult it must have been for Kevin, dealing with his loss and grief, to function as a soldier among men who might be either responsible for his brother's death, or suspect in covering it up. If Kevin had never brought up his concerns about Pat's death to Captain Scott, we never would have known about the first investigation. I marvel at the courage it took for him to confront General Jones, to tell him of the existence of Captain Scott's report, and to then insist that the general get testimony from Scott himself. Without Scott's testimony, we would not know how egregious the circumstances were, and we wouldn't have the substantial evidence we need to get justice for Pat. I reach for the binder that holds Captain Scott's testimony and start reading through it for the fifth time.

Captain Scott was summoned to testify on November 19, 2004, two days after Kevin gave his statement. He told General Jones he was verbally appointed by Lieutenant Colonel Bailey to investigate the facts of Pat within twenty-four hours of the shooting of his death. Bailey told him to begin right away. A formal order to investigate would come from the regimental commander, Colonel James C. Nixon, on April 29, 2004.

Captain Scott was based in Salerno when he conducted his witness interviews with soldiers, who testified under oath while facts were still fresh in their minds. Scott interviewed each witness individually. He sketched on a whiteboard where each soldier was during the incident, where they said each vehicle was located, where each serial was, the location of the villages, where every eyewitness was when the mission started, and where they were when Pat was killed.

After each interview, "I went back on the computer and started drawing up each individual's eyewitness [account] to the point where I could piece it all together," Scott testified. He noted that each Ranger provided his own perspective, and it was "really like piecing together a puzzle." Then he brought each witness back and they made sworn statements, which Scott entered into his computer. The point was for them to confirm what they said in relation to the other witnesses, "And they came back and all confirmed that, 'yes, that was indeed what happened based on my recollection,'" Scott said. He offered Jones copies of all of the sworn statements, which he said were still in his computer.

Captain Scott told Jones that he submitted his written report, including his recommendations, about "eight to ten days" after he began the assignment; it was recorded as completed on May 4, 2004, and went up Scott's chain of command to the regimental command. There, Scott testified, "They decided then that this was a little bigger than what we expected. I did confirm, based on my investigation, the conclusion that it was fratricide, based on the interviews and evidence and based on the photographs that were given to me."

Scott testified that after his report was submitted, the regimental JAG officer came to see him and suggested some changes in "military lingo" to make it easier for non-military people to read his report. The officer also suggested some "repackaging" and "formatting" changes, but nothing of major substance. Scott said, for example, in his original report, he did not have "exhibits" in parentheses, so the JAG officer recommended that format. Aside from these rather cosmetic changes, "the contents [were] still there. Nothing really was taken out," Scott said.

Scott then presented Jones with two documents that then were marked "Exhibit 1"—the rough draft of his report—and "Exhibit 2"—the final copy, whose only difference from the rough draft was an opening paragraph of background. It was Exhibit 2 that Scott said was submitted to regimental headquarters.

"I saw this original in the three-ring binder when I came back from Afghanistan. And now apparently we can't find it," Scott stated. "And so this is the only one that's out there, unless you have a copy."

Jones asked Scott: "This is the only copy left, correct?"

Scott responded: "I have it on my thumb drive, sir. I brought you a copy."[3]

Scott said his report's conclusion of fratricide was confirmed at regimental headquarters. A couple of days later, he was told that "You did a Battalion Level 15-6. Now we are going ahead and execute or initiate a Regimental 15-6." Scott said he determined that was being done because of the seriousness of the situation, that "based on my investigation . . . it was indeed fratricide," and he thought that it "could involve some Rangers that could be charged for criminal intent." He then told Jones: "I did bring an enclosure that shows my recommendation. And that was also sent up [to the regimental headquarters] as well. Mostly administrative recommendations, but, again, [I] brought that for your review."

The general then asked Scott if he had any physical evidence provided to him during his investigation. Scott replied that the morning after Pat's death, his MOLLE vest was shown to him. "It was in a brown trash bag. I got to see it. Got to take a look at it and it . . . had bullet holes. It was torn because of the fragments of bullets and different size holes." Jones asked if Scott saw fragments with green tips, or green markings on the MOLLE vest. (American rounds have green tips.) Scott said he could not recall, but other soldiers might.

Jones asked if there were any bullet fragments and if so, what hap-

---

3 Scott would later tell the Defense Department's Inspector General that he "deleted the files from the thumb drive after meeting with Brigadier General Jones."

pened to them. Scott said he thought there were some, but he could not recall what happened to them. Jones asked whether he was given a .50-caliber round, and Scott responded that it had been lodged in a boulder and that he couldn't recall what he did with it.

Jones turned to the incident itself and asked if there was "anyone in particular" who told Scott he called for a cease fire. Scott answered: "Up on the ridgeline, there were numerous Rangers yelling 'cease fire,' trying to call on the radio . . .[4] Staff Sergeant Weeks trying to call on the radio to tell him cease fire. [Private First Class Bryan] O'Neal yelling 'cease fire' as he—as soon as he learned that it was our guys shooting at their position. Numerous other Rangers, I can't recall their names. They're in here [his computer]. Pretty much all of them started yelling "cease fire" and using hand and arm signals at certain points.

Scott testified that the shooters were firing into the village and onto the ridgeline so indiscriminately and with such little restraint that they even came close to hitting soldiers in a vehicle behind them. And Scott had absolutely no doubt that they did hit the platoon leader and radio operator near the village.

Jones asked Scott what his recommendations were, and Scott, seeming to grow a bit frustrated, said, "Again sir, a copy of my recommendations [was] submitted along with my report. But . . ." He did not complete the sentence. Like his report, his recommendations also were obviously misplaced.

The regimental personnel lost Scott's original report and then his recommendations also. That had to have been the list Kevin saw when he transferred into Captain Scott's company. Thankfully, Scott then produced a draft version of his recommendations.

> SCOTT: Sir, my original recommendation or report that I submitted to regiment headquarters, one of my recommendations that is not on [this] draft was [that] I recommended that certain leaders

---

4 All names in the document were redacted. I inserted the names I could determine in brackets.

be investigated if this investigation continued because I felt that there was some stuff negligent on their part . . . I don't know if it was appropriate to do that because some of the persons that I interviewed were of the same rank and of higher rank than I. But that's what I submitted to—that's what I wrote on my final report was that these persons or persons that I listed, certain persons be investigated because of what I thought was some gross negligence.

When he talks of "certain leaders" who were grossly negligent he is presumably referring to the Cross Functional Team commander and Captain William Saunders, the officers who were involved in the order to split the troops, despite Platoon Leader David Uthlaut's vehement but futile warnings that it would be dangerous to do so. There was also the CFT commander's insistence that there be "boots on the ground" in Manah by dark, as if there were some real urgency that made putting the troops in jeopardy worth the risk.

> JONES: Do you remember specifically who that was?
> SCOTT: Staff Sergeant Baker was one of the individuals.
> JONES: And you said people of equal or higher rank to you?
> SCOTT: I interviewed [CFT commander] at the time, sir, and then Captain [William] Saunders. I also interviewed the . . . Executive Officer at the time.
> JONES: That was Captain [Kirby] Dennis?
> SCOTT: Yes, sir.
> LT. COL. MICHAEL HARGIS: Can we take a break here, sir?
> JONES: [To Scott] We're going to take about a two-minute break here. Could you step out for a minute?
> SCOTT: Yes, sir.

It is suspicious that a break is called now. Hargis is the JAG officer, the military's legal counsel in this investigation. He asked for a break just when Scott was implicating higher-ranking officers for negligence. The interview continued after the break.

JONES: I want to remind you that you're still under oath. One question I have is, Captain, is that you stated that, in your investigation, you are of the opinion that there were others that were potentially negligent. And you said Staff Sergeant Baker, you thought, in your opinion, demonstrated gross negligence. Is that accurate?

SCOTT: Yes, sir.

JONES: Were there others that demonstrated gross negligence?

SCOTT: Yes, sir, I believe the .50-cal gunner and the 240-gunner.

JONES: And their names?

SCOTT: . . . The .50-cal gunner was Specialist [Stephen] Ashpole and then the 240-gunner was Specialist Stephen Elliott.

JONES: Okay. You also said, though, you listed three other names, CFT commander Saunders, and Dennis. What specifically was the reference to those three?

SCOTT: That they were part of the interview process. So the sworn statements that I received from them were submitted with my original packet to the Regiment Headquarters.

JONES: Okay. But you had mentioned them right after you talked about Staff Sergeant Baker and negligence.

SCOTT: No. Okay, sir. That must have been my fault because they shouldn't be connected to the negligence. I think I was just referring to the fact that in my investigation, I had to interview those that are the same rank or higher in rank than I. I think that's what I was trying to portray.

I go back and reread what he had said just before the break: "I recommended that certain leaders be investigated if the investigation continued because I felt that there was some stuff negligent on their part . . . because of what I thought was some gross negligence."

Scott could not have been more clear, but then Hargis called for a break. Then, when Scott resumed interviewing, he appeared to have changed his testimony. I wonder if Jones or Hargis said something to him.

Scott then said that "I don't know if it was legal" to interview officers of higher rank than he. A few minutes earlier, before the break, he had said he did not know if it was "appropriate to do that" because of their rank. Did Hargis tell him it was illegal to have interviewed higher-ranking officers? Hargis and Jones outrank Scott. Were they trying to keep him from implicating officers at the TOC?

Scott then focused on the shooters, and started to get agitated: "I think Sergeant Baker demonstrated . . . gross negligence with the actions he took. One, he recognized that . . . the AMF soldier wasn't shooting in his direction but shot him and killed him anyways. And then I believe that he lost control of his vehicle, that he was responsible for number one, because he shot and killed that AMF soldier, and then two, again, the actions that everybody took within his vehicle."

He then turned his attention to Private First Class Trevor Alders, the 249-gunner, quoting from his interview with Alders: " 'I was shooting where the rest of the GMV was shooting.' He's referring to Corporal Tillman's location . . . 'As we were firing, I saw three or four arms pop up . . . They did not look like cease-fire hand-and-arm signals because they were waving side-to-side.' So at this point they weren't receiving any fire at all . . . No firing, no accurate firing, no effective firing , no firing at all except for what was coming out of the GMV [Baker's vehicle]."

Scott testified that there were many attempts made to signal to the shooters that there were friendly forces on the ridgeline—calling "cease fire," waving arms, Pat throwing a smoke grenade, and a sergeant on the ridgeline shooting a signal flare. Scott's testimony underscored the reality that Pat was killed in a senseless act by soldiers who were wildly and inexplicably out of control.

Jones asked if Scott had anything more to add before ending his testimony, and the captain certainly did, though he initially stumbled through his words.

> SCOTT: I just—this whole process—and I was going through the interview process, it was really—I think it's pretty easy to say that—probably the most difficult things, in fact, the most difficult things that I had to do since I've been in the Army. The other difficult thing, though, was watching some of these guys getting off . . . with what I thought was a lesser of a punishment than what they should've received. And I will tell you, over a period of time, you know, sir, you're like the third, fourth investigating officer to come in, [and] without the sworn statements, the stories have changed. They have changed to, I think, help some individuals.
>
> And I'm going to give you an example and I'm hoping this doesn't—this recording doesn't leave this room. But I was called in to the battalion commander's office. And the reason I'm saying this is because I disagree how this happened. But, during Staff Sergeant Baker's field grade[5] meeting and they had the entire chain of command [inaudible] . . . that were involved, the NCO,[6] the company commander, first sergeant, all sticking up for Baker.
>
> And the reason the battalion commander [Colonel Jeffrey Bailey] called me in was because the NCOs, [it] so happened, changed their story in how things occurred and the timing and the distance; in an attempt to stick up for their counterpart, [they] implied, insinuated that the report wasn't as accurate as I submitted it up the chain of command.
>
> And so instead of, really, an individual punishing or giving out the punishment to Staff Sergeant Baker, I was the one in there

---

5 Field-grade officers are commissioned officers senior in rank to a company officer but junior to a general officer; a major, lieutenant colonel, or colonel
6 Non-commissioned officer

saying, "No, this is accurate. They signed [interviews], sir, that were given to me." And that Staff Sergeant Baker did indeed show some gross negligence. So I kind of was the bad guy in front of the entire chain of command, sticking to the report, sticking to the conclusion.

And that probably should've been handled much differently than that, I think. I don't know if it was an attempt to put me in as a bad guy . . . The bottom line is, Staff Sergeant Baker was not chaptered out of the Army. I thought at a minimum that's what he should've received, but he did not. He received a field grade. Individuals Elliott [and] Ashpole were [inaudible] given company grades[7] and now are serving in a different unit.

Scott saw the shooters as careless, irresponsible soldiers who acted methodically, not out of control, in some sort of "fog of war" situation. They outrageously ignored many warnings that they were shooting at fellow soldiers. Scott felt that his investigation was accurate and was upset that his battalion commander, Colonel Jeffrey Bailey, apparently decided to go with the regimental officer's more lenient recommendations. Scott continued:

> SCOTT: And . . . you asked me if there's anything else. I guess that's really my frustration, is that I had to go through this, come up with a conclusion and then part of my recommendation was saying we need to look at these guys. Here are some individuals that could potentially, and have, demonstrated lack of control but more importantly the gross negligence . . . And then at the end I thought the investigation was complete. That they didn't get their due just punishment, and that they were just released; I guess

---

7 Company-grade officers are typically assigned to a company as a platoon leader or executive officer or as a commander; a second lieutenant, first lieutenant, or captain

that's why I was frustrated in how that all unfolded.

JONES: Let's go ahead and take a pause here, if you could, and just step out for a minute.

SCOTT: Yes, sir.

In the middle of crucial testimony, Scott is abruptly told to stop talking and step outside.

When the interview resumed, General Jones asked Scott about his opinion that witnesses had changed their stories from the time he interviewed them under oath in Afghanistan and later under questioning in the subsequent investigation conducted by the regimental officer. Scott explained that one key difference had to do with the time that elapsed while the shooters were attacking the ridgeline. He testified that based on his interviews with the eyewitnesses, he determined that the lead vehicle with Sergeant Baker "methodically came through [the canyon] and fired on the ridgeline in what I considered three volleys of fire."

The first was when they passed the jinga truck and they fired straight into the ridgeline. The second was when they fired on the Rangers on the hill, who at that point realized they were being fired upon by their fellow soldiers because they saw tracers from the weapons. The soldiers on the ridgeline were waving their arms and yelling "cease fire." Scott said it was at this point that Pat threw the smoke grenade, and the smoke started to build. The shooters, also at this same moment, stopped firing as their vehicle rounded a corner and their view became obstructed by a corral and a mud hut. When they stopped firing, Pat thought the smoke signal had worked because there was a lull in the fire. But soon the vehicle passed the hut, and Baker and his crew started firing again. The third and last volley, Scott testified, "would be onto the village itself."

Scott charged that the witnesses later tried to establish that "it was so quick that it was just one volley. It was during that one volley that Pat Tillman was killed . . . [T]hey were trying to say that it was under a minute to show that it was very quick . . . And I think in my investigation it was a little longer than that, so it was more methodically planned out."

The distinction was extremely important, as it helped drive Scott to the conclusion of gross negligence. He believed the shooters had enough time to assess the situation and " . . . these guys in the truck actually saw hands waving, could identify hands waving, could see movement up there, could actually see that . . . their weapons systems are not only firing up at the ridgeline but also firing on the backside of the ridgeline and also towards the village, which leads me to believe that these guys were similar in control." Scott said, ". . . I think what they were trying to show . . . the battalion commander was that this was a very short distance, very quick. It was very difficult to control anything. And I disagree with that." He believed they were in control, that their actions were methodical and they had plenty of time to assess the situation.

> SCOTT: And at that point, I went back to my office [and] told the battalion commander [Bailey] that if he's really confused about . . . the report versus what the NCOs are now saying, I could bring in the sworn statements. And I brought this [his thumb drive] in, loaded up on his computer and talked to the NCOs as a group. . . . And all of you [witnesses] in this room told me that everything that I back-briefed was very accurate. Now, you're coming back and saying that it is not accurate, which I totally disagree with and recommended [to] the Battalion Commander [Bailey] that "You need to stick with the original statements." And they didn't know I had the statements at that time. So it was very easy for me to refer to them. . . .

Scott was very distressed that testimony given to him under oath was changed. "[They] refit . . . the location of the AMF soldier, that he was in the prone position, when, in fact, he was standing up. I know that because that's what [Staff Sergeant Baker] told me, that he was standing up and [he] dropped him and actually saw him falling down after he shot him."

I vividly recall Bailey's "unofficial" briefing at my house when he said the Afghan soldier was standing when Baker killed him, and then at the official briefing at Ft. Lewis, where Bailey insisted that the Afghan soldier was prone when he was shot. He excused his change of story by saying he was "mistaken" when he was at my house. Now here was Captain Scott not only accusing these soldiers of changing their testimony on that point, but he has the proof—their original statements—and he is handing them to the investigators, literally.

Allowing or encouraging the witnesses to say the Afghan soldier was prone when shot, that the time that elapsed over the course of the barrage was much shorter, and that the distance between Pat and the shooters was greater than originally stated all seemed designed to paint a picture different from reality. It made it easier to excuse the shooters for not being able to identify their targets as friendly. It made it acceptable to let them off with lenient disciplines.

Scott complained that there were witnesses who testified in the regimental probe who he did not interrogate because they were not even on the scene when it happened. "Yet they were in there talking about the distance and the time . . . [it] led me to believe that these guys were coming in there just to stick up for Baker . . . doing whatever they could to retain him in the Army."

Scott regretted that a few days later, Baker told his commander that he was leaving the Army. "[T]hat really . . . was one of those things that kind of upset me, too," Scott said. "We had an opportunity to punish him, and now he leaves the system. . . ."

He seemed put on the defensive when JAG officer Hargis asked: "Captain Scott, were you present in the battalion commander's office when these NCOs—as you say—changed their story?"

"As you say?"

If the question was intended to unsettle Scott further, it worked. Scott said that the NCOs and his chain of command, including Captain William Saunders, were in the room when Colonel Bailey called him in, and it was clear he felt broadsided. Hargis then pressed Scott to identify which individuals in the room changed their testimony, and in what way. Scott said he could not recall specifically who said what—that was seven months before—but that but all six NCOs seemed to speak "with one voice."

> SCOTT: I think they all agreed . . . came in with one voice. I can't recall who was representing them and talking as the one voice. But again, refitting the distance, the time, the location, and the positioning . . . The battalion commander at the time, briefed me on, "Hey, these guys are saying this. You're saying this in your investigation and in your report. And I'm having a hard time figuring out, okay, who's telling the truth."
>
> And . . . that's kind of odd. And then you bringing me in front of . . . the entire chain of command. You're putting me on the spot. You're asking me if I told the truth on the investigation.
>
> The investigation, all the facts, are based on the sworn statements and in the interviews . . . And that's when I went back . . . got the PowerPoint presentation and the statements . . .

Jones completed his interrogation by telling Scott not to talk about his testimony, adding, "I appreciate your candor."

I close the binder and glance wearily over at Pat's picture on the bookshelf in the adjacent room. Pat was honest and incorruptible in life. He would be offended and outraged about the actions taken in the aftermath of his death. We owe it to Pat to find out who is behind these deceptions, and how high it goes.

15

*To know what is right and not to
do it is the worst cowardice.*

—Confucius

For more than a year, I have spent hours on the phone, every spare moment I have, talking to soldiers who served with Pat and Kevin, the medical examiner, mortuary affairs personnel, ballistic experts, investigative journalists, and the staffs of congressmen and senators. Since several months after Pat's death, I have been going through Senator John McCain's office to get answers to my family's mounting concerns. However, I sense Pat's case has become something of a political encumbrance to McCain. Gradually, I have turned to my congressman, Mike Honda, for help, while Patrick has relied on the support of Zoe Lofgren, his representative in Congress. The Jones investigation has uncovered valuable information, but it has answered few of our questions. If anything, the report raises more suspicions about what happened to Pat. Patrick has written a series of very powerful, and sometimes inflammatory, letters to military and Department of Defense personnel.

A few months ago, a letter he sent to General Jones came to the attention of the Department of Defense inspector general. Issues addressed in Patrick's letter, along with concerns raised by members of Congress, including Senator McCain, Senator Chuck Grassley, and Representatives Honda, Lofgren, Ike Skelton, Christopher Shays, and Dennis Kucinich, have prompted the inspector general to investigate Pat's death further.

In mid-September, I get a call from inspector general special agent Brian Grossman to set up an interview in several weeks. I arrange to have Mike, Richard, and Michelle at my house because they were present when Colonel Jeffrey Bailey came to tell us about the fratricide. I want the information we provide to be as accurate as possible. Kevin, who has been out of the military for three months, is in Hungary visiting friends and will have to be interviewed later. Agent Grossman also will interview Marie, who is living in New York, and Pat's father.

Because my house can be difficult to find, I arrange for Agent Grossman to meet me at my school after work to follow me home. He is accompanied by Air Force Colonel Elizabeth Adams. Once inside, we gather around the dining table, on which Grossman has placed a tape recorder. After some preliminary conversation, we begin to discuss the various meetings, briefings, and documents we have received since Pat died. We express our concerns about the autopsy, the field hospital report, the psychological evaluations Pat received, the grossly negligent conduct of the soldiers in the vehicle, and the irresponsible orders of the officers in the tactical operations center. We also discuss the significance of Captain Richard Scott's report and his testimony to General Jones. In the course of our discussion I mention that Kevin believes Major David Hodne did the 15-6 report after Captain Scott did the initial investigation. It is difficult to figure out all the players since the documents are redacted. Grossman corrects me and tells me it was Colonel Ralph Kauzlarich who did the 15-6 report.

I'm rather shaken by that, since Colonel Kauzlarich is the officer who makes disparaging remarks about our family not being Christian, and in his testimony to General Jones, he expresses disdain for Kevin for trying to get information about Pat's death. "It's coming to the point now where he's becoming a pain to [redacted] and [their] ability to do what they have to do train and deploy and fight and win." He also accuses Kevin of making verbal threats to soldiers. As I recall this, I become even more disturbed by what took place with Kevin seven months ago. About five months before his discharge, Kevin was given orders to deploy to Iraq attached to another unit. He had the option to decline because his brother had been killed, but he felt a responsibility to go, as he had made a commitment. However, when he learned he would be assigned to serve in a unit with soldiers involved in Pat's death, he went to his chain of command and said, "Sir, I'm being sent over there with guys who killed Pat; I'm a sniper, that's irresponsible, I'm not going." I find it disturbing that Kevin's superior officers were concerned about his behavior toward soldiers responsible for shooting Pat, yet they were willing to send him to a war zone with them.

Grossman goes on to tell us he and his staff will be thinking "outside the box." He says that in his brief exposure to the documents, he has come to believe Pat's death should have been examined with a great deal more scrutiny, especially since so many people apparently knew within hours it had been a suspected fratricide. He also says he has concerns about the snipers who were assigned to the second serial. He wonders why they were never questioned. We ask him if his staff is going to look at the orders given by the chain of command that day, and he indicates it will. He says if his people uncover anything that appears to be criminal on the part of the soldiers, his office will call for a criminal investigation.

He believes his review will take about a year.

Within a week of our interview, the *San Francisco Chronicle* publishes a well-written and quite comprehensive article, written by Rob Collier, about our family's search for truth and the inspector general's inquiry into Pat's death. Over the next few months I stay in close contact with Grossman. Once Kevin returns home from his trip to Europe, he also communicates regularly with the agent. In November, I ask Kevin if I can have the number of Bryan O'Neal, the young soldier who was next to Pat when he was killed. Kevin had offered me the number several times, but I had felt it might be too emotional for Bryan and me to talk too soon.

Dialing the number, I'm concerned the conversation will be awkward, but it's easy to talk to Bryan. I can understand why Pat was so fond of him. When I ask how he is doing, he tells me he has been treated very badly since Pat's death, something Kevin had learned months before. After Pat was killed, Bryan was whisked off to Ranger school so no one in the unit could talk to him. When he completed the school, he was assigned to the unit of Sergeant Kellett Sayre, the driver of Sergeant Greg Baker's vehicle. Sayre tried to convince Bryan that Pat was responsible for his own death, which appalls me.

Bryan then tells me that what disturbs him is that he is certain he saw three people out of the vehicle shooting, and he thinks Sayre may have been one of them. I tell Bryan that General Jones told us the vehicle never stopped moving once it exited the canyon. Bryan tells me that is not true. I ask Bryan how far away he thinks Baker's vehicle was from his and Pat's position, and he says thirty-five to forty yards. I let him know I had talked with Sergeant Matt Weeks, who was positioned fifteen yards behind O'Neal and Pat, about the distance of the vehicle from Pat's position, and he told me "about forty yards." I hesitantly ask Bryan if he thinks Pat could have been killed deliberately. He wavers but ultimately says no. The next day, I call Grossman and tell him about my conversation with Bryan. I let him know that he said the vehicle had stopped and he believed the driver was shooting at them from a distance of thirty-five to forty yards.

We have been trying for more than a year to determine who was the commander in Khost. None of the soldiers we talk to knows. Captain Scott would know, but he's in Iraq. Just before Christmas, I call Grossman from my classroom during lunch to find out if he can divulge to us that one redacted name. He tells me it was Kauzlarich.

"Kauzlarich! He was the commander whose orders basically got two men killed and two others wounded, and he did the investigation?"

"Yes, ma'am," Grossman says.

I tell everyone in my family the commander in Khost was Kauzlarich. Kevin is absolutely speechless. The next few months I continue to stay in contact with Grossman. Kevin and I have really grown to like him and trust him. We believe he is our ally.

In March 2006, I'm in Arizona to participate in a heart walk for a young friend, Emery Miller. While watching the news at Emery's house, we hear the inspector general announce that investigators have found evidence of possible homicidal negligence in Pat's death, and he orders the Army's criminal investigation division (CID) to investigate. Finally, Pat's death will be treated as a potential crime. I feel something will be done; Pat will get justice. However, a week or so later, Marie tells me she has spoken to Dale Jefferies, the lead inspector general for the CID in Pat's case. She tells me talking to him is awkward, and she doesn't feel he is very committed to getting at the truth. Not long afterward, I call Jefferies to discuss the field hospital report. I let him know I'm very suspicious about the reference to CPR. I also tell him I don't know why the doctor would write "transfer to ICU for cont. CPR." Jefferies tells me the hospital was very busy and was being fired upon. Things got stressful and confusing.

"What are you talking about? The field hospital in Salerno is a big hospital," I tell him. "I've seen pictures of it. It's not a MASH unit in Korea." After that conversation, I had no trust in Jefferies or any real hope that the CID would do the right thing.

In January, author Jon Krakauer contacted Marie, Patrick, and me about writing a book about Pat. Over several months Jon has met the whole family, and we have come to consider him a good friend. I told him I was already working on a book. He sent me an e-mail with an article attached, "Telling Transformative Tales: The Strange Post-Ranger Saga of Pat Tillman," by Stan Goff. The article reveals that Brigadier General Gary Jones was once Mr. Goff's battalion commander. Jones liked and trusted Master Sergeant Goff, and Goff respected him. However, events unfolded while the two were in Haiti that Goff said caused him to question the character of his commander and ultimately lose respect for him. Twelve years later, Goff learns that Jones has become an inspector general, put in charge of "making it appear that the Army will properly investigate itself in the case" of Pat's death. The most chilling part of the article reads:

> I don't know if Patrick Tillman Sr. and Mary Tillman know it, but their son was not only killed by friendly fire, which I'll describe momentarily, he was killed on a fake mission of fake vengeance by fake commanders. The whole thing was theater.

I immediately e-mail the editor of the site where it was published and ask Mr. Goff to contact me. Within several days, I have a phone conversation with Stan. He is a fascinating man and very knowledgeable about politics, the military, and life. He agrees to help my family get to the truth.

The inspector general and the CID investigations are dragging. Grossman told us that the investigation might be finished in September, but it's May and the investigation is not close to being closed. I trust Grossman, but I'm worried that nothing substantial will come of these efforts. I decide to start pushing for a congressional hearing in the event the two investigations lead nowhere. I contact the offices of Congressmen Honda and Kucinich and Senator Barbara Boxer, trying to impress on them the need to have the situation reviewed by Congress.

Pat and Kevin in Saudi Arabia, 2003.

Kevin, Steve White, Pat, and two other Navy Seals relaxing in Iraq, 2003.

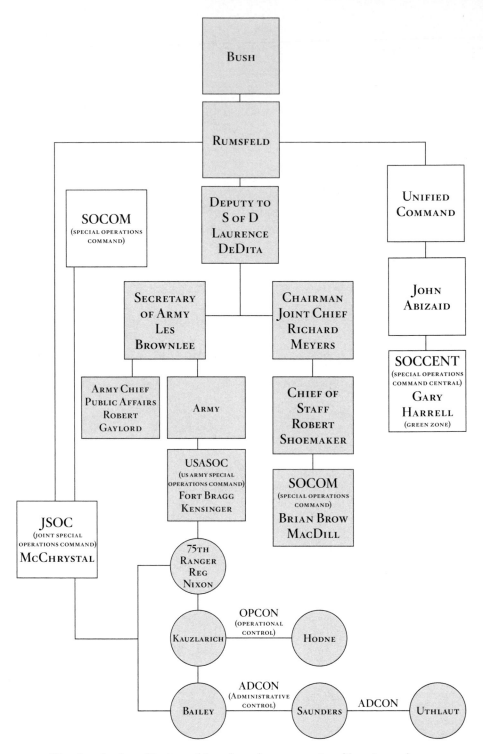

Handmade chart Kevin and I took to the congressional hearing to keep
the military chain of command straight.

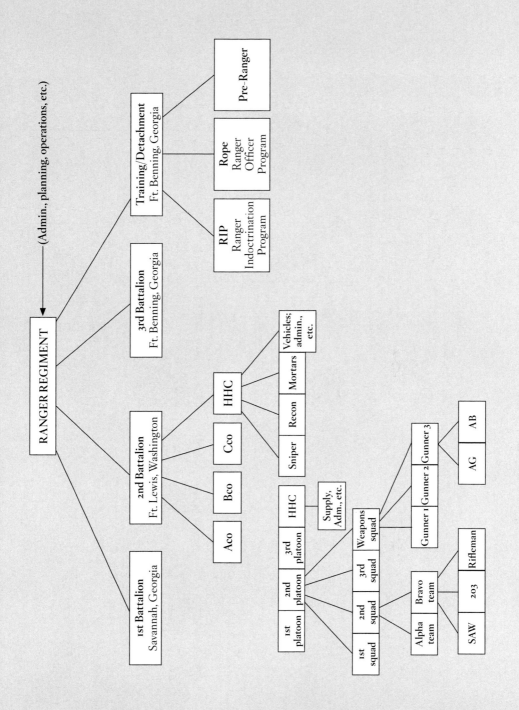

Provided during the Department of Defense Inspector General's briefing along with the criminal investigation division's briefing.

US ARMY SPECIAL OPERATIONS COMMAND — ORGANIZATIONAL CHART

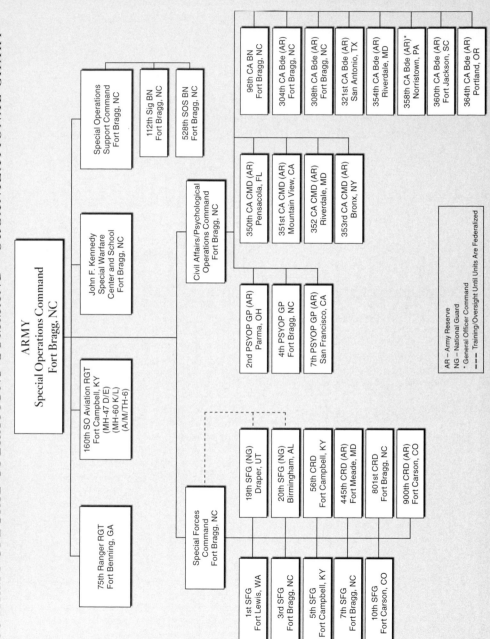

ARMY
Special Operations Command
Fort Bragg, NC

75th Ranger RGT
Fort Benning, GA

160th SO Aviation RGT
Fort Campbell, KY
(MH-47 D/E)
(MH-60 K/L)
(A/M/TH-6)

John F. Kennedy
Special Warfare
Center and School
Fort Bragg, NC

Special Operations
Support Command
Fort Bragg, NC

112th Sig BN
Fort Bragg, NC

528th SOS BN
Fort Bragg, NC

Special Forces Command, Fort Bragg, NC

Special Forces Command
Fort Bragg, NC

19th SFG (NG)
Draper, UT

20th SFG (NG)
Birmingham, AL

56th CRD
Fort Campbell, KY

445th CRD (AR)
Fort Meade, MD

801st CRD
Fort Bragg, NC

900th CRD (AR)
Fort Carson, CO

1st SFG
Fort Lewis, WA

3rd SFG
Fort Bragg, NC

5th SFG
Fort Campbell, KY

7th SFG
Fort Bragg, NC

10th SFG
Fort Carson, CO

Civil Affairs/Psychological Operations Command, Fort Bragg, NC

Civil Affairs/Psychological
Operations Command
Fort Bragg, NC

2nd PSYOP GP (AR)
Parma, OH

4th PSYOP GP
Fort Bragg, NC

7th PSYOP GP (AR)
San Francisco, CA

350th CA CMD (AR)
Pensacola, FL

351st CA CMD (AR)
Mountain View, CA

352 CA CMD (AR)
Riverdale, MD

353rd CA CMD (AR)
Bronx, NY

96th CA BN
Fort Bragg, NC

304th CA Bde (AR)
Fort Bragg, NC

308th CA Bde (AR)
Fort Bragg, NC

321st CA Bde (AR)
San Antonio, TX

354th CA Bde (AR)
Riverdale, MD

358th CA Bde (AR)*
Norristown, PA

360th CA Bde (AR)
Fort Jackson, SC

364th CA Bde (AR)
Portland, OR

AR – Army Reserve
NG – National Guard
* General Officer Command
---- Training/Oversight Until Units Are Federalized

Rules of Engagement

YOU MAY...

- Engage enemy forces committing **hostile acts** or displaying hostile intent.

- Engage persons actively assisting enemy or **deliberately interfering** with the mission.

- Engage enemy forces who are **fleeing with weapons.**

- Engage targets that pose a **likely and identifiable** threat to air assets.

- Use deadly force **to protect** designated third-country nationals or military forces.

- Use non-lethal riot control agents **(RCAs).**

- **Detain civilians** on target for intelligence exploitation.

- Conduct **electronic warfare.**

YOU MUST...

- **Positively identify** (PID) your targets.

Both charts provided during the Department of Defense Inspector General's briefing along with the criminal investigation division's briefing.

1. LOCATION	2. DATE *(YYYYMMDD)*	3. TIME	4. FILE NUMBER
Fort Bragg, North Carolina	2004/12/09 ~~10 AM~~	1430	

5. LAST NAME, FIRST NAME, MIDDLE NAME	6. SSN	7. GRADE/STATUS
Michael Hargis	███████	███

8. ORGANIZATION OR ADDRESS ███████

9. ████████ *Michael Hargis* ████████ WANT TO MAKE THE FOLLOWING STATEMENT UNDER OATH:

I was present for the interview by ██████████ *BG Jones* of ██████████ *Mt McChrystal* The interview was taped for the purpose of creating a verbatim transcript. A sworn statement, but upon playing the tape for transcription, it was determined to be defective and unintelligible. *McChrystal* *Jones* *McChrystal*

At the beginning of the interview, █████ *Jones* advised ████████ *McChrystal* that he had been appointed as an AR 15-6 investigating officer to look into the facts and circumstances surrounding the death of CPL Pat Tillman in Afghanistan. ████████ *BG Jones* then asked me to swear in ████████ which I did by asking him to raise his right hand and "Do you swear or affirm the statements you are about to make are the truth, the whole truth and nothing but the truth, so help you God?" to which he responded "Yes." ████████ *Jones* then asked the following questions, to which ████████ *McChrystal* provided the following answers:

1) • On what date were you first told that this was possibly fratricide?
~~No~~ I was in Qatar when I was told, about a day or two after the incident. No more than three days later. *3 days*

2) Who told you? What did they say?
████████ told me that they suspected fratricide at that time -- no later than 25 April. He gave me a brief overview of situation and told me that based on what he had heard, he believed there was a potential for fratricide and was investigating it. Id him that I concurred with him that an initial 15-6 investigation was appropriate.

3) Were you involved in any way in the initial notification to the family of the death?
No.

4) Were you involved in the initial decision to submit this soldier for a Silver Star? If so, how?
The Silver Star did come through me for recommendation. Based on all I knew, I believed that CPL Tillman's actions merited a Silver Star, so I concurred with the recommendation for award. Yes, at that time I did know that fratricide was a possibility.

5) Once you became aware that this was a possible fratricide, was there a conscious decision made to not tell the family of that possibility? If so, why?
There was a conscious decision on who we told about that potential because we did not know all the facts. I did tell the senior leadership ████████████ about that possibility prior to the Memorial Ceremony, because I felt they needed to know that before the Ceremony. I believe that we did not tell the family of the possibility because we did not want to give them some half-baked finding. *Acting Sec. Brownlee, Gen Abizaid, LTG Kensinger, Gen Brown*

7) Why not tell the family, within days of the incident, that this was possibly a fratricide and that a complete investigation was pending? If so, why?
I did not know there was a decision not to tell the family. They had another son in the firefight.

8) Which headquarters do you believe was responsible for telling the family that this was a fratricide?
Ranger Regiment was initially responsible for this, but then USASOC offered to backfill -- I'm not sure when that happened.

10. EXHIBIT	11. INITIALS OF PERSON MAKING STATEMENT ████	PAGE 1 OF __2__ PAGES

*ADDI*TIONAL PAGES MUST CONTAIN THE HEADING "STATEMENT _____ TAKEN AT _____ DATED _____

THE BOTTOM OF EACH ADDITIONAL PAGE MUST BEAR THE INITIALS OF THE PERSON MAKING THE STATEMENT, AND PAGE NUMBER MUST BE BE INDICATED.

Lieutenant Colonel Michael Hargis questioned General Stanley McChrystal on behalf of Brigadier General Gary Jones. The above statement is the result of that interview. Words and names blacked-out were redacted by the government. Other annotations on the document are those of the author.

STATEMENT *(Continued)*

Are you aware of anyone involved with this incident or the investigation thereof being reluctant to release that this was a fratricide? If so, who was it and what was the reluctance to release the information?

I am not aware of any reluctance of any kind on anyone's part to disclose that this was a fratricide.

10) Are you a General Court-Martial Convening Authority (GCMCA)?

I am not normally a General Court-Martial Convening Authority, although I might have been for this operation.

11) Who was your GCMCA on 22 Apr 04?

I am not sure who the GCMCA for us was at that time.

12) Do you know why the decision was made to initiate the AR 15-6 investigation at the Regimental level rather than at the GCMCA level? Nixon

▮▮▮▮▮▮ called me and told me that he was going to conduct an investigation into this incident. I told him that I agreed an investigation needed to be done and I was comfortable with his decision to do an investigation.

13) Are you aware of anyone being told not to discuss that this was a fratricide? If so, what was the reason for that instruction?

This was treated as any other incident involving a death. We did not want any speculation as to what happened, but I did not hear anyone say not to talk about this nor did I direct anyone not to say anything about this incident.

14) Were you involved in the family briefing once the 15-6 was approved? Did you provide any instructions to anyone / receive any instructions from anyone on what should be / should NOT be disclosed to the family?

I was not involved in the family briefing.

15) When was the 15-6 investigation submitted to your HQ? When did your HQ forward it to CENTCOM?

I don't recall when my HQ got the 15-6 not do I recall when we sent it to CENTCOM. My JAG would know that.

16) Is there any other aspect of this 15-6 investigation, award submission, release of information on the incident in which you have been involved?

I was not involved in the VTC regarding this incident that took place right before the press conference. No one has ever ▮▮d away from saying that this was a fratricide, but we did want to make sure we were correct before we said it. I did send a P4 ▮ssage to ▮▮▮▮▮▮▮▮▮▮▮▮▮ about this, telling them we suspected fratricide, which I can provide to you. Gen Brown, Abizaid, Kensinger

---

AFFIDAVIT

I, ▮▮▮▮▮▮▮▮▮ , HAVE READ OR HAVE HAD READ TO ME THIS STATEMENT WHICH BEGINS ON PAGE 1, AND ENDS ON PAGE 2 . I FULLY UNDERSTAND THE CONTENTS OF THE ENTIRE STATEMENT MADE BY ME. THE STATEMENT IS TRUE. I HAVE INITIALED ALL CORRECTIONS AND HAVE INITIALED THE BOTTOM OF EACH PAGE CONTAINING THE STATEMENT. I HAVE MADE THIS STATEMENT FREELY WITHOUT HOPE OF BENEFIT OR REWARD, WITHOUT THREAT OF PUNISHMENT, AND WITHOUT COERCION, UNLAWFUL INFLUENCE, OR UNLAWFUL INDUCEMENT.

(Signature of Person Making Statement)

WITNESSES:

Subscribed and sworn to before me, a person authorized by law to administer oaths, this 10th day of December , 2004
at Fort Brage, NC

_____

ORGANIZATION OR ADDRESS

(Signature of Person Administering Oath)

_____

(Typed Name of Person Administering Oath)

RGANIZATION OR ADDRESS

(Authority To Administer Oaths)

INITIALS OF PERSON MAKING STATEMENT

PAGE 2 OF 2 PAGES

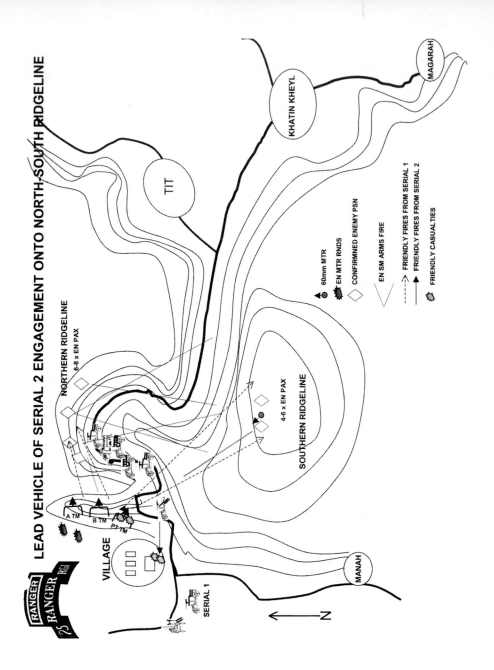

This map, provided by the Rangers, is of the region between Magarah and Manah, Afghanistan, where Pat and the AMF soldier "Thani" were killed. Serial One left Magarah 10 to 15 minutes ahead of Serial Two. Though the final position of the vehicles in Serial Two remains in dispute, the map depicts what is thought to have happened during the ambush. The positions of Pat and "Thani" are represented by two small bursts near the letters "PT TM." Bryan O'Neal was directly behind them. Lieutenant David Uthlaut and Special Jade Lane were wounded in the course of the incident, represented here by the two bursts in the village.

On June 23, 2006, I read in the paper that Iraqi trainees murdered Sergeant Patrick McCaffrey and Second Lieutenant Andre Tyson, both members of the California National Guard, on June 22, 2004. Patrick McCaffrey's mother, Nadia, and Andre Tyson's family were initially told insurgents killed their sons in an ambush. An Army investigation concluded in September of 2005 that the two soldiers were murdered for bounty; it has taken nine months for the Army to tell the families. I'm so sickened by this story. The Army continues to lie about the deaths of soldiers.

First Lieutenant Ken Ballard died on May 30, 2004. His mother, Karen Mcredith, was told he was killed in an ambush. Fifteen months later, she was informed that he was struck with a five-round burst from a 240-mm machine gun when a tree branch struck the weapon, which was mounted on a tank. It was well established that the gun killed Ken when it accidentally went off, but military personnel chose to lie to Ken's mother. It disturbs me that nearly all the mothers of fallen soldiers I have met or spoken to on the phone have lost their sons because of fratricide or, in Nadia's case, homicide. I also wonder if the reason the military lied to these parents is because Pat's fratricide was so high profile, and a cluster of them would be a public relations debacle. Ken Ballard died a day after Pat's fratricide was announced. Jesse Buryj died only days after that, and Patrick McCaffrey and Andre Tyson were killed exactly two months after Pat. Except for Jesse, all these soldiers were from California. Dolores Kesterson's son died in 2003, but technically her son's death was also a fratricide.

It's early August; I call Brian Grossman about the interview Kauzlarich did with journalist Mike Fish, in which he says that our family can't put Pat to rest because we're "not Christians" and suggests we have to think of Pat as "worm dirt" since non-Christians don't believe in an afterlife. During the conversation, I mention my dismay at Kauzlarich being the officer in command at the tactical operations center and the one who did the second investigation. Grossman stops me and tells me that Kauzlarich was not the commander at the TOC.

"But back in December when I asked you who was in charge at the TOC you told me Kauzlarich. I even had expressed shock that he was the commander *and* the investigator."

"I never said Kauzlarich was in command at the TOC," Grossman says. "Actually, Major Hodne was the commander at the TOC."

I'm certain he told me Kauzlarich was in charge because I immediately relayed that to my family and journalists working on stories about Pat; now I have to tell them I was wrong. Stan has written several Internet articles he needs to correct. I feel bad about this and wonder if Brian threw me off on purpose for some reason. He has always made me feel pretty comfortable, but this makes me uneasy. The only other time I felt that way was when he reprimanded me for trying to get in touch with General Jones. I made an attempt to call the general at Fort Bragg to see if he would talk to me. I learned that he had retired. I left my phone number so it could be passed along to the general. Instead of calling me, he called the inspector general, and Brian called and firmly chastised me for trying to get in touch with Jones.

I can't believe my family and I have believed for so long Kauzlarich was the CFT commander. It was Major Hodne. I had only heard his name mentioned when Kevin had believed he was the one who completed the regimental investigation. All this time we have concentrated on learning the actions of the wrong person. Major Hodne is the one who gave the order to split the troops, ignoring Uthlaut's insistence that splitting would be too dangerous. Major Hodne is the one who denied knowing the troops were split. Major Hodne is the man for whom Captain Saunders fell on the sword. It is important that the IG and CID investigators find out what happened with Major Hodne and Saunders at the TOC.

I have been so caught up in the investigation and teaching that I decide one day to get away and take a day trip with my friend Sherri to Half Moon Bay, about fifty miles away on the coast. While there, I get a call from a friend.

"Dannie, what are you doing?" she asks, sounding as if something is wrong.

"I'm in Half Moon Bay with Sherri."

"Kevin is going to kill me for telling you, but Dannie, you have to get on a computer and read Truthdig.com.

"What's going on? I don't have access to a computer," I tell her.

"Kevin has written the most amazing article in honor of Pat."

"I usually read Truthdig first thing in the morning, but we left early to come here. Can you read it to me?"

"Sure!" she says, and begins:

AFTER PAT'S BIRTHDAY

By Kevin Tillman

It is Pat's birthday on November 6, and the elections are the day after. It gets me thinking about a conversation I had with Pat before we joined the military. He spoke about the risks with signing the papers. How once we committed, we were at the mercy of American leadership and the American people. How we could be thrown in a direction not of our volition. How fighting as a soldier would leave us without a voice . . . until we got out.

Much has happened since we handed over our voice:

Somehow we were sent to invade a nation because it was a direct threat to the American people, or to the world, or harbored terrorists, or was involved in the September 11 attacks, or received weapons-grade uranium from Niger, or had mobile weapons labs, or WMD, or had a need to be liberated, or we needed to establish a democracy, or stop an insurgency, or stop a civil war we created that can't be called a civil war even though it is.

Something like that.

Somehow our elected leaders were subverting international law and humanity by setting up secret prisons around the world,

283

secretly kidnapping people, secretly holding them indefinitely, secretly not charging them with anything, secretly torturing them. Somehow that overt policy of torture became the fault of a few "bad apples" in the military.

Somehow back at home, support for the soldiers meant having a kindergartner scribble a picture with crayons and send it overseas, or slapping stickers on cars, or lobbying Congress for an extra pad in a helmet.

It's interesting that a soldier on his third or fourth tour should care about a drawing of a five-year-old; or a faded sticker on a car as his friends die around him, or an extra pad in a helmet, as if it will protect him when an IED throws his vehicle fifty feet into the air as his body comes apart and his skin melts to the seat.

Somehow the more soldiers that die, the more legitimate the illegal invasion becomes.

Somehow American leadership, whose only credit is lying to its people and illegally invading a nation, has been allowed to steal the courage, virtue, and honor of its soldiers on the ground.

Somehow those afraid to fight in an illegal invasion decades ago are allowed to send soldiers to die for an illegal invasion they started.

Somehow faking character, virtue and strength is tolerated.

Somehow profiting from the tragedy and horror is tolerated.

Somehow the deaths of tens, if not hundreds of thousands of people are tolerated.

Somehow subversion of the Bill of Rights and The Constitution is tolerated.

Somehow suspension of Habeas Corpus is supposed to keep this country safe.

Somehow torture is tolerated.

Somehow lying is tolerated.

Somehow reason is being discarded for faith, dogma, and non-sense.

Somehow American leadership managed to create a more dangerous world.

Somehow a narrative is more important than reality.

Somehow America has become a country that projects everything that it is not and condemns everything that it is.

Somehow the most reasonable, trusted and respected country in the world has become one of the most irrational, belligerent, feared, and distrusted countries in the world.

Somehow being politically informed, diligent, and skeptical has been replaced by apathy through active ignorance.

Somehow the same incompetent, narcissistic, virtueless, vacuous, malicious criminals are still in charge of this country.

Somehow this is tolerated.

Somehow nobody is accountable for this.

In democracy, the policy of the leaders is the policy of the people. So don't be shocked when our grandkids bury much of this generation as traitors to the nation, to the world and to humanity. Most likely, they will come to know that "somehow" was nurtured by fear, insecurity and indifference, leaving the country vulnerable to unchecked, unchallenged parasites.

Luckily this country is still a democracy. People still have a voice. People still can take action. It can start after Pat's birthday.

Brother and friend of Pat Tillman,

Kevin Tillman

I can barely speak. I'm so proud of Kevin. The piece is powerful, poignant, and honest, but it is also hopeful. I call him right away. I can tell he has been anxious to hear from me to get my reaction. I tell him

Pat would be in awe and that I believe it will impact the election. It's a poem with the power to incite. Kevin could make no greater tribute to his brother.

For several months Marie and Stan have tried to arrange for medical experts to view Pat's autopsy report, autopsy photographs, and medical documents in order to clear up concerns we have had about Pat's wounds. In November, Stan arranges to have forensic pathologist Dr. Robert Bux, the coroner of El Paso County, Colorado, and ballistic expert Dr. Vincent DiMaio, a retired Texas medical examiner renowned nationally for his textbook on gunshot wounds, meet him in Rockville, Maryland, headquarters of the Armed Forces medical examiner. Unfortunately, the Army will not permit Stan to accompany these experts to view the pictures or documents. However, Stan does get to meet with them prior to their appointment. I'm annoyed and a bit baffled when I learn that neither Dr. Craig Mallak nor Dr. James Caruso will be present for the experts to question. I can't help but wonder if they are purposely unavailable. Dr. Bux sends me a document with their conclusions.

> Dear Mrs. Tillman,
> This letter outlines our opinions regarding the death of your son, Pat Tillman, who was serving in Afghanistan with the 75th Rangers. They are based on our examination of the entire file presented to us at the Armed Forces Medical Examiner's Office. Our opinions are as follows:
> Based on fingerprints, dental records, DNA testing, the presence of ulnar deviation of the right little finger noted in autopsy photographs, as well as the in-theater identification of the body by SFC Jorge Escobedo, we believe that to a scientific certainty the body described and pictured in the autopsy report was that of your son Pat Tillman.
> Additionally there appears in the area of the right shoulder

joint two densities that we could not identify. It is possible that a radiologist reviewing this film might be able to offer an interpretation. Unfortunately at the time of the autopsy a CT scanner had not been deployed to the Dover facility which would have better characterized and thus resolved the significance or lack thereof to the case especially if this represents some type of change from the previous rotator cuff repair.

The cause of death of your son is three gunshot wounds to the forehead with destruction of the cranial vault and massive injuries to the brain. Because the entrance wounds were in a tight pattern, it is likely that they were produced by the same weapon, delivering full automatic fire at a relatively close range. The forehead entrance wound defects are small in diameter suggesting a small caliber weapon, i.e. 5.56 × 45. The injury pattern and the small entrance wound defects are not in keeping with a large caliber (7.62 × 51 or .50 caliber) machine gun.

Small metal fragments were removed from the head in the area of the wound tracts at the time of the autopsy and retained. Based on the chain of custody documents these fragments were signed over to the CID investigating this incident for analysis. It appears these fragments if analyzed should shed light on the caliber of weapon that struck Pat in the forehead and, therefore, could point to the individual who fired that weapon.

The wound in the left upper chest pictured in the photographs, in our opinion is a contusion/abrasion most likely caused by the body armor Pat was wearing and not due to CPR. Unfortunately the uniform and body armor that Pat was wearing was not available at the time of the autopsy in Dover for examination or photographs, as it was not sent with the body. We understand that instead it had been destroyed in the theatre by the unit. Therefore it is unclear to us if the body armor stopped an additional bullet or if the wound to the left chest occurred when he fell to the ground after being shot.

Sincerely,

Vincent J. M. DiMaio, MD, Robert C. Bux, MD

After reading the report of Dr. Bux and Dr. Di Maio, I become very angry. We were told there were no bullet fragments left in Pat's body, and all along they have been waiting for analysis. It is also clear that there is little discrepancy as to which caliber weapon killed Pat.

A weapon using 5.56 rounds killed him—the SAW gun. I'm sickened by the allegation that Pat was likely killed by a soldier Pat and Kevin had taken with them to Atlanta, to Judy and Neal McGrath's, on a weekend when he had nowhere to go—a soldier who wanted to be in a firefight.

Kevin had come to San Jose from Arizona for business in January. At around eleven thirty p.m. the phone rang. We figured it was Richard because he often calls late. Kevin answered the phone. I could tell immediately by the look on his face that it wasn't Richard. The person on the other end of the phone line was a young woman named Dawn Hellerman, whose husband, Staff Sergeant Brian Hellerman, was killed in Iraq on August 6, 2003. Dawn was told he was killed in an ambush. Months later she was told by another soldier that someone in his unit killed him.

Dawn has two teenage children who are devastated by their father's death. She has tried to find answers but has received no help from the Army or her representatives in North Carolina. Kevin and I give her the names of several investigative journalists, and I tell her we will talk to our congressmen about her situation. After we hang up, I make a note to call Stan in North Carolina the next day.

It is now late February. Ever since September, we have received calls from reporters or congressional aides telling us the inspector general and CID investigations are complete or almost complete. Finally, we learn we will be briefed in late March, about three weeks from now.

As the briefing gets closer, I have had several discussions with Brian Grossman and James Pavlik, the assistant inspector general, about bringing Stan to the briefing. At first they are adamant that he may not attend, but I explain that he has knowledge of military terms, procedures, and protocol that we don't have. I tell them we are at a disadvantage without his expertise. Mr. Pavlik agrees to allow him to attend. Just before the briefing, several things happened that we didn't expect. First, we thought we would be briefed before Congress and the press were, and we didn't expect any of the conclusions to be released prior to the briefing.

Just before the meeting with the inspector general and CID, there is a story in the media that nine officers, including four generals, will be investigated in regard to Pat's death. The article indicates the generals are retired brigadier general Gary Jones and retired lieutenant general Philip Kensinger, along with Brigadier General (formerly colonel) James Nixon and Lieutenant General Stanley McChrystal. The Washington, D.C., media and members of Congress will be briefed simultaneously with us.

Our briefing is held in a hotel in downtown San Jose. Patrick, Kevin, Richard, Marie, Stan, and I attend. Representatives from the Department of Defense Office of Inspector General, including Grossman and Pavlik, and CID investigators sit with us around a table in a conference room. A CID investigator presents first. I am expecting Dale Jefferies to be there, but the investigation must have been handed off to someone else. He makes it clear from the start of the presentation that they are not establishing who killed Pat or even what weapon killed him. The investigator suggests that a 5.56 or a 7.62 could have killed Pat, leaving room for the notion that the enemy could have killed him. When I point out what Dr. Bux's report stated, the investigator ignores me. I ask why

CID didn't analyze the bullet fragments left in Pat's body; I am given no answer.

Kevin becomes very angry when the investigator refers to the village houses as "barns." It is apparent he wants to negate the significance of Baker's men shooting at the buildings. It doesn't seem to matter that there were at least thirty to forty children in the structures. The CID concluded that no rules of engagement (ROE) were broken, even though soldiers didn't identify their targets and shot at waving hands and at buildings from which there was no threat, from which no one was shooting at them. The investigator explains that although reports indicate Pat's diary was missing, they have discovered that it was burned with his other equipment shortly after he died. We are told he had mission-specific information in the book. We are also informed that Pat's flashlight was recovered from a drawer weeks before the briefing.

No satisfactory explanation is given as to why Pat's flashlight would be in someone's drawer. The CID continues to claim Baker's vehicle never stopped. The investigator insists the vehicle came out of the canyon and opened fire on the ridgeline in a matter of seconds. The agent then tells us they have finally learned the name of the AMF soldier killed before Pat. For three years no one has been able to tell us the name of this soldier. We are told his name is Thani.

"Thani," Kevin says. "That's it?"

Just "Thani"? We all find that name to be unbelievable. It seems that most Afghans I know have many names. Thani is also a tribal name in that region. This may have been part of his name, but I don't think we are being told the truth.

At this point we are all very angry and realize the briefing is a total sham. Pavlik was orginally opposed to having Stan present, but he is the calmest presence on our side of the room. Faced with the wrath of my family, I'm certain Pavlik was now grateful he allowed him to come. At numerous points in the meeting Kevin and I look at Grossman, hoping he will stand up and do the right thing, but he doesn't. Patrick asks questions about the light conditions, Scott's "missing" investigation, and Sayre's actions that day. He asks why Sayre was not held accountable, but the investigator responds with a patronizing stare.

There are a lot of angry words about orders from the TOC, CID's inability to learn the AMF soldier's true identity, actions at the field hospital, and concerns about a cover-up, but no questions are answered and no concerns are assuaged. Stan is still the only calm presence on our side of the table. Pavlik provides a book that summarizes the inspector general's findings, and we're given CDs of the CID and Jones reports. We leave the meeting in a state of barely contained outrage. When we arrive at my house, Stan writes a statement to give to the press expressing our dissatisfaction with the investigations and the briefing reads in part: "The characterization of criminal negligence, professional misconduct, battlefield incompetence, concealment and destruction of evidence, deliberate deception, and conspiracy to deceive are not 'missteps.'"

Several days after the briefing, an Associated Press reporter is anonymously sent a copy of a P-4[8] memo written on April 29, 2004, by Major General Stanley McChrystal, who sent the high-priority memo to top generals warning them to inform POTUS—the president of the United States—to avoid mentioning the "devastating enemy fire" explanation written on the Silver Star award citation for their upcoming speeches due to the probability that Pat's death was caused by friendly fire.

We have been trying for some time to determine when the president or Donald Rumsfeld knew Pat was killed by fratricide, and neither one will talk about it; this memo could be a piece of that puzzle. Of course, the White House was quick to deny any knowledge of the memo. Two of the three recipients of the memo deny receiving it in a timely fashion.

---

8 High-priority "Personal For:" memo

One of those generals was Lieutenant General Kensinger, who attended Pat's memorial on May 3. He claims he was in transit to Pat's service on April 29 and never got the memo. This I question strongly; Kensinger was a three-star general, and there was a war going on. I find it hard to believe that message didn't reach him. General John Abizaid claims he was in Iraq and didn't get the memo until sometime in May. General Brian Brown said he got the memo but didn't think it was his responsibility to notify anyone.

After learning about this document, I looked up information on Stanley McChrystal, the only general named to be investigated who was unfamiliar to me, and found a rare article that had been written for *Newsweek*, June 26, 2006.

Lt. General Stanley McChrystal, West Point '76, is not someone the Army likes to talk about. He isn't even listed in the directory at Fort Bragg, N.C., his home base. That's not because McChrystal has done anything wrong—quite the contrary, he's one of the Army's rising stars—but because he runs the most secretive force in the U.S. military. That is the Joint Special Operations Command, the snake-eating, slit-their-throats "black ops" guys who captured Saddam Hussein and targeted Abu Mussab al Zarqawi.

JSOC is part of what Vice President Dick Cheney was referring to when he said America would have to "work the dark side" after 9/11. To many critics, the veep's[9] remark back in 2001 fostered his rep as the Darth Vader of the war on terror and presaged bad things to come, like the interrogation abuses at Abu Ghraib and Guantanamo Bay. But America also had its share of Jedi Knights fighting in what Cheney calls "the shadows." And McChrystal, an affable but tough Army Ranger,

---

9 Vice president

and the Delta Force and other elite teams he commands are among them.

After the Zarqawi strike, multinational forces spokesman General Bill Caldwell refused to comment on JSOC's role, saying, 'We don't talk about when special operating forces are involved." But when Bush revealed to reporters that it was McChrystal's Special Ops teams that found Zarqawi, Caldwell had to gulp and say (to laughter), "If the president of the United States said it was, then I'm sure it was."

McChrystal has checked all the right career boxes, serving as an unflappable military briefer during the Iraq invasion, and doing fellowships at Harvard and at the Council on Foreign Relations in New York (where he would run to work from Brooklyn, about six miles away). Still, the secrecy surrounding McChrystal's role worries some who note that Bush and Defense Secretary Donald Rumsfeld have given clandestine operations the lead in the war on terror—with little public accountability, including in the interrogation room.

Rumsfeld is especially enamored of McChrystal's "direct action" forces or so-called SMUs—Special Mission Units—whose job is to kill or capture bad guys, say Pentagon sources who would speak about Special Ops only if they were not identified. But critics say the Pentagon is short-shifting the "hearts and minds" side of Special Operations that is critical to counterinsurgency—like training foreign armies and engaging with locals. Special Operations Command spokesman Ken McGraw says the Pentagon is "significantly increasing" those units.) Experts like former Deputy Defense Secretary John Hamre are also concerned that Special Ops now has generic authority to deploy where it wants without case-by-case orders. Without proper civilian oversight, a Zarqawi-style success can easily become a "Black Hawk Down."

Keeping that from happening is McChrystal's most important mission.

After reading this article, I am convinced all parties received the memo, and I believe all parties warned the White House as cautioned. Major General McChrystal was/is clearly the "golden child" of Bush and Rumsfeld, and he is the head of JSOC. There is no way the generals who were meant to receive the memo didn't, and there is no way, once they got it, they wouldn't have warned the White House. I realize something else after reading the memo and the *Newsweek* article. Months ago I came across a testimony in the Jones report in which an individual whose name was redacted makes disturbing statements.

Question: *Once you became aware that this was a possible fratricide, was there a conscious decision made to not tell the family of that possibility? If so, why?*

Witness: *There was a conscious decision on who we told about that potential because we did not know all the facts. I did tell the senior leadership* [long redaction] *about the possibility prior to the Memorial Ceremony, because I felt they needed to know that before the Ceremony. I believe that we did not tell the family of the possibility because we did not want to give them some half-baked finding.*

On the next page of the document, it said:

Question: *Is there any other aspect of this investigation, award submission, release of information on the incident in which you have been involved?*

Witness: *I was involved in the VTC*[10] *regarding this incident that*

---

10 Video teleconference

took place right before the press conference. No one has ever shied away from saying that this was a fratricide, but we did want to make sure we were correct before we said it. I did send a P-4 message to [long redaction] about this, telling them we suspected fratricide, which I can provide for you.

The witness is McChrystal.

The following day, March 29, 2007, Tom Bohigian, assistant to Senator Barbara Boxer, sent me a copy of the P-4 memo.

> O 292234Z April 04
> FM Task Force
> To RUCAACC/USCENTCOM MACDILL AFB FL// CDR// INFO RUCQSAS/USSOCOCOM PP MACDILL AFB FL//CDR// RUEPVBT/TASK FORCE
> BT [REDACTION)] PERSONAL FOR CDR USCENT-COM CDR USSOCOM CDR USASOC
> DELIVER DURING NORMAL DUTY HOURS [REDACTION] DO NOT TRANSMIT VIA OPINTEL BROADCAST OPER/OEF// MSGID/GENAMIN/TASK FORCE
> //
> SUBJ/P-4 CONCERNING INFORMATION ON COR-PORAL TILLMANS DEATH//
> RMKS/SIR, IN THE AFTERMATH OF CORPORAL TILLMAN'S UNTIMELY YET HEROIC DEATH IN AFGHANISTAN ON 22 APRIL 04, IT IS ANTICIPATED HIGHLY POSSIBLE THAT CORPORAL TILLMAN WAS KILLED BY FRIENDLY FIRE. THIS POTENTIAL FIND-ING IS EXACERBATED BY THE UNCONFIRMED REPORTS THAT POTUS AND THE SECRETARY OF

THE ARMY MIGHT INCLUDE COMMENTS ABOUT CORPORAL TILLMAN'S HEROISM AND HIS APPROVED SILVER STAR MEDAL IN SPEECHES CURRENTLY BEING PREPARED, NOT INFORMING THE SPECIFICS SURROUNDING HIS DEATH. THE POTENTIAL THAT HE MIGHT HAVE BEEN KILLED BY FRIENDLY FIRE IN NO WAY DETRACTS FROM HIS WITNESSED HEROISM OR THE RECOMMENDED PERSONAL DECORATION FOR VALOR IN THE FACE OF THE ENEMY. CORPORAL TILLMAN WAS KILLED IN A COMPLICATED BATTLESPACE GEOMETRY INVOLVING TWO SEPARATE RANGER VEHICLE SERIALS TRAVERSING THROUGH SEVERE TERRAIN ALONG A WINDING 500-600 FOOT DEFILE IN WHICH FRIENDLY FORCES WERE FIRED UPON BY MULTIPLE ENEMY POSITIONS. CORPORAL TILLMAN DISEMBARKED FROM HIS VEHICLE, AND IN SUPPORT OF HIS FELLOW RANGERS AND DEMONSTRATING GREAT CONCERN FOR THEIR WELFARE OVER CARE FOR HIS OWN SAFETY ENTERED THE ENEMY KILLZONE INTO WHICH BOTH IMPACTED. I FELT THAT IT WAS ESSENTIAL THAT YOU RECEIVED THIS INFORMATION AS SOON AS WE DETECTED IT IN ORDER TO PRECLUDE ANY UNKNOWING STATEMENTS BY OUR COUNTRY'S LEADERS WHICH MIGHT CAUSE PUBLIC EMBARRASSMENT IF THE CIRCUMSTANCES OF CORPORAL TILLMAN'S DEATH BECOME PUBLIC. //

DECL/DERI:DRV FROM [REDACTION] /INST—[REDACTION]—// BT

CLASSIFIED BY:—[REDACTION]

REASON [REDACTION] DECLASSIFY ON:
[REDACTION]
CLASSIFICATION: [REDACTION]
CAVEATS: [REDACTION] TERMS: [REDACTION]

It's shocking to see how transparent this message is. McChrystal is covering his ass. No wonder Bush and Rumsfeld hold him in such high regard. Not only is he lying about the circumstances surrounding Pat's death, as enemy fire had ceased many minutes before the AMF soldier and Pat were killed, he is proposing false language for the Silver Star narrative. Silver Star awards are not customarily given to soldiers who die by fratricide. I have been told there are other awards for those situations. Since it was known within minutes that Pat's death was obviously a fratricide, the Silver Star was something given to him for public relations purposes and, in my opinion, to stir patriotic feeling. I know Pat's actions were honorable and heroic. The false narrative, which McChrystal clearly helped construct, diminished Pat's true actions. I'm also struck by the last line of the memo, which reads (underline is mine):

> I felt that it was essential that you received this information as soon as we detected it in order to preclude any unknowing statements by our country's leaders which might cause public embarrassment if the circumstances of Corporal Tillman's death become public.

First of all, if he wanted to warn the "country's leaders" as soon as they detected it was a fratricide, he should have done it at least three days earlier. There are statements in Brigadier General Jones's report by high-ranking individuals[11] that they knew Pat's death was a suspected

---

[11] It is clear they are high-ranking officers because in their testimonies Brigadier General Jones refers to each of them as "sir."

fratricide within three days. Second, McChrystal writes that he wants to prevent public embarrassment of our leaders "if the circumstances of Corporal Tillman's death become public." "*If.*" His statement indicates that no one had any intention of telling us, or the public, that Pat was killed by fratricide unless forced to do so.

They were forced to do so because the coroner refused to sign the autopsy report and because the Rangers in Pat's platoon were coming home and would start talking. Because Pat's death, based on testimony, was a suspected fratricide within minutes, we should have been told right away. There was already protocol on the books stating that if fratricide is suspected, family members must be told of that suspicion as soon as possible. McChrystal stated in his response to General Jones's question that he informed his superiors because he "felt [we] needed to know [the truth] before the Ceremony." Yet, his P-4 memo says he is informing his superiors so they can prevent the administration from being embarrassed "if" the truth becomes public. It is obvious he is selling a lie; I fear the lie will be bought.

Not long after receiving the P-4 memo, I go to hear retired general Wesley Clark speak. My friends Martha Kelley and Sherri Greer are with me. Clark is an articulate and seemingly compassionate man. At the end of his speech, the host asks him questions provided by the audience. "What do you think about the situation with our local hero Pat Tillman?" Pat's death and the circumstances of it have been in the news quite a bit the last several weeks, but I'm still shocked by the question.

Clark begins by explaining that friendly fire happens, and the military does its best to prevent such accidents. I clench my jaw, angry that he is addressing the question when he knows nothing about the situation. He then goes on to say he knows some of the generals who are being investigated, and he knows they would never be part of a cover-up.

The host moves on to the next question, but I don't even hear it. I'm furious that the former general would speak to something he knew nothing about. At the end of the presentation, I tell my friends that I have to talk to Clark. He is on a speaking tour; I don't want him speaking about Pat's death as an authority. I walk up to the stage where he is bent over shaking hands and talking to audience members surrounding him. I wait patiently as he speaks to people, but I become anxious that he will suddenly walk away.

"Excuse me!" I say loudly. He looks at me. "Excuse me, sir," I say with my voice lowered. "I'm Pat Tillman's mom." He shakes my hand and smiles then starts to turn away, but he turns back to look at me again. "What did you say? Did you say you're Pat Tillman's mom?"

"Yes, sir," I say, looking up at him. "General, I don't mean to be rude, but you know nothing of the circumstances of Pat's death. You really shouldn't be saying anything about it if you don't have any facts."

He crouches down closer to me. "You're right. Why don't you tell me about it."

At that point, his wife and the host of the event walk out from backstage to save him from me. He gently gestures to them that he's fine. "You know," he says, "I was asked a question about your son at last night's forum as well, and I'm afraid I responded the same way. Tell me more about it." Suddenly I remember Martha burned CDs of the CID and Jones reports and gave them to me before we left for the evening.

"Sir, I can tell you that a Brigadier General Kensinger was at Pat's memorial service, and knowing full well Pat's death was a fratricide, he let a false narrative be told by a speaker suggesting that Pat died in a gun battle."

He looks at his wife with a shocked expression. "I can't believe Phil would do something like that," he says. "We have known him for years."

"I have CDs of two investigations in my car. Are you serious about wanting to know more?"

"Yes, I'll wait here. Can you get them out of your car?"

"I'll be right back."

When I return, I hand him the CDs. He then asks for my phone number and tells me he will contact me when he has viewed the discs. I'm extremely grateful that the general is willing to look at the documents. I thank him and his very patient wife.

Several days later, while I'm in Arizona for Pat's Run, I find a message on my cell phone from Wesley Clark. He says he looked at the documents and would like to speak to me; he leaves his cell phone number for me to call. I call him back right away. He's in an airport waiting to catch a plane but says he has time to speak to me. He lets me know the documents are disturbing to him, and he understands our family's concern.

He says I must continue to pursue answers and tells me to call if I need anything. I let him know that I appreciate his time to look at the documents. I explain that I wanted him to know the truth because it hurts our efforts for him to give misinformation when he speaks to audiences across the country. Pat's death has become very controversial and political. I tell him I don't want Pat's situation to be an impediment to him politically. I just want him to speak about Pat's death with knowledge. He very graciously wishes my family and me luck.

We are soon informed that the Congressional Oversight and Government Reform Committee chaired by Henry Waxman will hold a hearing at the end of April. We spend the next several weeks preparing for the hearing, talking to committee staff attorneys to familiarize them with the documents. We are sent formal notification on April 17. I go through evidence and organize it in binders. Kevin prepares and practices the opening statement. On April 24, three years and two days after Pat's death, Kevin, Richard, Marie, Patrick, and I sit in a conference room in the Rayburn Building waiting for the hearing to begin. We are introduced to Jessica Lynch, a lovely and seemingly delicate young woman who obviously is quite honest, courageous, and strong, and Dr.

Gene Bolles, the doctor who treated her when she was taken to Landstuhl, Germany. We are finally called to go into the hearing room. Dr. Bolles, Jessica Lynch, Kevin and I take our seats at the table facing the congressional panel. Marie, Richard, and Patrick sit directly behind us. Steve White, who will be participating in the second panel later in the day, is seated next to Marie.

Kevin reads his powerful opening statement. Unnervingly, the thirty cameras in front of him flash in his face. I'm amazed at how well he keeps his composure and focus.

> I want to thank Congressman Waxman for holding this hearing and the members of the committee for attending.
>
> My name is Kevin Tillman.
>
> Two days ago marked the third anniversary of the death of my older brother, Pat Tillman, in Spera, Afghanistan.
>
> To our family and friends it was a devastating loss. To the nation it was a moment of disorientation. To the Military it was a nightmare.
>
> But to others in the government, it appears to have been an opportunity.
>
> The content of multiple investigations reveal a series of contradictions that strongly suggest a deliberate and careful misrepresentation. We appeal to this committee because we believe the narrative was intended to deceive the family and more importantly, the American Public.

Congress had titled the hearing "Misleading Information from the Battlefield." I called Congressman Waxman's attorneys before the hearing to let them know I thought the title of the hearing was misleading. My family and I believe the actions of the Army and, likely, the administration were far too heinous to be called misleading. I think Kevin's words establish that. Kevin also makes it clear that he is angry the government used Pat: "Pat wanted to leave a positive legacy, and he did. For the government to hijack his virtue and legacy is horrific."

He also tags the narrative that accompanied the Silver Star "utter fiction," saying the Army believed our family would "sink into our grief."

Jessica Lynch testified that "great tales of heroism" were told while she was recovering from her wounds: "My parents' home . . . was under siege by the media, all repeating the story of the little girl Rambo from the hills who went down fighting. It was not true.

"The bottom line is the American people are capable of determining their own heroes and they don't need to be told elaborate tales." Quite eloquently, she continues. "The truth of war is not always easy to hear, but it is always more heroic than the hype."

I make it clear that our family has serious questions about the circumstances surrounding Pat's death. We want to know why the troops were asked to move during daylight hours, why the vehicle had more significance than the mission troops, and why Pat's uniform was burned.

Kevin and I both indicate the family is disturbed by the field hospital report that states "CPR [was] performed" on Pat, then he was "transferred to ICU for cont[inued] CPR." Pat had been dead for nearly two hours, and most of his head was gone. I also tell the committee about the appalling remarks Colonel Kauzlarich publicly made about us not being able to accept Pat's death, saying we're not Christians.

I tell the committee that I believe Secretary of Defense Donald Rumsfeld knew Pat was killed by fratricide and permitted the cover-up. It is not believable that a man known for his propensity to micromanage would not want to know what happened to his most high-profile soldier. I inform the committee that Pat received a personal letter from Rumsfeld shortly after he and his brother enlisted, commending him for his commitment to serve. Pat was obviously in Rumsfeld's consciousness.

It is also not believable to me that General Abizaid didn't know about the P-4 memo McChrystal sent. He told the inspector general that he didn't get the memo until sometime in May because he was in Iraq. However, an American Forces Press Services news release dated April 30, 2004, indicates otherwise: "During a visit to Afghanistan April 29, Abizaid said he spoke to an Army Ranger lieutenant, Tillman's platoon leader, who was injured in the fight that killed Tillman. 'I asked [the lieutenant] yesterday how operations were going; I asked him about Pat Tillman,' Abizaid said."

At the time, Pat's lieutenant, David Uthlaut, was unaware that Pat was killed by fratricide or that he himself was wounded by "friendly" bullets. I let the committee know that what Uthlaut knew is not important. What's significant is that General Abizaid, the commander of the United States central command, was in Afghanistan when the situation in Iraq was calamitous. I don't believe Abizaid would have gone to see Uthlaut if he thought the enemy killed Pat, but he would go to see Uthlaut if he suspected Pat was killed by fratricide.

When our session with the committee comes to an end, we all go to watch the second panel on the television in the back conference room. We don't want to stay in the hearing room, in part because of the media, but also because we don't want to listen to the witnesses testify looking at the backs of their heads. Patrick does go sit in the hearing room shortly after the session begins. He wants to see them in person.

The second panel includes Kevin and Pat's friend, Navy Senior Chief Stephen White; Specialist Bryan O'Neal, the soldier who was with Pat when he was killed; Lieutenant Colonel John Robinson, who was a public affairs officer for central command when Pat was killed; Thomas Gimble, acting Defense Department inspector general; and Brigadier General Rodney Johnson, commanding general of Army criminal investigation command.

During O'Neal's testimony, he makes it clear that he was a hundred percent certain Pat was killed by fratricide. He says his battalion commander, Colonel Bailey, told him not to tell Kevin his brother was killed by friendly fire. He also says Colonel Bailey had him sit at a computer to write a statement about what happened the evening Pat was killed. He tells the committee the statement was changed without his consent and used to support Pat's Silver Star. The inspector general's investigation uncovered that Staff Sergeant Matt Weeks's statement was also altered, and neither statement from Weeks or O'Neal was signed.

Steve White testifies that he is haunted by the fact that he was the person who read the false narrative of Pat's death to the family and the public. "My role as far as at the memorial—it's a horrible thing that happened with Pat. I'm the guy that told America how he died basically, at that memorial, and it was incorrect. That does not sit well with me." It is repugnant tha the government would set up Pat's good friend, an honorable and decorated officer, a Navy SEAL, to decive the American public. He said he was the given the fraudulent accounting over the phone by someone he thinks was under Kensinger's command.

Committee members are outraged that the inspector general did not follow through to find out who falsified the documents. The investigators found evidence of a cover-up but made no attempt to find out who was responsible. Gimble appears humiliated. Waxman asks Gimble and General Johnson if any punishment was handed down to Kauzlarich for the rude remarks he made to the press about our perceived religious beliefs. They both indicated that nothing had happened to him with regard to his comments.

The committee closes the hearing by making it clear it is disturbed by the incompetence associated with Pat's investigations and indicates it will continue to examine the case. It is also apparent the committee is impressed by the integrity and courage Steve White and Bryan O'Neal displayed. As O'Neal testified, I could not help but be affected by the contrast between the poise and sincerity of the twenty-one-year-old soldier versus the newvous demeanor and disoriented testimony of the acting Inspector General, Thomas Gimble.

After the hearing I go to the hearing room to meet Bryan O'Neal for the first time. It is emotional for me. Bryan was the last person to see Pat alive. I hug him and I tell him what I had been thinking throughout his whole testimony: "Pat would be very proud of you."

Before I leave the hearing room, a woman named Liz Sweet approaches me. Her son Thomas Sweet was killed November 27, 2003. Thomas's death, like Pat's, was under suspicious circumstances. Her attempts to get answers have caused her more anguish. She confides in me that since she has started to get to the truth, the Army has informed her that her son committed suicide. She believes the Army told her that so she would go away. She tells me she hopes the hearing on Pat will open doors for her. I hope that, too.

My family and I meet in the conference room with Waxman's attorneys. They assure us they will continue to examine the documents and interview witnesses. Their hope is to have another hearing in several months. Patrick has to leave tonight to get back to San Jose; we go back to the hotel, where we sit in the lobby talking about the hearing until he has to catch his plane. We are very pleased with the outcome and look forward to the next one in hopes of getting more answers.

Kevin, Richard, and I have arranged to stay an extra day, but Marie has to leave tomorrow by one o'clock. After having coffee at the hotel, we catch a cab to the National Mall. We walk to memorials we're certain Pat visited when he was here. After Marie leaves for the airport, Richard, Kevin, and I go on a tour of the Capitol with two interns from Waxman's office, Matt and Bonnie. They are wonderful young people. Kevin and Rich appreciate that they each have a great sense of humor. Their tour was a perfect end to our visit.

One month after the hearing, Colonel Bailey sends O'Neal an e-mail critical of his testimony and accusing him of not being entirely truthful. O'Neal, who was next to Pat and could see who was shooting right at them, received this:

SPC O'Neal,

I'd like to set the story straight with you concerning CPL
Tillman. Your testimony before Congress was inaccurate . . . not
entirely untruthful but it was not accurate.

To be clear, I told you not to talk to Kevin about the cause of
Pat's death. As you should recall, we discussed it just before you
talked to Kevin on the phone (which was within forty-eight hours
of Pat's death). I told you not to speculate on the cause of death
because though you had one view of the battlefield you certainly
did not have all the facts. I further explained that there were 30
people who thought they knew what happened and that we would
conduct an investigation to determine the truth . . . and I empha-
sized that once the truth was determined by the 15-6 we would tell
the family every detail—withholding nothing. I allowed you to talk
to Kevin but asked you not to speculate by providing your views.

As you well know, what you saw of the incident was pretty
much exactly what happened. However, we did not know that to
be the case within a few hours of Pat's death . . .

I would like to speak with you upon receipt of this message.
COL Bailey

Within a few days of returning home, I begin looking at the CID and
Jones reports again. I want to have questions ready for Waxman's committee should we get another hearing. A week later, I get a call from
Meri Maben, Congressman Honda's assistant. She tells me Congress has
been successful getting the unredacted documents from the Department of Defense, and I can view them in Honda's office. Patrick gets a
call from Zoe Lofgren's office about the same time. He has access to the
documents she was sent. As soon as school gets out for the summer, I go
each day to Honda's office to read the unredacted documents and fill in
names and other information in my binders where that information is

blacked out. It's consuming and emotionally draining but very revealing. It takes weeks. There are days I become very angry that my family and I have to do this, just to get the truth that should have been forthcoming from the moment Pat died.

In July, we learn there will be another hearing on August 1. We are told Rumsfeld; and retired generals Kensinger, Abizaid, and Brown are being invited. We are also told Rumsfeld won't be coming and Kensinger probably won't, either. I know this is very significant; not only did Congressman Waxman have to push for this, but Minority Leader Tom Davis had to push hard as well. I become even more determined to gather information for Waxman's committee. Two weeks before the hearing, I type a narrative of the greatest discrepancies and our biggest concerns, which I then use as a basis for my presentation to Congress to help keep my facts straight.

THE AFTERMATH OF APRIL 22, 2004

Decisions made in Khost on April 22, 2004 were grossly irresponsible. It is appalling that Lieutenant Uthlaut was forced to split his troops when he so clearly gave sound reason for not wanting to do so. His greatest fear was a communication void which is precisely what led to the deaths of the AMF soldier and Pat and the wounding of Uthlaut and Lane. The decisions of the officers in the TOC are perplexing. Based on a conversation I had with Captain, now Major, Scott when he returned from Iraq last year, and testimony in the documents from Captain Saunders, First Sergeant Thomas Fuller, and Captain Kirby Dennis, everyone was very aware of Uthlaut's protest against splitting his platoon. I don't understand why Captain Saunders or Major Hodne didn't speak directly to Uthlaut so they would better understand the position he and his platoon were in that day. It is still unclear who actually gave the order to split the platoon. None of the investigators seriously tried to determine that. Dennis indicates in the Jones report that Uthlaut was very clearly seeking guidance. He states he agreed with Uthlaut's reasoning; I wish he had fought for him.

Saunders is very suspect to me. He drove the canyon twenty-four hours before the ambush. He must have realized the potential for danger in that canyon. Based on their testimonies, all the soldiers in the platoon saw the ambush potential as they entered the canyon. Captain Saunders tells Brigadier General Jones there was "No enemy, of course" in the region at the time he traveled through. He gives this as a reason for not being overly concerned about Uthlaut splitting the platoon, yet he knew the platoon had been stranded in Magarah for nearly six hours nursing a broken Humvee. I don't understand why he didn't speculate that locals would spread word to the enemy about the American presence. The region is prime Taliban country, right on the border of Pakistan. Saunders tells Jones that he assumed the platoon was going to split after maneuvering through the canyon because he spoke to members of the platoon when he dropped off the fuel pump on April 21, and they told him they would never travel the road from Tit to Magarah again because when they traveled it the first time nine or ten days earlier, it proved to be very dangerous. Yet, Uthlaut is very clear about his fears of splitting the platoon in the canyon. He also gave the intended routes of his elements to air support, which I've been told would go to the TOC as well.

In the e-mail Uthlaut sent to Dennis at 4:14 am on April 22, it is clear he intended to send the second element up the twelve-kilometer road, which is the route Serial Two was going to take until the jinga truck driver, through Sergeant Jeffrey Jackson, let the Platoon Sergeant Eric Godec know the road was too dangerous. Evidently, the jinga truck driver's reservations triggered Godec's memory about the road, and he agreed to take the road Serial One was driving.

It seems apparent to me the TOC knew the route Serial Two was intending to take. If Saunders had just spoken with Uthlaut, he could have assuaged the platoon leader's concerns by letting him know he could split once outside the canyon. Saunders made a statement in the Jones investigation that continues to haunt me. When Jones asked him about the Afghan soldiers, he tells him there were two cars of AMF soldiers. He said they stayed by the vehicles during the incident, except one, who "followed Corporal Tillman." Saunders said, "He was to be south of Corporal Tillman." This remark is significant—"was to be"—is not a typically used language convention. When it's used, it indicates the action was planned. It concerns me because it was the Afghan who drew fire to Pat. The Afghan is gone, just as Pat is gone. I have no idea who he was or why he was there. I don't like thinking ill of him, but from what I have read Afghan militia soldiers typically didn't get in combat situations with U.S. soldiers in 2004. They are very likely to fight alongside them now, but not at that time. The fact the CID could not give us a full name keeps me wondering.

Uthlaut was removed from the Ranger regiment, in part, because he "compromised the integrity of the platoon" because of the way he organized the serials, but the fact is he was basically told how to split the unit in an e-mail Dennis sent him April 22, at 4:32 am. The snipers and Sergeant Major Birch, he was told, had to get back to Salerno, and he was told which units were to have which mounted guns. He was also admonished for not ensuring his platoon had situational awareness; he says in the CID investigation that his platoon sergeant and his squad leaders were shown on a map which routes they were to take. It was the job of the squad leaders to inform their men. In looking at testimony, it appears Baker is the only squad leader in Serial Two who had no idea his serial was following the same route as Serial One, nor, he claims, did he know Serial One was ten to fifteen minutes ahead of them. Baker and the soldiers in his vehicle did not have situational awareness and they made no attempt to process what they were shooting.

Not once did Alders, Ashpole, Elliot, or Baker say they were scared, frightened, or confused. They said they were "excited," "I wish I had taken a split second to identify my target," and "I wanted to be in a firefight." These soldiers were not in a fog of war; they had a lust to fight. Baker testified to Scott he was out of the vehicle when he killed the Afghan, but he changes his statement when he is interviewed by Kauzlarich and Jones. O'Neal and Specialist John Tafoya said they saw Baker get out of the vehicle and shoot at them. However, Tafoya's statement is not included in the Jones investigation. His testimony is only found in the CID report. The Army does not want Baker's negligence to come out. If Baker was prosecuted for ROE violations, failing to identify targets, shooting at waving hands, firing into a village, he would have to testify about the reckless order to split the troops, and the false sense of urgency surrounding the mission to get "boots on the ground by nightfall."

The CID report is where the presence of a predator drone is first mentioned. Forward Observer Donald Lee called for air support when the ambush began and heard a predator drone overhead. He said that he also was told "by someone back at the TOC" that a predator flew over the platoon during the ambush. He testified that "Our air support was supposed to be three minutes out from my call in. He said at first he thought a C-130 had been sent to aid them, but it was the drone. I later was informed that every ground mission in Afghanistan, particularly through treacherous terrain, was supposed to have air support; the enemy, fearing retaliation, would be reluctant to attack with planes overhead ready to retaliate. What happened with this mission? Why wasn't there air support? Was it called off? If there was none available, why wasn't the mission delayed until there was air support?

There is documentation in the Jones report and in the CID report indicating that prior to December 2003, the uniforms and the equipment of fallen soldiers could only be destroyed if written authorization was given by medical personnel. After December 3, 2003, a memorandum was sent to the secretaries of the Army, Navy, and Air Force, as well as to the Joint Chiefs of Staff stating all uniforms and equipment of fallen soldiers is to be sent back to the medical examiner in Rockville to be used as evidence, especially in cases of suspected fratricide, homicide, or execution. I find it implausible that every officer in Pat's unit was unaware of this edict.

The excuse of burning Pat's belongings because they were a biohazard makes no sense. Pat's body was a biohazard. His uniform should have remained on his body and both could have been sent back to the states. The CID told us at our March briefing that there was no way to preserve the uniform because the facility in Salerno had no refrigeration capacity, yet the medical examiner states in his testimony to the CID, that Pat's body was very well preserved. If the uniform had remained on his body it would have been preserved. There was no need to take Pat's uniform off his body. He had no brain and he was dead; he had been dead for almost two hours before his body reached the field hospital. For the sake of argument, let's suppose the uniform was to be burned for sanitary reasons. Why wasn't it burned in a medical incinerator? Why was it placed in a tent for three days before it was burned? Why was his armor, valuable as evidence and in terms of determining equipment effectiveness, burned? Why was his journal burned? The notion that Pat had mission sensitive information in the diary is absurd. If that were the case, the military would collect everyone's diary or journal after each mission.

In the CID report, O'Neal, Fuller, and First Sergeant Peter Roethke said a large portion of Pat's brain and large pieces of his skull were on the ground after he was killed. Fuller and Roethke stated they picked up the remains and placed them in a plastic bag then put the bag in an ammo can.

Roethke gave the remains to Sergeant First Class James Schwartz, who then gave them to one of the chaplains to send to mortuary affairs. The remains never got to the medical examiner. The CID never asked Schwartz which chaplain received the remains. The brain and skull were important pieces of evidence. Dr. Mallak and Dr. Caruso stated in the CID report that if they had the brain and skull, they could have determined more accurately what happened to Pat.

We were told Pat died instantly once he was hit by what was apparently a three round burst. The medic said Pat's wounds were not compatible with life. He was bagged as KIA. No attempt was made to assist him at the site; it was too late to help him. This is why the field hospital report has always been so disturbing. The reference to CPR being performed and transferring him to ICU for continued CPR is not believable.

Why would anyone perform CPR on a man with no brain?

Why would a dead man be sent to ICU for continued CPR?

I believe this was done to make it appear as though an attempt was made to save Pat so there would be an excuse to destroy his uniform, as you can destroy the uniforms of wounded soldiers. The field hospital physician Dr. Anthony Foley told Marie and me over the phone that he didn't want it to appear as though he was ignoring Pat for the sake of the men who brought him in, but the soldiers who brought him in knew he was dead. Another thing that is very strange is that Roethke saw Pat's body half an hour after he was brought to the field hospital. Pat was still in his uniform, boots and RBA (body armor). No attempt was made to perform CPR. You can't perform CPR through armor. The second page of the field hospital report is dated April 25, 2004, and contains the notation "surgeon." It reads as though Pat died three days after he was brought in.

The redacted documents in the Jones investigation made it clear that high-ranking generals knew about Pat's fratricide within two days. Jones calls these particular witnesses sir, indicating they are a parallel rank or higher to Jones. Once I was able to view the unredacted documents in Honda's office I learned the generals' identities. General Brian Brown and Brigadier General Howard Yellen both testified to Jones that they knew Pat's death was a suspected fratricide within two days. General Brown stated he received a phone call from Major General McChrystal. If McChrystal called General Brown by phone two days after Pat's death, he probably called the other recipients of his P-4 message as well. Vice Admiral Eric T. Olson learned of the suspected nature of Pat's death from General Brown within a week. John Abizaid, Central Command commander must have been told. Based on Yellen's statement to General Jones, the Army was placed in a position to spin the narrative of Pat's death to benefit the Army, the administration, and the war effort. Yellen stated it was like, "Here is the [steak] dinner but we're giving it to you on a, you know, garbage can cover. You know, you got it, you work it." Why didn't any of these generals or the vice admiral step in to let us know Pat's death was a suspected fratricide? Because spinning Pat's death was part of a public relations effort during a period of "bad news." And because they were covering-up the role of emphasis on "showing progress in the unsound decisions made in Pat's death."

The standard operating procedure for notifying families is to tell them right away of the suspicion. If the White House/Pentagon is involved in covering up the fratricide then the White House/Pentagon is involved in covering up a crime. Covering up a negligent homicide is a felony. The first investigative officer, Scott, told Jones he believed there could have been "criminal intent" on the part of the soldiers in the vehicle. Yet, the partial report we have been given, that he supposedly wrote, states just the opposite. It may have been altered in places. The Army had no trouble falsifying the Silver Star. It is possible they also falsified Scott's report.

In the Jones report there are numerous e-mails that lead me to suspect the White House was aware of the circumstances of Pat's death fairly early. An e-mail dated April 28, 2004 indicates Rumsfeld's speechwriter and Bush's speechwriter wanted information about Pat's death. The P-4 memo from McChrystal, the number one spook in the land and Bush and Rumsfeld's golden boy, was sent on April 29, 2004. I suspect the president and Rumsfeld certainly were notified like the generals, within days that Pat's death due to a suspected friendly fire incident. The P-4 memo was simply confirmation. Colonel Hans Bush, chief of public affairs at Fort Bragg, claims he knew nothing about how Pat really died until May 28, 2004, yet he received an e-mail on April 30· 2004, with the subject title "CORPORAL Tillman's SS game plan." Why do you need a game plan for a Silver Star? On May 29, 2004, Robert Gaylord, chief of Army public affairs, sent out e-mails congratulating everyone for damage control in Pat's death.

I feel nauseous as I write this. I remember an interview Pat did that was aired on a program called *Biography*. Pat was talking about how he gets ready for a game. He said most of the really hard work, the preparation, is done during the week, then he said he'd start to wind down just before game time.

When the National Anthem came on he would pump up again. He said with a smile, "I have a patriot bone in me." Sadly, too few in his government do.

Within days of the hearing, I receive a copy of an interview the IG agents had with Commander Mallak and the medical examiner. A reporter who got it through the Freedom of Information Act sent it to me. It angers me that the interview was not given to us with the rest of the interviews. This interview is particularly revealing and upsetting. Commander Mallak tells the IG agent that within a day or two after Pat's autopsy, he and Dr. Carruso had concerns. Dr. Carruso contacted Human Resource Command.

IG AGENT: Okay. What were those concerns?

MALLAK: That the gunshot wounds to the forehead were atypical in nature and that the initial story that we received didn't, the medical evidence did not match up with the, with the scenario as described.

IG AGENT: And did he express those concerns just verbally or was it in writing or how?

MALLAK: It was just verbally at first. In fact, we were in this office and we called HRC from here and expressed our concerns.

IG AGENT: And HRC is?

MALLAK: Human Resources Command.

IG AGENT: And where is that?

MALLAK: Down at the Hoffman Building.

IG AGENT: And that's the United States Army?

MALLAK: Yes.

IG AGENT: Okay, and who did you talk to, do you recall?

MALLAK: [The name is redacted, but we know from reading

some unredacted documents that Dr. Carruso and Commander Mallak spoke to Brigadier General Gina Farrisee, the adjutant General], and there were a couple of other folks that she brought into the converstaion.

IG AGENT: And that was a day of so after the autopsy was performed?

MALLAK: Within a few days, I can't remember the exact date.

IG AGENT: Okay, what was their response?

MALLAK: They said they didn't think that our concerns were warranted at that time, that, that they had the story, that it made sense to them and they were going to proceed.

We fly into Washington the day before the August 1st hearing. Dave Rapallo, one of Congressman Waxman's attorneys, calls us just after we arrive to let us know that Rumsfeld will be coming. He also tells me that General Myers was in their office that day, and he was asked when Rumsfeld learned of Pat's death by fratricide. Myers responded by saying, "It was common knowledge in the Pentagon that Tillman was killed by friendly fire." I feel very hopeful that something may come of the hearing.

Republican Congressman Tom Davis makes a strong opening statement: "Testimony from our previous hearing, and the results of six separate investigations, all show the tragic truth can only fall somewhere between screwup and cover-up, between rampant incompetence and elaborate conspiracy."

Waxman reminds Myers about his testimony the day before in which he said most everyone at the Pentagon knew of Pat's fratricide. What a difference a day makes; he denies ever making the earlier statement.

Rumsfeld and retired generals Brown, Myers and Abizaid have great difficulty remembering what they knew and when they knew it. Someone sitting next to me whispers, "They have collective amnesia."

Rumsfeld was asked several times in various ways when he learned of

Pat's death, but he couldn't recall. Code Pink protesters chant "Donald Rumsfeld, you're a war criminal!" I dislike Code Pink's tactic, but I couldn't agree more.

Congresswoman Diane Watson asks him about the letter he sent to Pat right after he enlisted in which he praised him for his decision to serve. She also questions Rumsfeld about a memo he wrote to a colleague suggesting Pat was someone to watch because he was so special. She tells him she thought it strange that he took such an interest in Pat while he was alive but didn't even ask what happened to him when he died. He really doesn't respond to her. He says, "I know I would not be involved in a cover-up. I know that no one in the White House suggested such a thing to me. I know the gentlemen sitting next to me are men of enormous integrity and would not participate in something like that."

It strikes me that no one telling the truth would respond to a question that way. I know he is lying.

Brown, whom I know from the unredacted documents, knew about Pat's fratricide within twenty-four hours. He admits knowing about the likelihood of friendly fire shortly after April 22 but says it wasn't his responsibility to inform the White House or our family.

Abizaid claims he didn't learn of Pat's death until sometime in May. No one on the committee pressures him about the fact he originally lied about where he was on April 29 and April 30. He said he was in Iraq, but the Department of Defense Web site indicates he was in Afghanistan talking to Pat's platoon leader on April 28, 2004, and on April 29, the day the P-4 memo was sent, he was at CENTCOM headquarters in Qatar engaged in a teleconference with Pentagon reporters. Even though there is proof he was in Afghanistan, no one pressures him, and when he says he had better things to do that month than be concerned about Pat Tillman, no one gets in his face and says, "Exactly! Then what were you doing there talking to Tillman's platoon leader?" And no one asks him to explain how he could be at his headquarters in Qatar and not be able to receive a high-priority cable from a general issuing a warning for the president.

It is disturbing to me that the panel keeps blaming General Kensinger for the fact we weren't notified. I think Kensinger is culpable to a point, but he is not the ultimate bad guy. He would not have been the one to make the decision not to tell us. Just before the hearing, Wesley Clark went on Keith Olbermann's MSNBC program to discuss Pat's case. He said there is definitely an appearance of a cover-up and that cover-up wouldn't start at the three-star level. I don't understand why McChrystal was not punished more severely. His P-4 memo is extremely damning. None of the committee members seems to understand the significance of the memo. Everyone sees it as an attempt on McChrystal's part to do the right thing. However, I think the memo is transparently deceitful. He gives an example of how a false narrative can be written for Pat's Silver Star, and he indicates that no one had any intention of telling the family anything unless forced to do so. He wants to keep the leadership of the country from being embarrassed "if the circumstances of Corporal Tillman's death become public." "*If.*" No one presses the point. No one.

It's quite obvious that most of the Republican faction of the committee don't care what happened to Pat. Their indifference and, at times, disdain, is hurtful. I'm disgusted when Representative John Mica calls Rumsfeld a hero. It was inappropriate under the circumstances. Two Republican Committee members make it clear they feel too much time has been spent on Pat's death. Minutes later, one of those congressmen leaves his seat and walks over to my ex-husband, who is listening to crucial testimony, in order to give his condolences in front of the media. Patrick tells him to go away. Shortly after the congressman's retreat, another Republican member of the committee tries to speak with Patrick for the benefit of the camera. Patrick angrily tells him to leave as Waxman begins his final statement.

"You've all admitted that the system failed. The public should have known, the family should have known earlier," Waxman says. "None of you feel you personally were responsible, but the system itself didn't work."

In closing, Waxman harshly says, "The system didn't work, errors were made—that's too passive. Somebody should be responsible."

Yes, I say to myself. Someone should be responsible.

After the hearing we go to a back meeting room to talk to Waxman's attorneys. We let them know we are not happy with the hearing at all.

We have spent years gathering information and formulating questions with the hope of being in a forum like this, and we have been let down. Other than Minority Leader Davis, the Republicans on the committee are at best indifferent, but many of them are offensive. It was clear Pat—and the truth—didn't matter to them.

Most of the Democrats disappoint us as well. Their performance is not what it was in April. They are not prepared and they are unable to think on their feet. We expected more from Congress.

Waxman's attorneys apologize for the committee's poor showing and vow the next hearing, should there be one, will be better.

The following morning, Kevin, Marie, and I are driven to the Pentagon to talk to Secretary of the Army, Pete Geren, and Chief of Staff of the Army, General George Casey, about the inquiry into the conduct of military personnel involved in Pat's death and its aftermath.

We discuss the blatant lies in the investigations and question the insufficient disciplines meted out to the soldiers and officers involved in Pat's case. We are particularly upset with their denial that rules of engagement were broken, when evidence is clear to the contrary. Both men are extremely cordial, frustratingly so, as they insist there was no conspiracy in Pat's case, even though the inspector general cites evidence of suppression in his written report, and in April Congress judged there is indication of a cover-up.

At the close of our meeting we agree to disagree, but I promise them that we are not going away.

A young Marine is waiting to drive us to the airport. I look back at the Pentagon—one of the most renowned symbols of our American political system—eerily aware that our government is as insulated and protected as we are now, sitting in this black government SUV with bulletproof, tinted windows. It seems no one, no matter how determined, can penetrate the lies and deceptions that surround the Bush administration and its institutions. I'm saddened by how the government has betrayed not only Pat, but also the American public.

After more than three years of grueling and often painful research, and persistent pushing to get answers, our family has twice been heard before a congressional committee. The forum revealed publicly that there was suppression of evidence in reporting Pat's death and that there was a cover-up. I think of the Representative Henry Waxman's words at the close of the hearing:

> Our hearing today has been about two cases, the Tillman case, and the Lynch case, and in both cases, it seems like we have—we say deceptive—misleading information—it wasn't misleading information, we have false information that was put out to the American people. Stories that were fabricated and made up. In the case of Specialist Bryan O'Neal, his statement was doctored. It was rewritten by somebody. These aren't things done by mistake, there had to be a conscious intent to put out and keep with that story and eliminate evidence to the contrary and distort the record. In the case of Jessica Lynch, we have the *Washington Post* story saying they were told by the government officials. So it was attributed in the *Post* to government officials, and what we have is a very clear deliberate abuse, intentionally done. Why is it so hard to find out who did it? Why is it so hard to find out who's responsible and hold them accountable?

As I play that statement through my mind, it occurs to me that it's hard to find out who is responsible and hold them accountable because no one in a position of authority has the will or courage to do so.

Pat gave an interview in 2000 in which he discussed how he prepared for a game. He spoke about how he geared up all week, then he tried to remain calm and relaxed during the twenty-four hours before game time. He admitted, though, that he always felt a surge of energy and emotion at the point when the National Anthem was played. He chuckled and said, "I guess I have a patriotic bone in me."

The lack of respect Pat's government showed him for his patriotic commitment would break his heart.

Today, September 8th, is New Almaden Days, and it's my father's birthday; he would be seventy-six years old. This is also the day the community is dedicating a memorial to Pat. A big "Welcome to New Almaden" banner sways over the road and the flags roll with the warm breeze. A decorated golf cart, riders on horseback, fire trucks, and convertibles with honored guests and residents travel the short distance leading to modest Bulmore Park. The community and close friends and family gather around the stone-and-bronze monument, which is shaded with a canvas canopy and draped with a stars-and-stripes bunting. Standing before the crowd, in front of the monument she designed, my next-door neighbor and friend Peggy Melbourne speaks about the Pat she knew:

"We decided to dedicate this monument to Patrick because Patrick loved it here. This is what Patrick called home. This is our boy . . . We loved having him here. . . ."

Dutch Mapes, the ninety-one-year-old mason who painstakingly built the monument's brick base, pulls the bunting off, uncovering a simple yet skillfully crafted bronze plaque. The likeness in the portrait makes everyone smile. Many people in the crowd move closer to read the inscription with its fitting little grammatical flaw, and to touch Pat's face before walking across the bridge to the celebration. Barbecue, cold drinks, and ice cream are enjoyed by everyone. The kids have a water balloon launch, sponge toss, and treasure fishing, while grown-ups can sip on wine and beer while listening to the country tunes of the One-Eyed Jacks.

The sun starts to go down and the air is getting chilly. I walk past La Foret restaurant and across the bridge, stopping to look at the water. A vision unfolds in front of me: three little boys play in the creek, laughing with satisfaction that one of them caught a fish with his bare hands. Smiling, I walk over to the monument and look closely at the image smiling back at me. Touching Pat's cheek, I read the simple words that so earnestly describe his legacy:

PATRICK TILLMAN

November 6, 1976–April 22, 2004

Pat lived in New Almaden for most of his life. He came to love it for it's history and community spirit. He roamed the hills with his brothers as a kid, then hiked and trained in them as an athlete and soldier.

Pat was a loved son, brother, husband and faithful friend. He was a voracious reader, inquisitive scholar, civic volunteer, aggressive athlete and a patriotic and selfless soldier.

New Almaden and
the nation lost
Patrick Tillman
in Afghanistan on
April 22, 2004
in service to his country.

ACKNOWLEDGMENTS

At times our own light goes out and is rekindled by a spark from another person. Each of us has cause to think with deep gratitude of those who have lighted the flame within us.

—Albert Schweitzer

Mary Tillman

When I met Narda Zacchino in June of 2005, she and her husband, Robert Scheer, told me I should write a book to ensure that Pat's story is told completely and accurately. At that time I had no desire to write a book. I was preoccupied with researching documents and trying to make sense out of what happened on April 22, 2004. However, as the year passed, it became clear that nothing yet presented in newspapers, in magazines, on the Internet, or on television adequately brought to light the vast discrepancies and serious contradictions in the official accounts of Pat's death. When Narda continued to insist that revealing the truth of what happened to Pat was vital to the country, I was persuaded to take on the project.

We began working on the book in the summer of 2006. In the hours away from our jobs, we were almost constant companions. I spent many weekends in Narda's warm and welcoming home scrutinizing documents, researching information, and recounting events into a tape recorder for her to transcribe. Not only did Narda work with me, analyzing documents and researching military terms and procedures, she also organized many of my recorded memories into a detailed sequential narrative from which I could draw as I told Pat's story in my own words. When I completed each chapter, she then subtly and expertly edited the pages without disturbing my voice. I commend Narda for how persistently she has worked on this project, for how patiently she has dealt with me at times of great frustration, and for how loyally she stood by my family through two congressional hearings. I'm grateful for Narda's belief in our search for the truth and the tremendous support, expertise, and passion she provided.

Even before Narda and I intended to write a book, we spent countless hours examining the results of the official investigations. As we scrutinized the documents, however, we ran into formidable barriers in the form of redactions and impenetrable Army jargon that made it extremely difficult to make sense of what we were reading. We also were at a disadvantage because we knew little about military procedures and protocol. We needed an expert to interpret and demystify the military's insular culture. In May of 2006, we encountered such an expert in Stan Goff. Stan served in the US Army from 1970 to 1996. He served as a Ranger and as a Delta Force operator. He has spent countless hours reading the documents, researching, constructing timelines, interpreting military documents, and preparing a glossary of terms. Stan located forensics and ballistics experts and met with them in Rockville, Maryland, before they reviewed Pat's autopsy pictures and related material. In helping us, Stan spent many hours away from his family and forfeited other projects. I thank Stan for the personal sacrifices he made to improve this book and for his steadfast friendship to our family. I also thank his wife, Sherry, for being so patient and good-natured about the time she gave to Stan to help with this endeavor.

Robert Scheer devoted several extremely powerful newspaper columns to Pat's case in order to draw attention to the disturbing nature of his death. I'm thankful for his efforts, and for his wisdom and patience in supporting Narda and me through the writing process. I thank him, too, for sharing Narda with me when I know he wanted her to himself.

I'm grateful to Josh, Peter, Christopher, and Ben Scheer, for graciously sharing their home for two and a half years. I want them to know I appreciate it. I thank Josh for being so agreeable about helping his mother and me research obscure information; Peter, for talking me through setting up my new computer and fax machine; Chris, for assisting his mother with editing the book proposal; and Ben, for simply being Ben. I commend them, as well, for taking in stride the disruption brought to their lives by this project.

Narda and I asked Joanne Miller, Heidi Swillinger, Barbra Frank, Nikki McLaughlin, Caitlin Sullivan, and Chris Baron to assist in editing the book. I thank them for their thorough reading, constructive editing, kind praise, gentle criticism, and the gift of their time.

I often began writing about situations and events that were vague or unclear in my mind. At those points I invited individuals who were familiar with the circumstances to read portions of the book. They were extremely helpful in maintaining accuracy. Thank you to: James and Ginny Chapman, Alex and Christine Garwood, Sherri and Jim Greer, Jeff and Cindy Hechtle, Peggy and Syd Melbourne, Carmen Navarro, and Paul and Bindy Ugenti.

My many readers read the manuscript to critique tone, construct, and voice. They validated, heartened, and inspired me. I extend my appreciation to all of them: Janice Aron, Marcelle Chapman, Diane Delbridge, Jean Farrington, Julie Filippini, Pat Frisch, Sherri and Jim Greer, Kari Hansen, Elahe Hajazi, Joanne Howell, Michelle Jannone, Martha Kelley, Dolores Kesterson, Linda and Larry Marmie, Greg Martin, Don McCloskey, Liz and Keith McDavit, Kandi Owens, Karen Pelosi, Terri Peterson, Annie Purinton, Lori Rausher, Adele Shepard, Lannie Spalding, Katie and Tom Stoddard, Janette Supp, Joan Tillman, Kevin Tillman, Marie Tillman, Patrick K. Tillman, Richard Tillman, Julie Melbourne-Weaver, and Bonnie Wohl.

I want to sincerely thank the community of New Almaden, and the administration, staff, students, and parents of Bret Harte Middle School.

I thank Sergeant Bryan O'Neal and Navy Senior Chief Stephen White for supporting my family and me in our search for the truth. I thank them for their unwavering friendship, and I admire them for their integrity and courage.

I thank Russell Baer and Tamara Wright for assisting and supporting us during the most stressful and traumatic time of their lives.

I extend my gratitude to Peggy Buryj, Dawn Hellerman, Dolores Kesterson, Nadia McCaffrey, Karen Meredith, and Liz Sweet. They have touched my life with their stories and have supported our search for the truth, so they might find answers of their own.

Thank you to Dr. Robert Bux and Dr. Vincent DiMaio.

I want to thank my agent, Steve Wasserman, for his belief in this story and for his persistence in making certain it would be told, and Jill Kneerim, for her wisdom, patience, and guidance during those frightening early stages of writing.

To my editor, Leigh Haber, I am grateful for your faith and confidence in this book, for your skilled yet light touch, and for your very open mind.

I am privileged to have many wonderful people in my life who support and care about my family and me. Their expressions of kindness, generosity, encouragement, and understanding—great and small—are valued and will never be forgotten. However, since I began writing this book, there are certain individuals—colleagues, neighbors, and friends—who have been particularly supportive, assisting, motivating, and inspiring me on nearly a daily or weekly basis. To them, I offer a special thanks:

Cathy Bagan, Marcelle Chapman, Diane Delbridge, Jean Farrington, Carolyn Fortino, Pat Frisch, Sherri and Jim Greer, Elahe Hajze, Kari Hansen, Joanne Howell, Katrina Kalman, Mary Kearny, Martha Kelley, Don McCloskey, Nick and Sam Miller, Syd and Peggy Melbourne, Scott Murray, Elizabeth Navarro, Tiara Nelson, Karen Pelosi, Annie Purinton, Adele Shepard, Debbie Stanley, Amy Wagner, Rhonda Weltz, Nancy Witt, Bonnie Wohl, and Sandy Yokota.

To Carman Navarro, whose assistance, serene presence, and wisdom were invaluable. Thank you, Carmen.

To Gale Resz, who predicted I was carrying Pat before I knew it myself. Thank you for the love, patience, and support that thirty-two years of friendship entails.

To Kevin Young and Jane Frost, I extend my heartfelt appreciation for your understanding and assistance.

I thank my mother, Victoria Spalding. If I have any gift for telling a story, I owe it to her.

Thank you to my brother Mike Spalding, one of my best friends and staunchest advocates. For him, this book is a necessity.

Gratitude to my brother Richard Spalding, for his big heart, for being so supportive of my efforts with the book, and for being so confident that it will make a difference.

My heartfelt gratitude to Michelle Jannone for the gracious way she has stood by us.

I want to thank Patrick K. Tillman, for the sons we share, and for trusting me, and so staunchly supporting me, as I have written this account of Pat's life and death.

To Mary Badame, thank you for being there for Pat's father, for your unwavering encouragement, and for being a friend.

To Kandi Owens, thank you for the sunshine.

Pat has been gone for four years. I miss his physical presence, and I always will, but his energy is all around me. It lives in my vivid memories of him, in the earnest and loving letters he left behind, and in the stories shared by his friends and acquaintances. Most of all, it lives in his brothers, Kevin and Richard, and in his wife, Marie.

Marie, I'm grateful that Pat had you in his life. Just as I see in you some of the steel and spirit I recognized in him, a relaxed gentleness developed from the friendship, love, and respect you provided. I appreciate how watchful you are of Pat's legacy. Thank you for your trust throughout this project.

Richard, you were the first person to defy the stereotype that was becoming Pat. You had the courage to plant the seed at his memorial service, informing the public that he was a man who followed his own head and heart; for that I will always be grateful. Your unfaltering faith in me, and in the book, has been a source of tremendous confidence and pride.

Kevin, I thank you for persistently going after the truth of what happened to Pat, and I commend you for bravely facing your chain of command in order to uncover the one testimony that would expose the first layer of cover-ups and lies. Without your dogged determination, our suspicions could not have been substantiated. While you were in the Army, you were Pat's right-hand man; after his death, you became mine.

Narda Zacchino

Mary Tillman is a force of nature. Clearly, military officials had no idea what would hit them when they lied to this family about how Patrick Tillman was killed. From the first time I met her, I knew this mother would let nothing stop her in getting at the truth of her son's death. I started working with Mary as an editor for the *San Francisco Chronicle* and was impressed with her keen intelligence, total lack of inhibition in confronting authority, and her ability to separate her deep emotions

from the often ghastly accounts of her son's last moments to reach a dis-
passionate analysis of the facts.

She led her family in questioning all of the government's highly suspect investigations and specious conclusions, never willing, even now, to
settle for less than the truth. As a former investigative reporter, I was
impressed that nothing in the thousands of pages of government documents we read escaped her meticulous eye. As we grew to work closely
together, first for the *Chronicle* stories and later on the book, I witnessed
a more personal side: the strength of her character, the purity of her
integrity, the simplicity of what made her content—and I got an understanding of who Pat was.

I discovered Mary to be a very fine writer, her opening pages of the
book one of the best beginnings of a nonfiction work I have read. Her
evocative style made the book a pleasure to edit. She was an inspiration
to other mothers who lost sons and were lied to by the military; they told
me she empowered them to question the government in their own
cases.

I thank her for the hard work, the laughs, even the tears as she
shared stories of Pat, and for introducing into my life her warm and
remarkable family—sons Richard and Kevin, Pat's widow Marie, his
uncle Mike, Mary's former husband Patrick, her mother, Victoria—and
of course, Pat.

Once Mary cleared the way (as one put it, "I will do anything Mrs.
Tillman asks me to"), Pat's agent, Frank Bauer, and three of his coaches—
Larry Marmie, Dave McGinnis, and Lyle Setencich—all together gave
me hours of time and my earliest nonfamily insights into the young man
who touched their lives, and I thank them.

I share Mary's gratitude to our agent and friend Steve Wasserman
for his vision and patience, and to Jill Kneerim for kick-starting the book
proposal. I want to add to Mary's comments about Stan Goff by expressing gratitude for his humor, patience, and empathy for our nation's

soldiers. My introductory call to him was interrupted when he was needed to help talk a young soldier returning from Iraq out of committing suicide; when the crisis was averted, Stan called me right back.

My friends Barbra Frank, Heidi Swillinger, and Anne Weills provided not only editing skill and feedback but were there for me in too many ways to mention.

A loving thank you goes to my sons Josh, Peter, and Christopher, and grandson Ben for keeping me humble. Above all, I thank my husband, Robert, for introducing me to Mary and for his understanding, tolerance, and support for the last year and a half.

SOURCES & CREDITS

156–160: Eulogy reprinted by permission, courtesy of Jim Rome.

161–162: Eulogy and personal letter reprinted by permission, courtesy of Maria Shriver and Governor Arnold Schwarzenegger.

162–163: Eulogy reprinted by permission, courtesy of Senator John McCain.

164–166: Eulogy reprinted by permission, courtesy of Stephen White

166–169: Eulogy reprinted by permission, courtesy of Jake Plummer

169–174: Eulogy reprinted by permission, courtesy of Alex Garwood.

174–175: Eulogy reprinted by permission, courtesy of Richard Tillman.

175–176: Excerpt from Dan Bickley's article "Memorial Adds to Legend: In death, Tillman's life has become symbol of freedom" (May 4, 2004), reprinted by permission, courtesy of the *Arizona Republic*.

177–179: Eulogy reprinted by permission, courtesy of Lyle Setencich

180–181: Eulogy reprinted by permission, courtesy of Dave McGinnis.

182–183: Eulogy reprinted by permission, courtesy of Larry Marmie.

184–185: Eulogy reprinted by permission, courtesy of Terry Hardtke

185–189: Eulogy reprinted by permission, courtesy of Zach Walz.

219–221: Excerpt from Brian Cloughley's article "Lies Upon Lies Upon Lies: US Military in Crisis" (June 12, 2004) from counterpunch.com reprinted by permission, courtesy of Brian Cloughley.

221–223; 225–226: Excerpts from Brian Cloughley's personal letters and www.briancloughley.com reprinted by permission, courtesy of Brian Cloughley.

280: Excerpt from Stan Goff's article "Telling Transformative Tales: The Strange Post-Ranger Saga of Pat Tillman" (April 5, 2006) on fromthewilderness.com reprinted by permission, courtesy of Stan Goff.

283–285: Excerpt from Kevin Tillman's article "After Pat's Birthday" (October 19, 2006) from truthdig.com reprinted by permission courtesy of Kevin Tillman.

292–294: Excerpt from Michael Hirsh and John Barry's article "Military: The Hidden General Exposed: Stan McChrystal runs 'black ops.' Don't pass it on." (June 26, 2006) reprinted by permission, courtesy of *Newsweek*.

INDEX